BEST PRACTICE IN MOTIVATION AND MANAGEMENT IN THE CLASSROOM

ABOUT THE AUTHORS

DENNIS GENE WISEMAN holds the Ph.D. and M.A. degrees from the University of Illinois (1974, 1970) and the B.A. degree from the University of Indianapolis (1969). He is Special Assistant to the President for University/Schools Collaboration and Associate Provost at Coastal Carolina University, Conway, South Carolina. His teaching specialization areas are curriculum and instruction, social studies education, and educational psychology. Dr. Wiseman has taught with both the Champaign, Illinois, and Indianapolis, Indiana, public school systems. He is co-author of *Effective Teaching: Preparation and Implementation, The Middle Level Teachers' Handbook: Becoming a Reflective Practitioner,* author of numerous articles in professional journals, and actively involved in collaboration activities between K-12 and higher education.

GILBERT HARRISON HUNT holds Ph.D. and M.Ed. degrees from the University of North Carolina (1975, 1971) and the B.S. degree from Campbell University (1969). He is Dean of the College of Education at Coastal Carolina University, Conway, South Carolina. Dr. Hunt taught at the middle level with the Harnett County, North Carolina, public school system. He is co-author of *Effective Teaching: Preparation and Implementation, The Middle Level Teachers' Handbook: Becoming a Reflective Practitioner,* author of numerous articles in professional journals, and is a member of Phi Delta Kappa, Kappa Delta Pi, National Middle School Association, and Association of Teacher Educators.

BEST PRACTICE IN MOTIVATION AND MANAGEMENT IN THE CLASSROOM

By

DENNIS G. WISEMAN, Ph.D.

and

GILBERT H. HUNT, Ph.D.

*Coastal Carolina University
Conway, South Carolina*

Charles C Thomas
PUBLISHER • LTD.
SPRINGFIELD • ILLINOIS • U.S.A.

Published and Distributed Throughout the World by

CHARLES C THOMAS • PUBLISHER, LTD.
2600 South First Street
Springfield, Illinois 62794-9265

©2001 by CHARLES C THOMAS • PUBLISHER, LTD.

ISBN 0-398-07237-X (hard)
ISBN 0-398-07238-8 (paper)

Library of Congress Catalog Card Number: 2001037864

Printed in the United States of America
CR-R-3

Library of Congress Cataloging-in-Publication Data

Wiseman, Dennis.
  Best practice in motivation and management in the classroom / by Dennis G. Wiseman
and Gilbert H. Hunt.
      p. cm.
  Includes bibliographical references and index.
  ISBN 0-398-07237-X (hard) − 0-398-07238-8 (paper)
      1. Motivation in Education. 2. Classroom management. 3. Effective teaching. I. Hunt,
Gilbert. II. Title.

LB1065.W57 2001
371.102'4−dc21   2001037864

This text is dedicated to the thousands of students who enter schools each day and bring with them, or encounter there, problems in motivation and management and to the dedicated teachers who continue to seek ways to meet the personal and learning needs of these students.

PREFACE

Teachers today are called on to provide services to their students, schools, and communities that would never have been considered and/or discussed even ten years ago. Likewise, teachers today are being held accountable for their own performance and the performance of their students in ways and through means that also would not have received serious consideration ten years ago. This demand for additional services and higher levels of performance and accountability comes at a time when the challenges that teachers face each day in their schools and classrooms are greater than at any previous time in the history of the teaching profession.

There is no question that teachers must have an in-depth understanding of the subject matter that they teach. Students cannot be expected to achieve nor will they achieve at high levels without teachers who are expert themselves in the content that they teach. Knowledge of subject matter alone, however, is not sufficient to ensure that teachers will be effective and that students will achieve at high levels. Teachers interact on a daily basis with students who often see little value in what they are being taught and feel uncomfortable or out of place in the schooling environment that frequently is so very different from that of their homes and communities. Many of these students have difficulty controlling their own behaviors and attending to what is expected of them in the classroom. Many bring with them a host of issues and concerns about who they are today as well as who they will be in the future.

In addition to the great need to have a deep understanding of the subject matter that they teach, teachers have an equally great need to be able to teach this subject matter in ways that their students find interesting, relevant, engaging and understandable. If students do not see what they are learning as interesting, if they do not recognize it as being relevant to their lives either now or in the future, if they are not meaningfully connected to it, and if they do not view it as being understandable to the degree that they can be successful, they will not achieve at their greatest potentials. In today's classrooms and schools, teachers are expected to achieve at high levels in getting their students to learn, and students are expected to achieve at high levels in demonstrating what they have learned.

To be effective, teachers must have an understanding of their students' interests, styles of learning, and backgrounds. Teachers cannot meet the unique needs of their students if they do not know their unique needs. Having the ability to manage the learning environment, motivate students in the learning environment, and offer instruction that itself is motivating and that contributes to students learning what they need to learn and acquiring skills they need to acquire characterizes effective teachers. To meet the expectations held for them, teachers clearly must have highly developed skills as instructional specialists, motivators, managers, and problem solvers.

This text offers practical information and vicarious practice for both beginning and veteran teachers to become more knowledgeable, skilled, and therefore effective in their work. Through study, application of what has been studied, and the analysis and evaluation of the end result of this application, teachers who care to improve can improve. And, teachers who are already successful in their teaching can be even more successful. Effective teachers are also active learners themselves; this text provides a specific context and focus for this learning in the areas of student motivation and classroom management, which are considered critical for best practice in teaching in classrooms today.

DENNIS G. WISEMAN
GILBERT H. HUNT

CONTENTS

ix

BEST PRACTICE IN MOTIVATION AND MANAGEMENT IN THE CLASSROOM

Chapter 1

MOTIVATION AND MANAGEMENT: TWO SIDES TO THE SAME COIN

When a classroom population ranges from twenty to forty students from disparate backgrounds, peaceable and productive learning environments depend on the management of explicit standards and expectations to which all adhere. Schools need to set up management structures that promote prosocial behaviors and educators must be prepared to teach replacement behaviors that are prosocial. A major flaw in school management has been that of erasing negative behaviors without teaching prosocial replacement behaviors. (Froyen & Iverson p. 6, 1999)

The knowledge base of motivation is so extensive that the crucial factor is making the best choice for a particular problem. If we have not learned the extensive motivational knowledge base, then our choices are limited. (Alderman p. 13, 1999)

THE INTER-RELATEDNESS OF MOTIVATION AND MANAGEMENT

Annual polls conducted by the Gallup organization in conjunction with Phi Delta Kappa for years have identified concerns with classroom management among the most critical of those held by veteran and novice teachers. From 1968 to 1986, *discipline* was identified as the most important problem that teachers face. From 1986 to 1992, *discipline* ranked third only to *drugs* and *inadequate funding* as the most significant educational problem. In 1994 and 1995, *discipline* again was the number one problem (Elam & Rose, 1995). Since that time, *discipline* was second to *drug abuse* in 1996 (Elam, Rose, & Gallup, 1996), tied for first with *lack of financial funding* in

3

1997 (Rose, Gallup, & Elam, 1997), second to *fighting/violence/gangs* in 1998 (Rose & Gallup, 1998), first again in 1999 (Rose & Gallup, 1999), and second to *lack of financial support* in 2000 (Rose & Gallup, 2000). With the ongoing question asked in the Phi Delta Kappa/Gallup Poll being, "What do you think are the biggest problems with which the public schools of your community must deal?" and the answer consistently being *discipline* and now *violence*, educators must give greater attention than ever before to addressing what is clearly a significant national issue. Problems of discipline in schools and classrooms are no longer problems of only public perception but of teacher recruitment and retention as well. It is popularly believed that the problems teachers face associated with student behavior are related to the teacher shortage problems now being faced by states and school districts, because these problems have contributed to the reduction in the number of teachers entering the profession. Such problems are also believed by many to be one of the reasons for the shorter periods of time that many teachers now stay in the profession. Whether from a student achievement or school staffing perspective, student behavior is a problem of critical importance to the teaching profession today.

Facing potential student problems with respect to classroom management . is also one of the most important concerns held by pre-service teachers or those preparing to enter the teaching profession. Historically, pre-service and beginning teachers have felt least well prepared to deal with issues related to classroom management and discipline (Kher-Durlabhji, Lacina-Gifford, Jackson, Guillory, & Yandell, 1997). Over the past few years, managing student behavior has gone beyond being an issue only associated with engaging students in effective instruction to now represent an issue associated with classroom and school safety. School-based tragedies across the country involving student violence have captured the national attention with outcries for immediate action and demands for safer schooling environments. Beginning teachers are faced with the daunting challenge of offering instruction of high quality in what are often very unpredictable environments. Clement (1998) reports on the ten most common problems faced by first-year teachers. Student motivation and classroom management and discipline are first and third on the list, respectively. The entire list is as follows:

1. student motivation

2. handling students' social and emotional problems

3. maintaining classroom management and discipline

4. overenrolled classrooms

5. book and supply shortages

6. uncomfortable classroom environments (size, temperature, cleanliness)

7. working with special education or inclusion students

8. grading students' work

9. communicating with parents

10. school or district administration

Although problems of student behavior in schools today are easily documented, the major tenet of this text rejects the identification of managing student behavior as a stand-alone issue. Problems of managing student behavior must be looked at more broadly to include related issues associated with student motivation. It is not advisable to separate concerns of student management from concerns of student motivation. Efforts to do so only serve to oversimplify the understanding of each area as important concerns for teachers related to establishing best teaching practice in classrooms and schools. Although it is possible to study student management separately from student motivation, and vice versa, treating the two in isolation from one another misdirects the most meaningful investigation and understanding of either one. Their understanding and importance to school settings go together and, in fact, rely on one another.

All too frequently, the problems that teachers have in the area of managing student behavior are more fundamentally problems with student motivation or, at least, management and motivation problems occurring simultaneously. This text will explore student management and student motivation as they directly relate to each other, and influence each other, rather than as discretely separate elements of the teaching/learning process. No teacher should leave school at the end of the day lamenting how difficult it was to manage students without also exploring how he or she might become better able to motivate them. In most cases, though perhaps not in all, the presence of problems in managing student behavior occurs concurrently with the absence of needed levels of student motivation.

ESTABLISHING A COMMON LANGUAGE FOR THE STUDY OF MOTIVATION AND MANAGEMENT

Because the relationship between student motivation and student management is so important, having a clear understanding of both constructs as they relate to the work of the teacher in the classroom is essential. Although the terms are used frequently in education circles today, they are often used in different ways with different meanings by different individuals. It also is important to address *discipline* in this discussion, because the term discipline is often used interchangeably with *management*. This is unfortunate for the two are not the same. As clear communication and understanding are key to effective teaching practice, so are they key to the successful understanding and study of that practice.

The following are popular definitions of the concepts *motivation* and *management* found in the literature today:

Motivation

a force that energizes, sustains, and directs behavior toward a goal (Baron, 1992; Schunk, 1990);

an energizing or activating of behavior, a directing of behavior, and a regulating persistence of behavior (Alderman, 1999);

the forces that account for the selection, persistence, intensity, and continuation of behavior (Snowman & Biehler, 2000);

an internal state that arouses one to action, pushes one in a particular direction, and keeps one engaged in certain activities (Elliott, Kratochwill, Cook, & Travers, 2000);

an internal state that arouses, directs and maintains behavior (Woolfolk, 2001).

Management

strategies that create and maintain an orderly learning environment (Eggen & Kauchak, 2001);

all things that a teacher does to organize students, space, time, and materials so that instruction in content and student learning can take place (Wong & Wong, 1991);

the teacher's ability to cooperatively manage time, space, resources, and student behavior to provide a climate that encourages learning (Alberto & Troutman, 1986);

the use of rules and procedures to maintain order so that learning may result (Elliott et al, 2000);

the conscientious and active control of classroom environmental conditions and antecedents to prevent the occurrence of behavior problems (Harlan, 1996).

The definitions presented here identify that *management* may be looked upon as an action or actions that the teacher takes in relation to the classroom environment to make optimum levels of student achievement possible. *Motivation* may be seen as that which the teacher initiates or seeks to bring about so that students become and stay positively engaged in the learning experiences found in the classroom environment. Management does not necessarily precede or follow motivation. The two go hand in hand. For the purposes of this text, **management** is defined as *a system of organization that addresses all elements of the classroom (i.e., students, space, time, materials, and behavioral rules and procedures) to reach optimum levels of instruction and learning.* **Motivation** is defined as *an internal state that arouses students to action, directs them to certain behaviors, and assists them in maintaining that arousal and action with regard to certain behaviors important and appropriate to the learning environment.*

Following these observations, how does classroom or student discipline relate to student motivation and management? The following are common definitions of the concept *discipline* found in the literature today:

Discipline

- teacher responses to student misbehavior. (Eggen & Kauchak, 2001);

- the required action by a teacher or school official, toward a student (or group of students), after the student's behavior disrupts the ongoing educational activity or breaks a pre-established rule or law created by the teacher, the school administration, or the general society. (Wolfgang, 1999);

- what teachers do to help students behave acceptably in school. (Charles, 1999);

- the process of enforcing standards and building cooperation so that disruptions are minimized and learning is maximized. (Jones, 1987).

These definitions suggest that discipline is what the teacher engages in when efforts to motivate students and manage the classroom have not been completely successful. **Discipline** may be defined as *action taken on the part of the teacher to enforce rules and respond to student misbehavior.* Behavior that is considered to be inappropriate is referred to as misbehavior. Charles (1999) identifies that classroom misbehavior occurs intentionally, not inadvertently. In exhibiting misbehavior, students do things on purpose that they know they should not do. Five broad types of misbehavior are identified here as noted by Charles (1999) in descending order of seriousness:

1. **Aggression:** physical and verbal attacks on the teacher or other students.

2. **Immorality:** acts such a cheating, lying, and stealing.

3. **Defiance of authority:** refusal to do what the teacher requests.

4. **Class disruptions:** talking loudly, calling out, walking about the room, clowning, tossing objects.

5. **Goofing off:** fooling around, out of seat, not doing assigned tasks, dawdling, daydreaming.

Although it is important for the teacher to be prepared for discipline problems when they arise, it should be recognized that when the teacher uses strategies to discipline students, the teacher is in more of a reactive than proactive mode of behavior. As with the delivery of good teaching practice, the teacher needs to be poised, confident, capable, and focused when using discipline strategies in response to student misbehavior. When the teacher needs to use discipline strategies, however, it is observed that one likely reason for this is that the teacher's approaches to motivation and management were less than fully effective.

BEST PRACTICE IN MOTIVATION AND MANAGEMENT

Teachers who are able to maximize student learning minimize student misbehavior. Acknowledging this, the relationship between best practice in teaching and best practice in motivation and management cannot be ignored. Why is it that effective teachers typically have a minimum number of discipline problems to address compared with ineffective teachers? The primary reasons for this are not overly complicated, and the answer to this question lies in the teacher's attitude, readiness and preparedness, and ability to offer meaningful and relevant instruction to all students and manage the learning environment. Teachers who are well prepared for teaching, motivating, and managing have fewer classroom problems than those who are not.

In a classic study, Kounin (1970) identifies that effective teachers are really no different from ineffective teachers in their ability to respond to and deal with student misbehavior *after the misbehavior has occurred.* The study reported, however, a significant difference in the behaviors of effective and ineffective teachers *before the student misbehavior took place.* Kounin found that it was the ongoing behavior of teachers in carrying out their instruction that determined whether teachers were effective or ineffective. Kounin's research pointed out that ineffective teachers simply were not fully ready for all of what was expected of them or needed to occur in the classroom. Lack of readiness led to confusion, confusion led to uncertainty, uncertainty led to mixed messages with lack of clarity in communication and understanding of expectations, and all of these in total led to student misbehavior. The ineffective teachers, virtually daily, became more and more stressful, disorganized, frustrated, negative, and held others responsible for the problems that they were experiencing. Kounin concluded from his research that the key to maintaining orderly classrooms lies in the teacher's ability to prevent behavior problems from occurring rather than in the teacher's ability to handle inappropriate student behavior once it happens. This observation led to the separation of the concept *classroom management*, which represents the teacher's strategies used to create and maintain an orderly learning environment and the concept *discipline*, which represents the teacher's reactions to and ways of dealing with student misbehavior.

Effective teachers are prepared for the many things, some expected and some unexpected, that come into play in the job of teaching. The classroom is ready, meaningful learning experiences are ready, and the students are ready to learn when they enter the classroom. Effective teachers are so well prepared through their prior practices that they are able to prevent most student misbehaviors, certainly most serious misbehaviors, from ever occurring. It, perhaps, sounds all too simple. The reason that effective teachers are effective is that they have fewer student behavior problems and, consequently, are better able to get their students to work (be engaged), stay on task, and achieve. In turn, effective teachers incur less stress as a consequence of having to deal with fewer behavior problems. They are able to leave school each day having been more productive and feeling more satisfied with their work than those teachers who are seen as not being effective. These conclusions by Kounin have been validated over the years on more than one occasion (Brophy & Evertson, 1976; Evertson, 1980).

Most textbooks on teaching methods include a section on the need for the teacher to be prepared and ready when entering the classroom. Being ready for teaching is often explored with respect to the teacher being well planned to teach lessons to students. The term *plan* is typically presented in the context of the teacher's plan for instruction. It is important, however, to expand this outlook toward planning to not be limited to only instructional planning. Three additional types of plans should be considered. These are (1) the teacher's motivation plan, (2) the teacher's management plan, and (3) the teacher's discipline plan. Although it may sound awkward to think of the teacher as a discipliner, it is not awkward to think of the teacher as a motivator and a manager. The effective teacher is a motivator with a plan to motivate and a manager with a plan to manage. The effective teacher is also someone capable of dealing with student misbehavior or discipline problems if they arise. Following this line of thought, then, the effective teacher is someone with a plan to discipline. Not only do effective teachers have these plans, they also have the ability to implement them and be successful in their use.

THE TEACHER AS A MOTIVATOR

Many different qualities come to mind when thinking of the characteristics of effective teachers. Effective teachers are organized, flexible, informed about the subjects that they teach, clear in their communications, task-oriented, enthusiastic, and dynamic in their work. Included in such a listing is reference to the teacher's ability to create positive learning environments where students become actively engaged in their own learning. Educational research identifies that effective teachers are able to motivate students or establish environments in which motivated students are the end result. Effective teachers are believed to be motivational in their approaches to teaching. Sternberg (1999, 1985) notes that the main constraint in assisting students to achieve is not with respect to some fixed capacity that they bring with them to the classroom or school but with respect to the degree to which they are purposefully engaged in working on their learning. And, this also involves the degree to which their teachers are engaged in helping them. Working toward achievement involves experiences with effective instructional practices, active participation on the part of the student, role modeling on the part of the teacher, and reward. Sternberg identifies a model for developing expertise and achievement in students with five key elements: (1) metacognitive skills, (2) learning skills, (3) thinking skills, (4) knowledge, and (5) motivation. All of these elements depend on the context for learning that has been established. At the center, driving the elements, is motivation. In the absence of motivation, nothing happens. Motivation drives the development of metacognitive skills, which then activates learning and thinking skills. Learning and thinking skills then provide feedback for the further development of metacognitive skills enabling the student's level of understanding to increase. Motivation is the key to this process.

Elliott and colleagues (2000), however, suggest that one of the myths associated with motivation is that teachers really do motivate students. The best that teachers can do, some believe, is establish conditions for learning that are as attractive and stimulating as possible and match learning tasks to student abilities. When these conditions have been established, students will be motivated. It is the conditions, then, that create the motivation, not the teacher. Regardless of the source of the motivation, whether students are motivated by the conditions found in the environment or by the teacher in the process of teaching and in establishing the conditions, motivation is considered to be a critical part of the learning process.

Eggen and Kauchak (2001) identify the learner-focused classroom as representing the kind of environment most suitable for promoting student motivation. The authors do not suggest whether the teacher or the environment is the actual motivator of students. This, in fact, may not be an important point or distinction. The important consideration is, however, on the relationship between the learner-focused classroom and student motivation. Student motivation increases when teachers establish classrooms that are focused on their students. The following four elements and their accompanying teacher tasks are present in the learner-focused environment:

Self-Regulated Students

- **Setting goals:** students have meaningful opportunities to set goals for themselves and participate in the goal setting in the classroom.

- **Monitoring goals:** students have and are expected to take responsibility for monitoring their own progress.

- **Metacognition:** students are aware of the way they study and learn, monitor the effectiveness of their efforts, and adapt when necessary.

- **Strategy use:** students learn and use learning strategies that are effective and that assist them in the learning process.

Teacher Characteristics

- **Personal teacher efficacy:** the belief that teachers can have an important positive effect on students; the more this is believed, the more it will happen.

- **Modeling and enthusiasm:** teachers present information enthusiastically, resulting in increased student self-efficacy, attributions of effort and ability, self-confidence, and achievement and through their own behavior display or project a positive learning model.

- **Caring:** teachers empathize with, and invest in, the protection and development of the student.

- **Positive expectations:** teacher expectations tend to be self-fulfilling; the expression of low expectations by differential treatment can inadvertently lead children to believe less in their abilities and perform more poorly.

Climate Variables

- **Order and Safety:** students see the learning environment as physically and psychologically safe.

- **Success:** achievement on meaningful and appropriately challenging tasks is essential; opportunities for student success are maximized.

- **Task comprehension:** students understand what they are to learn and why they are to learn it.

- **Challenge:** success occurs in moderately difficult or challenging tasks.

Instructional Variables

- **Introductory focus:** lesson beginnings attract student attention and offer a framework for the entire lesson.

- **Personalization:** lessons and topics are seen as personally meaningful and intellectually and/or emotionally relevant.

- **Involvement:** instruction actively involves students in the learning activity.

- **Feedback:** students receive information on their own personal progress and receive this information on a regular basis.

Snowman and Biehler (2000) offer six recommendations for teachers in motivating students to learn. These include certain teacher behaviors, student perceptions, and environmental concerns. Each recommendation, it is noted, is presented in terms of a teacher behavior. The teacher should:

1. Use behavioral techniques to help students exert themselves and work toward remote goals.
2. Make sure that students know what they are to do, how to proceed, and how to determine when they have achieved their goals.
3. Do everything possible to satisfy deficiency needs, defined by Maslow (1970) as physiological, safety, belongingness, and esteem needs.
4. Direct learning experiences toward feelings of success in an effort to encourage an orientation toward achievement, a positive self-concept, and a strong sense of self-efficacy.
5. Try to encourage the development of need achievement, self-confidence, and self-direction in students who lack these qualities.
6. Try to make learning interesting by emphasizing activity, investigation, adventure, social interaction, and usefulness.

Woolfolk (2001) also provides an overview of strategies for teachers to use to bring about student motivation in learning. The focus of each strategy, once again, is on what the teacher does to establish student motivation. The end result of using these strategies and in displaying certain behavioral characteristics is a classroom environment where students are motivated to learn. The teacher is responsible for his or her teaching behaviors and, in fulfilling this responsibility, for the development of the learning environment.

Fulfill Basic Requirements

- **Provide** an organized class environment.
- **Be** a supportive teacher.
- **Assign** challenging work, but not too difficult.
- **Make** tasks worthwhile.

Build Confidence and Positive Expectations

- **Begin** work at the students' level.
- **Make** learning goals clear, specific, and attainable.
- **Stress** self-comparison, not competition.
- **Communicate** that academic ability can be improved.
- **Model** good problem solving.

Show the Value of Learning

- **Connect** the learning task to the needs of the students.
- **Tie** class activities to the students' interests.
- **Arouse** curiosity.
- **Make** the learning task fun.
- **Emphasize** the use of novelty and familiarity.
- **Explain** connections between present learning and later life.
- **Provide** incentives and rewards, if needed.

Help Students Stay Focused On the Task

- **Give** students frequent opportunities to respond.
- **Provide** opportunities for students to create a finished product.
- **Avoid** heavy emphasis on grading.
- **Reduce** task risk without oversimplifying the task.
- **Model** motivation to learn.
- **Teach** learning tactics.

Glasser (1997) identifies that the foundation of poor student motivation may be found in problems in the relationship that exists between the teacher and the student. A positive student-teacher relationship rests, in part, on the perception held by the student as to whether the teacher actually cares for him or her. Students who are destined to fail, and in many cases destined to be unmotivated, often believe that no one (in this discussion their teachers) cares about them as individuals. This is based on their analysis of the teacher behaviors that they observe.

In the text *Positive Classroom Management*, DiGiulio (2000) offers a fine explanation of the relationship between motivation and management in noting that teachers make success definite when they make failure impossible. Teachers can help to ensure success when they know their students including their strengths, their weaknesses, what interests and what does not interest them, and when they establish a positive relationship with them. Three axioms are offered as a guide for ensuring student success:

- Students who feel successful are seldom behavior problems.
- To feel successful, students must actually be successful.
- To actually be successful, a student must first do something of value.

THE TEACHER AS A MANAGER

It would be naïve to suggest that if a teacher has a plan for establishing a well-managed classroom, this will guarantee that no student behavior problems will ever occur. No such guarantee is possible. Nevertheless, teachers can establish and manage the learning environment in such a way as to greatly diminish the possibility of problems with student misbehavior. To do this, teachers must be able to develop as well as implement well-conceived management plans. The effectiveness of such plans and their implementation rests to a large degree on the teacher having a good understanding of the characteristics of such environments and acquiring the necessary skills to create them. McCaslin and Good (1998) note that classroom management historically has been seen largely as controlling students and getting them to respond to teacher demands, needs, and goals. Control of student behavior remains for many teachers the primary foundation of classroom management. Although this view may still be quite prevalent, it is not the proper foundation for classroom management. Rather than focus on control of the environment, teachers should focus on promoting the goal of students developing their own capacity for self-regulation. Self-regulation was one of the four components of the learner-focused environment presented earlier in conjunction with student motivation. Students should not behave in certain ways or be regulated merely as a response to a control system that the teacher has created.

In describing the classroom environment with respect to student management, Gathercoal (1993) addresses the importance of teachers being proactive in their work and able to clearly define and communicate the expectations that they hold for their students. Clarity and consistency in communicating rules and expectations are of significant importance. If students do not know what their teachers expect of them, there is little reason to believe that they will be consistent in exhibiting those behaviors that their teachers desire.

Rules help to clarify the expectations that teachers have for students and the clear statement of even a few important rules of conduct can prevent many student behavior problems. Henson and Eller (1999) offer eight guidelines with respect to identifying and listing classroom rules:

1. Establish the list during the first few class meetings.
2. Keep the list short.
3. State each rule simply in language the student can understand.
4. Include only those rules that are considered necessary and be prepared to explain why each rule is needed.
5. Involve students in setting rules.
6. Focus on student behavior needed to achieve lesson goals.
7. State consequences for breaking rules so that students will know what will happen if rules are broken.
8. State rewards for following rules.

Wong and Wong (1991) observe that the characteristics of a well-managed classroom need to be agreed on by students and teachers and not complicated to understand. Simplicity in the characteristics is seen as a strength. They identify four key characteristics of a well-managed classroom:

1. Students are deeply involved with their work, especially with academic, teacher-led instruction.
2. Students know what is expected of them and are generally successful.
3. There is relatively little wasted time, confusion, or disruption.
4. The climate of the classroom is work-oriented but relaxed and pleasant.

Wong and Wong further note that the well-managed classroom has a positive climate and is physically arranged to facilitate productive work. Students are on task, cooperative, and respectful of one another. All of these dimensions are within the sphere of control of the teacher and should be established early in the school year.

In their analysis of common teacher problems in establishing well-managed classrooms, McCaslin and Good (1998) conclude that students, and the classroom in general, often suffer from inconsistent messages that teachers send students. Teachers frequently manage for obedience while professing to be teaching for exploration and risk taking.

> Educators have created an oxymoron: a curriculum that urges problem solving and critical thinking and a management system that requires compliance and narrow obedience. The management system at least dilutes, if not obstructs, the potential power of the curriculum for many of our students. Students are asked to think and understand, but in too many classrooms they are asked to think noiselessly, without peer communication or social exchange. And the problems they are asked to think about must be solved, neatly, within (at most) forty-five minute intervals. In the problem-solving curriculum, in too many cases, the teacher sets the performance goals, identifies relevant resources, establishes criteria for evaluation, and eventually announces winners and losers. Students generally gain recognition and approval by paying close attention to recommended procedures and by taking few academic risks (e.g., reading and extensively footnoting fifteen secondary sources rather than venturing their own informed opinions). (McCaslin & Good, p. 173, 1998)

The conflict seen in this observation between what teachers say and what they do is obvious. If teachers desire that students develop successful work habits and certain behavioral characteristics, it is necessary for them to have the opportunity to meaningfully think about and explore how they learn and to actively participate in their own learning.

It is clear that the relationship between classroom management and discipline is a close relationship. Teachers are reacting to student behavior problems when they engage in the use of discipline strategies and seeking to prevent them when they develop their systems of management. Wong and Wong (1991) identify the following Principles of Effective Discipline as a framework for both addressing student problems and establishing an environment to prevent their occurrence. The principles themselves reinforce this relationship.

- Treat students with dignity and respect.
- Effective teaching reduces discipline problems.
- Students need a limited say in what happens in the classroom.
- It takes time to develop an effective discipline plan and style.
- Teachers create most of their discipline problems by how they teach and treat people.
- Bored students become discipline problems.
- Lack of self-esteem is the major reason why students act up.
- No one wants or likes to fail; a student would rather be bad than be stupid.

- Anything a teacher can do to make students feel good about themselves will help to minimize discipline problems.
- Students who feel powerless will find ways of expressing their lack of power (e.g., not knowing what has been assigned to them).
- Teachers deny most the students who need to learn responsibility by denying them the experience to have responsibility (e.g., student council, athletics, music).

Koenig (2000) notes that, to be effective, teachers must have their own individual plan for handling management or discipline problems in the classroom. Not having an effective plan will stymie the teacher in reaching the primary goal in teaching, this being to assist his or her students as they advance in the learning process. When management problems emerge, they stand in the way of the teacher being successful in meeting this goal. It is interesting to note that three of the five elements of the plan deal specifically with motivating students. To be effective, a plan for handling student behavior needs to do the following:

1. Be individualized to fit each teacher's teaching style and personality.
2. Prevent misbehaviors and encourage cooperation.
3. Motivate a student to stop disruptive behaviors.
4. Motivate a student to want to learn.
5. Be quick and easy to use.

It is important for teachers to carefully analyze the characteristics of student motivation, classroom management, and discipline as they prepare to be effective teachers and problem solvers in their classrooms. Danforth & Boyle (2000) observe that behavior management ultimately is represented by teachers understanding and appropriately selecting from an array of interventions created to help them influence the behavior of their students and teach them to behave in positive and safe ways. It will be, in the end, the ability to resolve problems (instructional, motivational, and managerial) that determines the measure of the teacher's effectiveness, in particular as successful resolutions to problems inform the teacher's practice, thus reducing the likelihood of similar problems occurring in the future.

THE TEACHER AS A REFLECTIVE PRACTITIONER

Wilen, Ishler, Hutchison, and Kindsvatter (2000) observe that teachers make assumptions about teaching and learning and depend on what they know and believe as they carry out their daily teaching activities. Assumptions tend to be more informal when beliefs are more structured.

Both develop from one's experiences. The more that teachers have learned from their experiences, the better grounded their assumptions and beliefs will be. As professional educators, teachers must make decisions and take action based on the most current information that is available and continually seek to add to their information base. For teaching to be viewed as a profession, teachers must look on their work as knowledge or information based and develop habits of deep, substantive thinking and reflection (Darling-Hammond & Goodwin, 1993). Shavelson (1973) identifies that decision making is the most significant teaching skill. It is difficult to argue, given the challenges of instructing, motivating, and managing children in schooling environments, that this is not the case.

There is no doubt that teaching involves highly complex processes. Effective teachers must be well informed regarding current teaching principles and able to make use of this information to strengthen and advance their practice. As reinforced throughout this book, teachers must be able to make sound decisions on a daily basis, and, in fact, many times each day. These decisions need to be based on the most current information available. Reasoned, reflective decision making is at the heart of good teaching and, when developed, will help ensure the highest possible levels of effective practice (Wilen, Ishler, Hutchison, & Kindsvatter, 2000).

Even if a teacher has a deep understanding of the concepts of motivation and management and plans for each, this will not ensure that students will always be well motivated and the classroom will be well managed. The teacher must know how to make use of this knowledge and use sound decision making skills in applying it. Although teachers need to know how to establish positive learning environments, they also need to be able to make adjustments to these environments when needed, in particular when problems with student behavior arise. A critical element here is the teacher's ability to reflect and be an informed decision maker. Whether an issue is one of motivation, management, or both, it is essential that the teacher has the ability to make sound decisions based on relevant and accurate information so that, when made, these decisions will result in effective classroom instruction, motivated students, and a well-managed environment. If effective instruction is not occurring and if student motivation and management are not as they are desired, the teacher must be able to alter what is taking place in the classroom in some meaningful way so that this will be the end result.

McEwan (2000) notes that a one-size-fits-all approach to management cannot appropriately serve teachers who seek to create calm and safe learning environments in their classrooms and, in so doing, meet the needs of all of their students. Albert (1996) suggests that the key to establishing positive classroom behavior is in determining exactly what students expect from teachers and what teachers expect from students. When students elect to relate to teachers through misbehavior, teachers need to be able to recognize the purpose or the goal of the misbehavior and know how to respond to it immediately and in the long term. Teachers have enormous power in influencing student behavior. Albert (1996) identifies that Cooperative Discipline is one approach to student behavior management that can bring about the type of learning environment that is needed and that both teachers and students desire. Emphasis is placed on cooperation, and through it two important achievements are possible. First, the classroom environment is a safe, orderly, and an inviting place where teachers can teach and students can learn. Second, student self-esteem increases, which is necessary if teachers desire for their students to behave responsibly and achieve academically. Cooperative discipline offers a process for management that is corrective, supportive, and preventive. Regardless of the approach adopted or developed, the key for the teacher when dealing with instances of student misbehavior is in determining the cause of the behavior being exhibited, deciding knowledgeably what to do about it, and then taking appropriate action.

The following case studies adapted from Brubaker, Case, and Reagan (1994) represent first-year teachers who are faced with decisions to make based on problems of student behavior that they have experienced in the classroom.

Seth's Confidence

Seth is a first-year teacher in a first-grade classroom. He completed his student teaching last year in a neighboring school with an experienced teacher near the end of a long, excellent career. Although Seth respected her, he often felt she was rather old-fashioned and knew less about modern techniques than he himself knew. By the end of his student teaching experience, Seth rarely took advice from anyone; he was confident that he knew what there was to know about teaching first-graders. He found, though, that he still had much to learn. On one particular day early in the year, the children were especially disruptive, and in spite of his many efforts, the noise level in the classroom continued to grow. It seemed as though the children were consistently up and doing things that were inappropriate. This type of behavior frustrated Seth, and he began making mistakes as a result. At one point, the students even teased him and laughed at his clumsy errors. After school, he went home and shared his day with his wife, who was sympathetic and soothing. Seth began to feel better about things and even laughed at his own silly mistakes. He felt sure that he would do better the next day and that the children would settle down more as the school year progressed. He felt it would help if he tried to be more humorous while teaching. Seth decided that the best thing for him to do was to take each day as it came, because worrying about it would only be extra stressful on him and take away from his ability to do his best.

Susan's Problem Ownership

Susan also did her student teaching last year, in a ninth-grade setting, where she taught pre-algebra and algebra I. However, this year she was hired in the same school system but was assigned to teach sixth grade in a middle school on the other side of the district. Susan liked the area, so she took the new position thinking that she could soon transfer to another school with more mature students when such a position became open. Susan had had a few difficult days early on, but today was an absolute disaster. Students were talking out of turn and not cooperating as she taught. Soon the conditions in the classroom deteriorated to the point at which some students were actually arguing with one another across the room and in one case a student even showed defiance to Susan. Susan lost control of herself as a result of what she considered her students' petty, childish behavior. She made several threats about after school detention and parent conferences, but, by the day's end, had failed to follow through on any of them. As she drove home, she thought about her unfortunate circumstances during the day. It was obvious that her mentor teacher and her principal were not helping her enough. The parents of her students were, in her opinion, not doing their jobs either. The school district itself had made a mistake, she felt, in even assigning her to a position teaching such immature students. By the time she arrived home, she had begun to feel better. She felt that things would work themselves out and, if they didn't, she would find a position elsewhere next year where the students behaved as they should and really wanted to learn mathematics.

Jenn's Planning and Analysis

Jenn is a first-year art teacher in the same high school where she had completed her student teaching the year before; in fact, she was hired to replace her former cooperating teacher, Ms. Smith, who moved with her family to another state. Ms. Smith and Jenn had become very close, yet Ms. Smith was a very strong individual who made most of the decisions in the classroom unilaterally. Ms. Smith, who had excellent control of her classroom, was almost more like a mother to Jenn than a mentor or team leader. On this particular day, Jenn had set up sixteen workstations in her classroom complete with easels, paint, and other necessary materials. She had arranged the stations neatly, giving each student adequate space to prevent students from interfering with one another while working. Ms. Smith had correctly taught her the importance of having everything prepared before the students' arrival so as not waste valuable instructional time. When the first class began, Jenn was ready to teach; however, some problems arose almost immediately. Tom and Becky had been feuding all week, and Tom came into the classroom and selected the workstation closest to the one where Becky was working. Very soon Tom and Becky were arguing, and everyone was watching them instead of working on their projects. Bill, who liked Becky, walked past Tom's station and bumped into it knocking Tom's supplies on the floor. Two of the other boys in the classroom had to separate Tom and Bill to prevent a fight. Sally, another student, began laughing and making loud remarks. This was too much for Jenn who raised her voice and scolded Sally in front of the entire class. Finally, the bell rang and the students left; Jenn was totally depressed. During her planning session, she got out her lesson plans and made some diagnostic notes, which was one of the techniques that she had learned from Ms. Smith. As she reflected on the class that she had just finished, Jenn realized she had made some mistakes that needed correcting. She listed each mistake she could think of and then wrote beside each error what she could do to correct it in the future. For example, when you know certain students do not get along well together, you should assign their workstations in such a way as to avoid the kind of problem she had had with Tom and Becky. She felt that she needed to have a conference with her first-year mentor, who might have some additional ideas to help her avoid some other problems she noted in terms of motivating her students to stay on task. She wondered if some type of a reward system might help. Finally, she was concerned that she had mishandled the situation with Sally in front of the class. The next day she would make a point of interacting positively with Sally where all other students could see.

• • •

These three case studies provide real-life situations for analysis and represent three different ways that the teachers involved in them chose to approach the problems that they were having with student behavior in their classrooms. Each took a different approach, with only one, Jenn, taking an approach that was systematic in terms of breaking down the events of the day for specific review, acknowledging ownership of the problem and of the responsibility for seeking a solution, and preparing a strategy or plan to follow when the class next met. Seth took a general and less thorough approach to analyzing the problems he encountered by talking to only one other individual (his wife) about them and concluding that he should try to be more humorous in the classroom and not to worry but take each day as it came. A plan for problem resolution was not developed. Susan appeared to feel no responsibility for the problems that had developed and was prepared to return to the classroom the next day without recognizing the need for any specific adjustments in her approach to teaching her students or managing her classroom. She held others responsible for the problems that she was having. Like Seth, she also did not develop a plan for problem resolution nor did she see a need to do so. Jenn was the only one of the three teachers who accepted responsibility for the problems that had occurred, specifically analyzed them, and formulated a plan to deal with them.

The Model for Reflection and Inquiry in Figure 1.1 is offered as a guide for teachers to   systematically analyze both motivation and management problems in the classroom. The teachers identified in the three case studies just presented would find using the model beneficial as a strategy to improve their respective classroom situations. The model can play an important role in helping teachers make decisions concerning the use of initial strategies and plans to motivate students and manage the classroom. It can also be beneficial in analyzing problems related to motivation and management once they have occurred. The model represents a logical problem-solving process for teachers to follow in reflecting on and making decisions in a variety of areas regarding student motivation and classroom management. Although the use of the model will not guarantee motivated students or well-managed classrooms, its use will ensure that the teacher will be approaching issues in these areas in a logical and reasoned way. This, in turn, will enhance the likelihood of a higher level of student motivation and a better managed classroom in the future.

Figure 1.1
Model for Reflection and Inquiry

---

1. Statement of the Problem

The problem is identified and clarified; the problem should be meaningful and manageable.

2. Development of a Hypothesis(es)

A hypothesis or educated guess regarding a solution to the problem is formulated; there may be more than one hypothesis.

3. Collection of Relevant Data

Data or pertinent information relevant to the problem is collected and/ or identified; references or sources of information are considered and reviewed.

4. Analysis of Data

Clarifications are made as to information collected; sources of data are considered and perhaps reconsidered. Relationships should be identified among data collected and data should be clearly organized and analyzed as to how this information relates to the problem.

5. Interpretation and Reporting of Results, Drawing Conclusions and Making Generalizations

Conclusions should be drawn and relevant generalizations made related to the accuracy of the original hypothesis.

Many see solving student behavior problems in the classroom as a process of trial-and-error decision making. If this is the case, and to some degree when dealing with problems associated with human beings it is, this makes the use of a model such as the Model for Reflection and Inquiry even more important. The model can serve to guide the teacher's thinking processes and problem-solving efforts by ensuring the use of more systematic decision making with respect to what problem-solving strategies are used. Over time, a better match between typical problems and effective solutions will develop. This, then, will reduce the "starting from the beginning" approach that many teachers often follow who have not systematically observed and learned from their past efforts. In becoming more knowledgeable with respect to what problem-solving strategies to use in certain situations, the teacher will be able to more quickly and effectively solve problems of student motivation and classroom management when called on to do so. Classrooms will run more smoothly and efficiently. Students will see themselves more positively as learners, and teachers will see themselves as being more effective as teachers. All of this will result in greater attention being given to the instructional program that the teacher has established, and higher levels of student learning taking place.

CLASSROOM PROBLEMS ANALYSIS

Read through the following situations and (1) identify the problem; (2) decide whether the problem identified is primarily one of student management, motivation, or both; and (3) formulate an initial hypothesis that could apply to successful problem resolution.

Jeremy and David are students in the third grade who sit next to each other at the back of the classroom. Day after day both boys seem to continually talk to each other when the teacher is teaching the class. Neither boy becomes involved in small group activities nor in individual seat work when this strategy is used.

Tammy is an eighth grade student who frequently seems uninterested in becoming involved in the activities of the class. During class activities, she typically either stares out the window of the classroom or draws in her notebook. She seldom turns assigned homework in to her teacher and often seems to be far away in her thinking, although she is physically in the classroom.

Clarice is in the eleventh grade for the second year and seems to have all but given up on ever graduating from high school. She rarely brings books or writing utensils to class. When the teacher is trying to teach, she often speaks out loudly to those around her or even directly interrupts the teacher during the lesson. The teacher seldom calls on her for fear of what she might say or how she might say it.

Jamal is a fifth grade student who has been identified as very capable academically. However, he only infrequently answers questions when they are asked in class. When he is returning from lunch, sharpening a pencil, or going back to his seat from the teacher's desk, he often punches students as he walks by them or even marks on their papers or desks. Jamal does not associate with any particular student in the class and keeps to himself most of the time.

Trevor is in the ninth grade and has only been in his present school for a few weeks. When the teacher is conducting the lesson, he often calls out answers to questions without being called on or makes comments about what the teacher has said. When he does this, other students turn to him and make derogatory comments. This, in turn, results in Trevor making derogatory remarks back to them. He seems to have no friends.

Whether classified as representing a motivation or management problem, or both, each of these situations represents problems found frequently in schools today. Each also illustrates the difficulty in identifying situations as being grounded in only student motivation or management issues. The Model for Reflection and Inquiry can help to direct the teacher to more immediate and effective solutions to problems such as these by offering a systematic approach to analyzing each situation. The first step in using the model involves clearly identifying and understanding the nature of the problem. Consider each situation and identify the problem that the teacher is dealing with. Then go to the second step of the model and hypothesize what the teacher might try to do about it. The purpose here is not to "solve" any individual problem but to explore the interplay between motivation and management and accurately identify the problem and a possible approach to its resolution.

In the first situation, Jeremy and David obviously represent a management problem. They are inattentive to the teacher as they continually talk to one another while the teacher is teaching and do not become involved in the teacher's planned activities. It also can be observed that neither boy is motivated by the learning tasks that the teacher has used. Both boys are more motivated by their desire to interact with each other than they are to engage in the activities that the teacher has planned. Recognizing this, the teacher might begin to solve the problem by no longer allowing the boys to be seated next to each other and to begin to work with them individually to get them involved in the classroom activities.

In the second situation, Tammy's behavior appears initially to represent more of a motivation problem than a problem of management. She does not get involved in the activities of the class but does not outwardly cause trouble either. The teacher, however, should not conclude that Tammy's behavior might not also represent a problem of management just because she is not misbehaving. Tammy's situation represents a motivation problem, because she is not engaged in the academic life of the classroom and a management problem for this same reason. It is recommended that the teacher set up a time to personally meet with and "interview" Tammy with respect to what interests her and what she likes to do when not in school. The teacher needs to get to know Tammy better and should also take the time to ask her how she thinks the class is going and what she thinks about the activities that have been used.

In the third situation, Clarice's behavior reflects a management problem for the teacher in that she is verbally loud and not involved in the teacher's instructional activities. Given that she is repeating the eleventh grade for a second time, she also represents a motivational challenge. Perhaps not, but Clarice may have concluded that her graduation from high school is unlikely. If this is the case, the classic strategy used by many teachers to motivate. students, their receiving good grades or moving from grade to grade, may be less effective in this situation. The teacher should be mindful of the views held by William Glasser (1997) and take the time to establish a personal relationship with Clarice. Many students have problems in large part because they feel that no one cares about them personally. The teacher should find out what Clarice hopes to do after she finishes high school. In doing this, the teacher will help Clarice see that she cares about her, but it will also allow the teacher to discover more about Clarice's interests and the problems that she has encountered earlier in her high school career.

In the fourth situation, Jamal's misbehavior is clear but may really reflect that the teacher's primary difficulty is in motivating him. His lack of involvement in, or possibly disinterest in, the activities of the class has led to management problems. Although Jamal is identified as academically able, he has not become involved in the lessons and activities that the teacher has presented, and his behavior has become a management concern because of this. The teacher should recognize that a part of the problem could be that Jamal does not find what goes on in the classroom challenging and/or interesting. The teacher needs to know how Jamal truly sees what is taking place in the classroom in terms of how and what the teacher teaches.

In the final situation, Trevor exhibits the typical management problem of a student who does not feel connected to the classroom or the student group. Given that he is new to the school and has not established any meaningful friendships, he has selected attention-getting behaviors to be recognized.

Trevor has presented management problems for the teacher in that he exhibits inappropriate behaviors in the classroom. The teacher should review the instructional activities that have been used to determine whether it might be possible for cooperative learning or group activities to be implemented if they have not been. Trevor's problems, to some degree, rest on his not having close relationships with any of his classmates. These problems could partly be addressed by the teacher making sure, through the use of certain instructional activities, that he meets and gets to know more students and works with them in a mutually reliant way.

Specific plans can and should be developed to address each of these situations. After clearly identifying the problem(s), the teacher must then formulate an idea or a plan with strategies for problem resolution. Initial ideas (hypotheses) have been made here. As a part of doing this, the teacher needs to learn more about the individual students involved, their interests, their styles of learning, their strengths, what distracts them, what successes they value, etc. With this knowledge and having a clear understanding of the problem, the teacher can then develop a workable plan for each situation so that each student becomes more motivated and connected to the learning experiences in the classroom and feels more successful when involved in them.

Problem solving to improve student motivation and classroom management is difficult and at times uncertain work. Without using a systematic approach to it, however, the success of the teacher in meeting individual student needs will be even more uncertain. The Model for Reflection and Inquiry offers a system for reflecting on, logically analyzing, evaluating, and developing solutions for problems of student motivation and classroom management and, if applied consistently, will result in improved learning conditions for students and improved teaching conditions for teachers.

CONCLUSION

Chapter 1 has stressed that problems of student motivation and management are best considered simultaneously rather than as separate and isolated issues. The chapter provided a number of definitions popularly used for both classroom management and student motivation. The concept of discipline also was introduced and defined as what the teacher is engaged in when efforts at management and motivation have not been successful.

The chapter stressed that teachers need to be well prepared by having a well-thought-out instructional plan, management plan, and motivation plan. Teachers also need to have discipline plans in place and feel comfortable and confident in their use when behavioral problems arise. No pilot would leave an airport without a flight plan nor would a coach enter a contest without a game plan. Likewise, no teacher should enter the classroom without having plans to instruct, motivate, manage, and deal with student problem situations should they occur.

Finally, the chapter emphasized the necessity of the teacher being a logical decision maker or reflective practitioner in addressing problems of student motivation and management. The Model for Reflection and Inquiry was introduced to guide the teacher in the decision-making process. Without a logical approach to making decisions, the teacher will not be able to establish and then maintain a well-managed classroom with motivated students. Nor will the teacher be able to effectively solve problems after they have occurred, or possibly even fully understand how problems were solved after conditions have improved.

QUESTIONS/ACTIVITIES FOR REFLECTION

1. If a student consistently fails to complete homework assignments, how might you address the problem as a management concern as well as a motivation concern? What steps would you take or follow in dealing with the problem?

2. Kounin (1970) found effective teachers to be no better than ineffective teachers when responding to student misbehavior after it had occurred. Analyze Kounin's finding; why do you think that he drew this conclusion? Based on your observations of teachers, do you agree? Explain.

3. In the case study of Seth, it was stressed that Seth was highly confident; but his confidence may actually have been overconfidence and then became a flaw. As far as being a manager and motivator of students is concerned, what are some of the reasons for and ways to show confidence? What are some of the pitfalls associated with being or appearing overconfident?

4. The position is taken that to be an effective manager and motivator a teacher must be a reflective practitioner. How would you describe a reflective practitioner? Describe a classroom situation illustrating how a teacher who is truly a reflective practitioner might handle a behavior problem associated with students calling out in class when the teacher is teaching a lesson.

5. Develop a list of at least five management rules for the classroom along with related consequences for students when the rules are broken. Identify what classroom purpose each rule serves. In your own classroom, how would you proceed to develop your list of management rules?

REFERENCES

Albert, L. (1996). *Cooperative Discipline.* Circle Pines, MN: American Guidance Service, Inc.

Alberto, P., & Troutman, A. (1986). *Applied Behavior Analysis for Teachers.* Columbus, OH: Merrill.

Alderman, M. (1999). *Motivation for Achievement: Possibilities for Teaching and Learning.* Mahwah, NJ: Lawrence Erlbaum Associates, Publishers.

Baron, R. (1992). *Psychology* (2nd ed.). Needham Heights, MA: Allyn & Bacon.

Brophy, J., & Evertson, C. (1976). *Learning from Teaching: A Developmental Perspective.* Boston: Allyn & Bacon.

Brubaker, J., Case, C., & Reagan, T. (1994). *Becoming a Reflective Educator: How To Build a Culture of Inquiry in the Schools.* Thousand Oaks, CA: Corwin Press, Inc.

Charles, C. (1999). *Building Classroom Discipline* (6th ed.). New York: Addison-Wesley Longman, Inc.

Clement, M. (1998, April 8). *Beginning teachers' perceptions of their stress, problems, and planned retention in teaching.* Paper presented at the meeting of the Midwest ATE, Urbana, IL.

Danforth, S., & Boyle, J. (2000). *Cases in Behavior Management.* Columbus, OH: Merrill.

Darling-Hammond, L., & Goodwin, A. (1993). Progress toward professionalism in teaching. In G. Cawelti (Ed.), *Challenges and Achievements in American Education.* Alexandria, VA: Association for Supervision and Curriculum Development.

DiGiulio, R. (2000). *Positive Classroom Management* (2nd ed.). Thousand Oaks, CA: Corwin Press, Inc.

Eggen, P., & Kauchak, D. (2001). *Educational Psychology: Windows on Classrooms* (5th ed.). Upper Saddle River, NJ: Merrill Prentice Hall.

Elam, S., & Rose, L. (1995). The 27th annual Phi Delta Kappa/Gallup poll of the public's attitudes toward the public schools. *Phi Delta Kappan,* 77(1), 41–56.

Elam, S., Rose, L., & Gallup, A. (1996). The 28th annual Phi Delta Kappa/Gallup poll of the public's attitudes toward the public schools. *Phi Delta Kappan,* 78(1), 41–59.

Elliott, S., Kratochwill, T., Cook, J., & Travers, J. (2000). *Educational Psychology: Effective Teaching, Effective Learning* (3rd ed.). New York: The McGraw Hill Companies, Inc.

Evertson, C. (1980, May). Effective classroom management at the beginning of the school year. *Elementary School Journal,* 219–231.

Froyen, L., & Iverson, A. (1999). *Schoolwide and Classroom Management.* Upper Saddle River, NJ: Prentice-Hall, Inc.

Gathercoal, F. (1993). *Judicious Discipline* (3rd ed.). San Francisco: Caddo Gap.

Glasser, W. (1997, April). A new look at school failure and school success. *Phi Delta Kappan,* 596–602.

Harlan, J. (1996). B*ehavior Management Strategies for Teachers.* Springfield, IL: Charles C. Thomas Publisher.

Henson, T., & Eller, B. (1999). *Educational Psychology for Effective Teaching.* New York: Wadsworth Publishing Company.

Jones, F. (1987). *Positive Classroom Discipline.* New York: McGraw-Hill.

Kher-Durlabhji, N., Lacina-Gifford, L., Jackson, L., Guillory, R., & Yandell, S. (1997, March). *Preservice teachers' knowledge of effective classroom management strategies.* Paper presented at the annual meeting of the American Educational Research Association, Chicago.

Koenig, L. (2000). *Smart Discipline for the Classroom: Respect and Cooperation Restored* (3rd ed.). Thousand Oaks, CA: Corwin Press, Inc.

Kounin, J. (1970). *Discipline and Group Management in Classrooms.* New York: Holt, Rinehart & Winston.

Maslow, A. (1970). *Motivation and Personality* (2nd ed.). New York: Harper & Row.

McCaslin, M., & Good, T. (1998, Summer). Moving beyond management as sheer compliance: Helping students to develop goal coordination strategies. *Educational Horizons,* 169–176.

McEwan, B. (2000). *The Art of Classroom Management: Effective Practices for Building Equitable Learning Communities.* Upper Saddle River, NJ: Prentice-Hall, Inc.

Rose, L., & Gallup, A. (1998). The 30th annual Phi Delta Kappa/Gallup poll of the public's attitudes toward the public schools. *Phi Delta Kappan,* 80(1), 41–56.

Rose, L., & Gallup, A. (1999). The 31st annual Phi Delta Kappa/Gallup poll of the public's attitudes toward the public schools. *Phi Delta Kappan,* 81(1), 41–56.

Rose, L., & Gallup, A. (2000). The 32nd annual Phi Delta Kappa/Gallup poll of the public's attitudes toward the public schools. *Phi Delta Kappan,* 82(1), 41–58.

Rose, L., Gallup, A., & Elam, S. (1997). The 29th annual Phi Delta Kappa/Gallup poll of the public's attitudes toward the public schools. *Phi Delta Kappan,* 79(1), 41–56.

Schunk, D. (1990). Introduction to the special section on motivation and efficacy. *Journal of Educational Psychology,* 82, 1–6.

Shavelson, R. (1973). What is the basic teaching skill? *Journal of Teacher Education,* 24, 144–151.

Snowman, J., & Biehler, R. (2000). *Psychology Applied to Teaching* (9th ed.). New York: Houghton Mifflin Company.

Sternberg, R. (1985). *Beyond IQ: A Triarchic Theory of Human Intelligence.* New York: Cambridge University.

Sternberg, R. (1999, Spring). Ability and expertise: It's time to replace the current model of intelligence. *American Educator,* 10–13, 50–51.

Wilen, W., Ishler, M., Hutchison, J., & Kindsvatter, R. (2000). *Dynamics of Effective Teaching* (4th ed.). New York: Addison Wesley Longman, Inc.

Wolfgang, C. (1999). *Solving Discipline Problems* (4th ed.). New York: John Wiley & Sons, Inc.

Wong, H., & Wong, R. (1991). *The First Days of School: How to be an Effective Teacher.* Sunnyvale, CA: Harry K. Wong Publications.

Woolfolk, A. (2001). *Educational Psychology* (8th ed.). Needham Heights, MA: Allyn & Bacon.

Chapter 2

UNDERSTANDING MOTIVATION AND MOTIVATING ENVIRONMENTS

Chapter 1 provided an overview of the concepts of *motivation* and *management* as related to students and classrooms. It was emphasized that motivation and management are closely interrelated in terms of their relationship to the behaviors that students exhibit in the classroom. Definitions were given for both concepts with the following definition being identified for *motivation*:

Motivation: *an internal state that arouses students to action, directs them to certain behaviors, and assists them in maintaining that arousal and action with regard to certain behaviors important and appropriate to the learning environment.*

Three key elements comprise this definition. Motivation is an internal state that:

1. Arouses students to action.
2. Directs them to certain behaviors.
3. Assists them in maintaining that arousal and action.

MOTIVATION

Many teachers who understand the meaning of the term "motivation" are still unable to motivate students or establish truly motivating environments in their classrooms. Knowing is one thing, and doing is another. The definition provided here represents an important foundation for understanding the concept of motivation and a natural starting point from which to develop the ability needed to motivate students in schools and classrooms.

Teachers have at least three important questions to answer when dealing with questions of student motivation. First, "What can I do to arouse my students so that they will be engaged in the learning activities that I have planned and motivated to learn the subject matter that I am teaching?" Second, "What can I do to help my students become focused on and display the learning behaviors that I desire?" Third, "What can I do to assist my students in maintaining their arousal over and action in the learning activities of the classroom?" The Model for Reflection and Inquiry introduced in Chapter 1 can be helpful in finding answers to these questions.

Part of the answer to these important questions lies in the knowledge that teachers have of their students. "What interests do they bring with them to the classroom?" "What issues do they bring with them to school each day?" "What are their lives at their homes like?" "How do they really learn best in terms of their learning styles?" "What are their aspirations?" "What has their past record of academic performance been like?" The list of questions and needed answers reflecting knowledge of students could be lengthy. However, questions such as these must be asked, and answered, if teachers hope to be able to establish high levels of student motivation in their classrooms. Beyond this knowledge of students, it is also critical that teachers have a solid knowledge of motivation itself. "What is it?" "What causes it?" "How can it be established and then maintained?" Students choose to do many different things every day in many different situations and for many different reasons. In exploring the concept of motivation in the context of influencing student behavior in the classroom, it is helpful to break down the concept into its component parts and systematically focus on the *motives* behind the actions that students take. Teachers need to know the reasons underlying their students displaying or not displaying certain behaviors or becoming or not becoming involved in the learning activities of the classroom to be able to motivate them.

Read over the following comments made by students regarding their learning experiences and analyze them against what you already know about the concept of motivation. Continue to think about them as important points of reference as you read further in this chapter.

Joey (fifth grade): "That activity was really fun. I really didn't think that we had spent so much time on it, and it's already time to stop."

Sarah (ninth grade): "I've tried it and tried it and just can't get it. I don't see the point in trying again."

Bailey (seventh grade): "I thought I understood it, but I guess I didn't. I'm really not very good in that area. I don't really like doing this."

Matt (second grade):   "My teacher really spent a lot of time with me today. Maybe she thinks that I can't get it on my own."

Alexis (eleventh grade): "If my friends wouldn't talk so much when I am trying to listen, I would understand things better. I don't know why the teacher can't explain things more clearly."

Effective teachers not only understand what motivation is, they also know how to apply this understanding to motivate students in their classrooms. Serving as a guide to their teaching and their own personal and professional motivation, they also know what effect motivation has on student learning and behavior. Effective teachers recognize how motivation relates to successful learning for their students and how it relates to their own behaviors as individuals charged with the responsibility of guiding this learning. Ormrod (2000) offers six specific effects that motivation has on students in their learning. Understanding these effects can be helpful to teachers in working to establish their own motivating classroom environments.

1. MOTIVATION DIRECTS BEHAVIOR TOWARD PARTICULAR GOALS. It helps to determine the specific goals toward which students will work and that affects the choices that they make.
2. MOTIVATION INCREASES EFFORT AND ENERGY EXPENDED TOWARD THESE GOALS. It helps to determine the extent to which students pursue tasks enthusiastically and wholeheartedly or apathetically and reluctantly.
3. MOTIVATION INCREASES INITIATION OF, AND PERSISTENCE IN, ACTIVITIES. It helps to determine the level at which students will, on their own, initiate and stay involved in activities.
4. MOTIVATION ENHANCES COGNITIVE PROCESSING. It influences what and how information is processed; for example, motivated students are more likely to pay attention, try to understand material, and seek help on a task when they need it.
5. MOTIVATION DETERMINES WHAT CONSEQUENCES ARE REINFORCING. The more motivated students are to achieve in certain areas (e.g., athletics, academics, and social interactions), the more they value the rewards that come from this success.
6. MOTIVATION LEADS TO IMPROVED PERFORMANCE. As a result of the aforementioned effects, motivation generally leads to increased performance; students who are motivated to learn tend to be the highest achievers in the school.

Elliott, Kratochwill, Cook and Travers (2000) identify what some have referred to as myths associated with motivation. For example, some teachers believe that failure is a good motivator. For most students, this definitely is not the case. It is popularly thought that experience can be a valuable teacher and that all students can learn from their mistakes. However, a student who experiences chronic or persistent failure may become trapped in a failure cycle from which he or she cannot escape. Some failure can lead to more failure and more and more failure can lead to helplessness. Feeling that success simply is not possible may, ultimately, be the end result (Seligman, 1975). **Learned helplessness** is *the belief held by students that no amount of effort on their part will produce success and that events and outcomes in their lives are beyond their control* (Weiner, 1992). Chronic failure leads to more failure unless a better pathway to success is found. Success, even in small amounts, is a more potent motivator for most students than failure, especially those with any pattern of failure in their past.

Another view of motivation is that teachers motivate students. It was introduced in Chapter 1 that possibly the best that teachers can do is establish the classroom climate and create the most likely conditions in which motivation will be the end result. Teachers may really just set the stage for motivation to occur by managing the learning environment in such a way as to increase the likelihood of students exhibiting certain behaviors. Only indirectly, in terms of creating the climate and establishing the conditions, might one say that the teacher motivated the students.

A third belief is that threats or coercion increase student motivation. Teachers threaten students with detention, retention, low grades, or calling their parents in anticipation that these actions will "get the students' attention" and that they then will be motivated. Although the use of such strategies from time to time may result in a short-term positive effect or change in behavior with some students, they generally are not productive in the long term. The use of such strategies frequently reveals how little some teachers actually know about their students, what interests them, what they enjoy and do not enjoy, and, basically, what moves them. It also reflects a lack of understanding of important knowledge about student motivation itself. For example, a student who has grown accustomed to receiving low grades typically will not be motivated by the threat of receiving more low grades. Likewise, a student who has often been made to stay after school for detention or has had his or her parents called by the teacher usually will not see the continuation of such actions on the part of the teacher as motivating. This point will be explored in greater detail later in this chapter.

Actions that teachers take or certain behaviors that teachers exhibit that motivate some students will not motivate others. In the language of motivation, some actions will have *potency* for some students and not for others. **Potency** is *the strength or the power of a reinforcer, reward, praise, or even criticism* *to change behavior.* The most effective teachers are those who have learned what works and with whom and who have a knowledge of each student's past history of success and failure.

INTRINSIC AND EXTRINSIC MOTIVATION

In the perfect world, students are eagerly involved in all of the activities planned by the teacher simply because they find enjoyment in learning. Observation verifies that there is no perfect world. And yet, some students do seem to enjoy learning very much and want to experience more and more of it. Others only seem to do what the teacher asks them to do after considering what they will receive if they complete the task or what will happen to them if they do not. These two different observations of learner motivation are often described as representing the concepts of *extrinsic* versus *intrinsic* motivation. **Intrinsic motivation** is *motivation to become involved in an activity for its own sake.* **Extrinsic motivation** is *motivation to become involved in an activity as a means to an end.* Intrinsically motivated students become active in their learning just because they see the task as important and/or enjoyable. Intrinsically motivated students do not engage in learning activities for concrete rewards or incentives but because they find the activities themselves or the learning that comes from them rewarding and pleasurable. Extrinsically motivated students, on the other hand, become active in their learning because they understand that they will receive something of value in return if they do what the teacher desires or something that they dislike if they do not. They represent a large part of the student population who wants to know "what's in it for me" when deciding whether to be involved in or not be involved in or complete or not complete a learning task. This "what's in it for me" outlook toward life seems to represent a large part of the societal population as well. Brophy (1983) observes that many activities or tasks that characterize school environments today are not intrinsically motivating to students. Many students do not find them naturally enjoyable, personally rewarding, or even see the point in them. As a response to this, many teachers approach their challenges of student motivation by relying on extrinsic incentives such as praise, tokens, and special recognitions (e.g., Student of the Month) to get students to do what they want them to do (Alderman, 1999). Students, in many cases, become accustomed to this reward-giving approach to learning and conditioned to receive rewards as a natural part of the schooling process. They make the association that completing schoolwork on their part produces the giving of rewards on the part of their teachers. Once this cycle begins, and students, in effect, learn to anticipate some type of reward for the completion of their assignments, it becomes a difficult pattern of behavior to break.

Brophy (1998) suggests that it is unrealistic for a teacher to expect to routinely produce what might be considered ideal motivation in the classroom in each and every lesson taught. Intrinsic motivation does exist, but teachers cannot count on students being intrinsically motivated on every task that they present before them. Working to produce a state of *motivation to learn* is a more realistic and reachable goal. Motivation to learn differs from extrinsic or reinforcement-oriented motivation and intrinsic or pleasure-oriented motivation. **Motivation to learn** is *motivation represented by the quality of a student's cognitive engagement in a learning task or activity.* It is seen as a realistic goal for teachers to develop and then sustain their students' motivation to learn from academic activities. This will be based, in part, on their tendency to find the academic activities meaningful and worthwhile, along with their ability to be successful with them and to value the benefits derived from them.

A fundamental question for teachers to ask in studying student motivation in the classroom is, "What will arouse students to action, direct them to engage in or exhibit certain behaviors, and assist them in maintaining this arousal and direction?"

Motivational theories that address this question can be categorized much like theories of learning: *behaviorist, cognitive, or humanist* (Lefrancois, 2000). An understanding of these theories of motivation is beneficial in exploring this question. Figure 2.1 provides an overview of how motivation is defined in each theory.

Figure 2.1
Synopsis of Theories of Motivation

Definition of Motivation

Theory

Behaviorism:	Motivation is the result of responses to reinforcement. The effective use of reinforcers, either present internally within the student or externally as influenced by the teacher, is critical to behavioral approaches to motivation.
Cognitive Theories:	Motivation results from students attempting to find order or balance, predictability, and an understanding of the world. Students have a natural motivation to understand their world and bring into balance irregularities that they may experience. These are needs that students have, and they are motivated to satisfy them.
Humanism:	Motivation results from students attempting to fulfill their full potential as human beings. Individuals have an innate tendency to develop their talents and to grow and enhance themselves. There is no such thing as an unmotivated learner.

BEHAVIORISM AND MOTIVATION

The behaviorist theory of learning emphasizes observable behavior changes that take place as a result of experience. Behaviorism does not focus on what necessarily may have changed in the learner's mind, but on that which may be seen. This view of learning, especially as it relates to motivation, raises a number of interesting and debatable points.

Behaviorism is popularly associated with the giving of reinforcement or the use of reinforcers. A **reinforcer** is *something given or a consequence that adds to the frequency or influences the length of a behavior.* An important question to be answered in the behaviorist theory of motivation would be, "What are the best reinforcers, and when should they be used?" The answer to this question is actually very complex and not without some controversy and criticism (Harter & Jackson, 1992; Kohn, 1992). In spite of this controversy and criticism, the giving of reinforcers, (e.g., popcorn, soft drinks, watching favorite videos, free time, teacher praise, grades, class positions, and responsibilities) is common in schools today, especially in elementary classrooms. The use of reinforcers has not been found to be as effective for middle or high school students and underachieving students in general. Some reinforcers, as suggested earlier, are more potent or have greater impact than others. What may have potency for one student in one situation may not have such potency for another in even a similar or comparable situation. A reinforcer that may be potent for a student at one point may be less potent or not potent at all at a later point. This could be brought about by inappropriate or overuse of the reinforcer. Eggen and Kauchak (2001) report four criticisms of the use of reinforcers.

1. THE USE OF REINFORCERS MAY DECREASE INTRINSIC MOTIVATION. Offering reinforcers for engaging in intrinsically motivating tasks can decrease student interest in such tasks. The problem with reinforcers can involve how a behavior is rewarded. Rewarding students for simply completing tasks rather than for making progress in learning may ultimately detract from motivation.

2. THE USE OF REINFORCERS CAN NARROW THE STUDENT'S FOCUS. Reinforcers themselves can become the goals of learning rather than the beauty of or interest in learning itself. As opposed to adding to the breadth of the learning experience, reinforcers can have the impact of narrowing that experience. The reinforcer can become the reason for the student's motivation to learn, just so the reward can be received. In such a case, the student would be learning for the reward, not because of it.

3. THE USE OF REINFORCERS OFTEN CREATES LOGISTICAL PROBLEMS. Using reinforcers demands time, energy, and sometimes even money; in addition,

rewards given to some students may cause resentment in other students who do not receive them. This can bring about an inconsistent use of rewards by the teacher, with the end result actually being a lower level of student motivation.

4. THE USE OF REWARDS IGNORES STUDENT COGNITIONS. The use of behaviorism as an approach to motivate students is often criticized from the view that it focuses on the application of reinforcers (rewards) and ignores learners' perceptions and beliefs about themselves and about learning. As an example, praise is a common reinforcer, and its use seems easily understood. This is far from the case because the use of praise can be misunderstood. Older students may see praise as reward for effort as opposed to an accomplishment. Such students may interpret praise for performance on easy tasks as a statement that the teacher sees them as having low ability. Although intended as a reinforcer, the praise really may be perceived negatively.

Finally, behaviorist approaches to motivation tend to emphasize extrinsic reinforcers (e.g., reward and praise). These reinforcers may be seen as being either primary or secondary in nature, and both can be used to strengthen or influence behavior. Examples of **primary reinforcers** are *food, water, and safety that meet basic physiological needs.* Examples of **secondary reinforcers** are *praise, grades, and money that may address a student's psychological needs.* The behaviorist theory of motivation rests on the belief that students are motivated through the desire to receive something for their actions. Interestingly enough, this can include love of learning (Henson & Eller, 1999).

COGNITIVE THEORIES OF MOTIVATION

Cognitive theories of motivation are grounded in the belief that individual behavior is influenced by the way people see themselves and their environment (Snowman & Biehler, 2000). Students have a need for order and predictability and an understanding of things around them. When order and understanding are present, they seek to maintain it. When order and understanding are lost, they seek to regain it. Order and understanding represent an important balance for students and, therefore, predictability. Greeno, Collins and Resnick (1996) posit that children are naturally motivated to learn when they encounter experiences that are inconsistent with their current understandings. They seek to establish or perhaps reestablish this consistency when it is absent. They also are naturally motivated to learn when they encounter information that is not yet found in their already-held definitions and ideas of the world. When this type of situation occurs, they seek to acquire an understanding of this information and incorporate it into their individual ways of seeing the world.

The work of Piaget (1952) is applicable to this discussion of motivation and a student's need for order and understanding. Although well known in the study of learning processes, Piaget's concept of equilibrium is important here in that it represents a need that all individuals possess. **Equilibrium** is defined as *a state of balance.* When students experience **disequilibrium**, or *a state of being out of balance*, they seek to regain their balance. *The process of searching for order or balance and, in so doing, testing one's understanding against the real world* is referred to as **equilibration**. Certain amounts of disequilibrium are actually believed to be desirable, and teachers can carefully create them and use them to their teaching advantage to motivate their students. As students encounter out-of-balance situations, they are motivated to regain their balance, and they grow in their learning through this process as they strive to reestablish a state of equilibrium. Extreme disequilibrium, however, can be counterproductive, creating too much frustration and anxiety. When learning activities or teacher actions create out-of-balance situations that are too severe, students may perceive that no amount of effort on their part can bring about a return to balance. Success cannot be achieved. A result of this perception may be the student pulling away from or displaying misconduct toward the learning task, the teacher, or both.

Self-Efficacy

Most teachers have seen students who appear quite motivated and those who seem virtually impossible to motivate. A close observation of these two types of students reveals many things. One thing that it could show is how drastically different the two types of students may really view themselves. Cognitive theories of motivation consider beliefs and expectations as two important personal factors. Atkinson (1964) and Feather (1982) discuss the role of expectations in the *expectation X value theory* of motivation. The **expectation X value theory** is *the theory of motivation that suggests that students are motivated to engage in learning tasks to the extent that they expect to succeed on the tasks and the degree to which they value achievement on the tasks or other potential outcomes that may come as a result of task achievement.* The challenge to the teacher here is twofold. The teacher must create legitimate learning experiences in which students can find success, and the success that they achieve must be on activities that they see as being of value. If students do not necessarily see the task as being of value, it is important that they see value in other outcomes that are associated with successful task attainment. The expectation X value theory of motivation creates a new way of looking at motivation for some teachers in that many believe that student success is the key factor in motivation. In the expectation X value theory, success is nec-

essary but not sufficient in establishing motivation in students. Success coupled with seeing the value in what is attained or at least in some other outcome that will be forthcoming are key to student motivation. Being successful at a task that holds little value will have limited positive motivational
impact, at least in the long run.

Schunk (1994) notes that when students are successful on tasks that they
value they develop higher *self-efficacy*. **Self-efficacy** is *one's beliefs about the
capability of succeeding on specific tasks*. Students who have high self-efficacy
believe in their abilities and see themselves as capable of making genuine
progress toward worthwhile goals. Such students are able to sustain their
work effort longer, because they anticipate that they will be successful at the
end of the task. Students who have low self-efficacy see themselves as having limited ability and as likely not being successful when engaging in learning activities. Students with high self-efficacy try hard while holding on to
the belief that they can succeed; students with low self-efficacy hardly try.
Figure 2.2 provides an analysis of some of the characteristics of students with
high and low self-efficacy.

Figure 2.2
Analysis of Students With High and Low Self-Efficacy

	High Self-efficacy	Low Self-efficacy
Task Orientation	Accepts challenging tasks.	Avoids challenging tasks.
Effort	Expends high effort when faced with challenging tasks.	Expends low effort when faced with challenging tasks.
Persistence	Persists when goals are not initially reached.	Gives up when goals are not initially reached.
Beliefs	Believes they will succeed.	Focuses on feelings of incompetence.
	Controls stress and anxiety when goals are not met.	Experiences anxiety and depression when goals are not met.
	Believes they are in control of their environment.	Believes they are not in control of their environment.
Strategy use	Discards unproductive strategies.	Continues the use of unproductive strategies.
Performance	Performs better than low-efficacy students of equal ability.	Performs more poorly than high-efficacy students of equal ability.

Adapted from Bandura (1993); Schunk (1994); Eggen and Kauchak (2001).

An understanding of self-efficacy is important to an understanding of the potential for the motivation of any student. It is also important to an understanding of the motivational state that a student might be in as related to any given learning task. Although having an understanding of self-efficacy is important, being able to recognize a particular student's level of self-efficacy is more important. What is of even greater value is being able to influence students with low self-efficacy to increase their self-efficacy and to influence students with high self-efficacy to either maintain or even increase their self-efficacy. The teacher's role, therefore, is twofold. First, the teacher must diagnose or otherwise gain an understanding of his or her students as to their levels of self-efficacy. Second, the teacher must take appropriate action with this knowledge in hand to motivate his or her students in their learning and, in so doing, increase their levels of self-efficacy. Bandura (1986) recognizes four factors that influence students' beliefs about their ability to perform.

1. **Past performance:** how a student has done in the past on a particular task influences how he or she will do on a similar task in the future.
2. **Modeling:** being able to see someone else perform a particular task successfully influences the observer to do the same.
3. **Verbal persuasion:** verbal encouragement offers a tangible way for the teacher to communicate to the student the belief that he or she can be successful.
4. **Psychological state:** the teacher must be able to recognize and, if possible, positively influence the student's psychological state; a student who is anxious, tired, fearful, or hungry will experience a lowered level of self-efficacy.

HUMANISTIC VIEWS OF MOTIVATION

Like cognitive theories, the intrinsic motivation of students is also important to humanistic views of motivation. Humanists see motivation as an attempt to fulfill the total potential of a human being (Hamachek, 1987). The humanistic theory of motivation represents a reaction against the belief that reduces human behavior to either a response to the environment or to internal instincts. Contrarily, the humanist view of motivation looks at the entire physical, emotional, interpersonal, and intellectual qualities of an individual as they impact on what that person chooses to do. According to the humanist, there is no such thing as an unmotivated student. All students are motivated. It is possible, however, that some students could be motivated to do things other than that which the teacher desires for them to do.

The now-classic Hierarchy of Needs theory of Abraham Maslow (1970), called the father of the humanistic movement, is frequently referenced when exploring the question of student motivation as influenced by need. Maslow identified student needs as being in one of two categories: *deficiency needs* and *growth needs*. **Deficiency needs** are *needs at the lower levels of the hierarchy including survival, safety, belonging, and self-esteem.* They are needs that must be fulfilled or met for the student to move to the upper or higher levels. **Growth needs** are *needs at the higher levels of the hierarchy including intellectual achievement, aesthetic appreciation, and self-actualization.* These needs are never fully satisfied. Growth needs expand and evolve as individuals have experience with them. Efforts to satisfy growth needs only lead to further development within them. Individuals who are intellectually stimulated, for example, will seek additional intellectual stimulation. Individuals who engage in the pursuit of beauty, through art, music, etc., will seek to continue in this pursuit. Maslow's highest level of the hierarchy is identified as self-actualization. **Self-actualization** is explained as *the full development or use of one's potential.* Achieving self-actualization represents an ongoing evolution and is never fully reached.

Applications of Maslow's hierarchy to the work of the classroom teacher are obvious. Students who are hungry and tired will not learn and develop to their fullest potentials as long as these conditions are present. Students who do not feel safe and accepted in the learning environment will not be able to reach their fullest potentials in their learning until they feel safe and accepted. Students who have low self-esteem will not move forward at an optimum rate in terms of either their intellectual achievement or their full understanding of themselves until their self-esteem is strengthened. Figure 2.3 offers a representation of Maslow's hierarchy.

Figure 2.3
Maslow's Hierarchy of Needs

GROWTH NEEDS

Self-Actualization: meets and uses one's full potential

Aesthetic: goodness, beauty, truth, justice, order

Intellectual (cognitive) achievement: knowledge, understanding, symmetry

DEFICIENCY NEEDS

Self-esteem: recognition, respect, approval, feeling of adequacy

Belongingness and Love: affection, acceptance from family and peers

Safety: security, absence of physical and emotional threat, psychological safety

Physiological: food, sleep, drink, shelter, warmth

FACTORS THAT AFFECT STUDENT MOTIVATION

Having a sound theoretical base in understanding the concept of motivation is critical for teachers to be able to motivate students in classroom learning environments. Additional considerations also are important. Factors such as *attribution, locus of control, goals (performance and learning), teacher expectations, anxiety, and environment* all affect the teacher's ultimate understanding of, and ability to establish, high levels of student motivation.

Attribution

Attribution is a *cognitive theory that represents a student's view of the causes of outcomes or an event and how this view influences his or her future expectations and behaviors* (Alderman, 1999). In looking at why he or she was or was not successful, the student may pose the question, "To what may I attribute my success or failure?" The answer that the student gives to this question has significant bearing on how the student approaches, or actually may choose to not approach, a learning task. Heider (1958) suggests that there are two primary reasons that people use to explain their performance: *can* and *try*. **Can** speaks to whether a person has the ability to do a task, and **try** speaks to how much effort a person puts forth. If a student fails at a task, the student's expectations for future success will differ depending on whether the student attributes the failure to a lack of effort (**try**) or to not having the ability (**can**) to succeed on the task.

Weiner (1990, 1992, 1994a, 1994b) reports that one of four reasons are generally given by students as the cause of success or failure in school settings:

Ability: the student might say, "I was successful because I am just good at that," or the student might say, "I was not successful because I just don't have enough ability to be successful."

Effort: the student might say, "I was successful because I really tried hard," or the student might say, "I know that I could have been successful if I had tried harder and put more time in it."

Task Difficulty: the student might say, "I was successful because the assignment was really easy," or the student might say, "I was not successful because what the teacher wanted was just too hard."

Luck: the student might say, "I don't know why I was successful. It must have just been my good luck," or the student might say, "I don't know why I couldn't get it right. It just must not have been my lucky day."

Ability and effort have been found to be the most frequent reasons given by students for their success or failure in schooling settings.

The causes of success or failure have also been classified into three different dimensions:

1. Internal versus external.
2. Stable versus unstable.
3. Controllable versus uncontrollable.

The internal versus external and controllable versus uncontrollable dimensions are especially important to teachers as they explore ways to motivate their students. Teachers need to be able to identify how students see themselves and how they perceive the reasons for their success or lack of success. Knowing this will enable teachers to address their learning needs more completely and, in so doing, better motivate them.

Although many teachers might not realize it, most students, at least to themselves, frequently do think about or try to understand and explain the reasons for their failures. When students who are usually successful are unsuccessful, they typically identify internal and controllable reasons (attributions) for their lack of success. Such students may claim that they did not study hard enough or did not understand a particular assignment and had not prepared correctly for what was expected of them. When students who are normally successful are not successful, they generally attribute the reason for their lack of success to controllable causes and believe that they will be successful the next time they attempt the task. Students who perceive themselves as having sufficient ability and being in control of the situation usually do not pose major motivational problems for teachers.

Students with a history of repeated failure and who attribute their learning difficulties or lack of success on learning tasks to uncontrollable, external forces often represent the teacher's greatest motivational challenge. These students usually attribute their failure to conditions out of their control. They tend to perceive themselves as helpless, are often depressed and/or anxious about their learning, and doubtful of their abilities. They characterize themselves overall as more unsuccessful than successful and concentrate more on their own inadequacies. Lack of future effort is a common reaction to failure for such students, because they believe that their situation is not likely to change. They also are less likely to seek help, because they do not believe that they can be helped (Ames & Lau, 1982). When students attribute the learning outcomes that they are experiencing to controllable causes, their motivation to learn remains encouraged regardless of whether they have histories of failure or success. When they attribute the outcomes or results to uncontrollable ones, their motivation to learn tends to lessen (Woolfolk, 2001). Students of this latter type often see themselves as inadequate in learning situations and can represent major motivational problems for teachers.

Locus of Control

Locus of control refers to *the degree to which students perceive that both positive and negative events that impact their lives are under their control* (Bernhard & Siegel, 1994). Locus of control is an important aspect of the attribution theory described earlier. Some students have more of an **internal locus of control,** which is indicated *when students feel that they are responsible for what happens to them.* Others have more of an **external locus of control,** which is indicated *when students feel that forces external to or outside themselves control their lives.* Students who hold the view that success comes as a result of skill and not luck or chance believe that they have control over their own destinies. Students who hold the view that success comes as a result of luck or chance and not skill assume that they have little control over their own destinies. How students see themselves, as successful or unsuccessful learners, has bearing on whether they, in fact, will be successful or unsuccessful. Knowing how students see themselves will help their teachers be more successful in motivating them to higher levels.

A great deal of research has been done on the concept of locus of control, in particular as it affects students and their learning as well as teachers' attitudes toward students. Some of the findings in this area are relevant to the work that teachers do in motivating their students and are included in Figure 2.4.

Figure 2.4
Locus of Control and Motivation

1. Teachers often look on students who have an external locus of control more negatively than those who have an internal locus of control; interestingly, students who have an external locus of control frequently look on their teachers more negatively than do students who have an internal locus of control.

2. Students who have an external locus of control perform better when they receive specific comments with respect to their teachers' expectations.

3. Students with an internal locus of control are more effective than those with an external locus of control in recognizing and using available information.

4. Students with an external locus of control are less successful in competitive situations than are students with an internal locus of control.

A student's view regarding what causes him or her to be successful or not successful influences the student's motivation in different situations. If students believe that they are responsible for their own successes, they are referred to as *internals.* If they believe that something or somebody other than themselves is responsible, they are referred to as *externals*. External students often have higher levels of anxiety than internal students, because they see themselves as having less power over their surroundings (in this case their classroom and their learning) and what happens to them. Internal students generally have more confidence in themselves, are greater risk takers, are more curious, and anticipate success rather than failure when they enter into learning activities.

Locus of control, however, can change. As teachers assist students in gaining greater levels of confidence with respect to their abilities and potentials, their sense of having more internal control increases. Their anxiety in learning decreases, and their performance increases. Wigfield (1994) reports that as students become older and more mature and as they experience more successes in their learning, their beliefs about the causes of these successes becomes more internal. Teachers can enhance this change through the appropriate use of learning activities (e.g., active learning and cooperative learning are much preferred over passive learning and individual and isolated learning), rewards, and approaches to instruction that ensure that students are able to achieve higher levels of success.

Goals–Performance and Learning

One might wonder how the teacher's goals or desired outcomes can have a specific impact on a student's motivation. What teachers establish as their desired instructional outcomes or goals for students, in fact, does have the potential to have a tremendous effect on a student's level of motivation. Teachers communicate in many ways what they value and what they want their students to value. One way they do this is in their selection of the goals that they would like for their students to attain. A **goal** is identified as *that which an individual is striving to achieve or accomplish* (Locke & Latham, 1990). Teachers should remember that they frequently identify goals for their students that their students do not identify for themselves. In terms of best instructional practice and best student motivation in the classroom, teachers' goals are of limited value when students are not striving to achieve or accomplish them. How can a teacher create higher levels of student motivation so that the students will strive to achieve their goals? The answer to this question, at least in part, lies in the kinds of goals that teachers select for their classrooms. This is especially true to the degree that students accept these goals as their own and see them as being achievable and important.

Goals are often divided into two categories or types: *performance goals* and *learning or mastery goals*. **Performance goals** are *goals that emphasize the demonstration of high ability and the avoidance of failure*. **Learning goals** or

mastery goals are *goals that emphasize the challenge of learning and the mastery of a task.* Woolfolk (2001) notes that the point of a learning goal for the student is to improve and learn, no matter how many mistakes may be made. In performance goals, the focus for the student is on looking smart or informed and displaying accomplishments without failure. The teacher's primary responsibility is to get students to learn, not perform.

Goals that are specific, seen by students as being of at least moderate difficulty and that can be attained in a reasonable period of time, and as having value, tend to enhance student motivation and persistence (Stipek, 1996). Specific goals provide greater clarity as to the teacher's expectations and standards for evaluating student performance. This quality, coupled with reasonableness of difficulty and time involved, contributes to increased levels of student motivation (Pintrich & Schunk, 1996). With respect to self-efficacy, students' beliefs about their abilities to be successful also have impact on their engaging or not engaging in learning tasks and their levels of persistence to stay with them once engaged. Because learning goals focus on mastery of information without great concern for or overemphasis on mistakes, they contribute to increased levels of student motivation. Performance goals, in which the focus is on performing, looking good, and not being seen as failing, contribute more to decreased levels of motivation. The learner or learning-focused classroom presented in Chapter 1, as opposed to the performer or performance-focused classroom, is recommended for its positive relationship to student motivation as related to goals established.

Teacher Expectations

At times, students may not be certain as to what teachers expect of them in the completion of particular learning tasks. They frequently do understand, or at least think they understand, however, what their teachers' expectations are of them in terms of their ability to be successful in completing these tasks. Two important concepts here are *teacher expectation* and *teacher efficacy.* **Teacher expectation** refers to *what teachers expect or think students will be able to accomplish.* **Teacher efficacy** refers to *the teacher's belief in his or her ability to be successful in getting students to learn.* Both concepts are closely related to each other. When teachers have high expectations for their students' learning potentials, they have a greater belief that they will be able to be successful with them. When they have low expectations of their students' abilities, they have greater doubt (lower teacher efficacy) that they can be successful with them. Students themselves have their own views of how their teachers see them as being successful or not successful. This student view has an important relationship to the level of motivation that the student exhibits.

Ormrod (2000) identifies that teacher expectations (1) influence how teachers treat students, (2) tend to perpetuate themselves, and (3) affect student's self-concepts. Teachers tend to treat students in ways consistent with the expectations that they hold for them. This point can become a serious concern when teachers predict or hold the view that certain students are destined to have problems or even fail to learn altogether. When teachers expect students to achieve at higher levels, they typically do. Conversely, when they expect them to not achieve at higher levels, they typically do not (Rosenthal & Jacobson, 1968). This has been referred to as the **self-fulfilling prophecy** or the *phenomenon that a student's performance is greatly influenced when a teacher holds certain beliefs about the student's ability to perform.* When teachers anticipate or prophesy a higher level of student performance, they will generally receive it. When they predict a lower level of student performance, this is also what is usually found. As a correlate to this, a student's motivation responds to what the student perceives as being the prophecy held by the teacher. A student's behavior also responds to what the student perceives as being the belief held by the teacher.

The relationship between expectation and performance is now a part of the supporting argument on a national scale that teachers should have higher expectations for their students. When teachers expect more, they generally will receive more. Teachers, like the population as a whole, are likely to maintain their expectations about their students once they are developed. This can be positive or negative for the student, depending on how he or she is viewed by the teacher. Positive views more normally result in higher levels of performance; negative views more normally result in lower levels of performance. For example, many teachers underestimate the capabilities of students from minority and low-income backgrounds and maintain these expectations (Garcia, 1994; Knapp & Woolverton, 1995). This expectation can be devastating in terms of the impact on the achievement levels of such students. Again, when teachers expect less, they get less. A key part of this dynamic that also must be acknowledged is how students view themselves as influenced by how they perceive their teachers view them. If students identify that their teachers see them as capable of only low achievement, they will often perceive themselves of being only capable of low achievement. Their individual self-concepts will respond in a like manner. In the end, the level of motivation of such students is frequently low, because it has been negatively influenced by what their teachers believe about and expect of them. On the other hand, if students feel as though their teachers have confidence in them as learners and that they can succeed on the learning tasks that are assigned, this influences the students to be better motivated, which, in turn, has a positive influence on their achievement. Good and Brophy (2000) outline a six-step process in describing the effect of the self-fulfilling prophecy.

1. Early in the year, the teacher forms differential expectations for student behavior and achievement.
2. Consistent with these differential expectations, the teacher behaves differently toward different students.
3. This treatment tells students something about how they are expected to behave in the classroom and perform on academic tasks.
4. If the teacher's treatment is consistent over time, and if students do not actively resist or change it, it will likely affect their self-concepts, achievement, motivation, levels of aspiration, classroom conduct, and interactions with the teacher.
5. These effects generally will complement and reinforce the teacher's expectations, so that students will come to conform to these expectations more than they might have otherwise.
6. Ultimately, this will affect student achievement and other outcome measures. High-expectation students will be led to achieve at or near their potential, but low-expectation students will not gain as much as they could have gained if taught differently.

Each child is different. Although all teachers know this, they often overlook the differences and focus on the similarities that exist among young people. Young people may share a common blood type or ethnic background, speak a common language or share a particular religious upbringing. Despite these similarities, each human being is different. At times, both teachers and students in schools feel isolated. With so many children being at risk, and sometimes not only because of socioeconomic circumstances, perhaps the entire culture is at risk as well. For students and parents not socialized in the ways of education, it is easy not to realize that something is amiss. The raw power of education is so strong that many children and their families often feel left out (Strother, 1991). These feelings manifest themselves in a number of different ways. Some students are silent and sullen, some make lots of noise, some become the class clown, some turn to violence, some get high on drugs, and some are just absent a lot. All of these are ways that they use to defend themselves against the feeling of not belonging. Sadly, they are also all ways of failing.

Teacher efficacy, the belief held by the teacher as to his or her capability of being successful with students, has a powerful influence on student motivation. When teachers believe students are capable of only low levels of performance, this has already influenced the way they approach their teaching with them. Students who are believed to be more capable are challenged more, taught with greater energy, involved in more dynamic lessons and activities, and receive a richer set of learning experiences than those who are not seen in this way.

Anxiety

Who reading these pages has never had an anxious moment or felt worry or concern? Lefrancois (2000) defines **anxiety** as *a feeling of apprehension, worry, tension, or nervousness.* Hansen (1977) identifies **anxiety** as *a general uneasiness with a sense of foreboding and feeling of tension.* Although some may believe that being anxious from time to time is not such a bad thing, research on the effects of anxiety on student achievement has consistently identified a negative correlation between anxiety and school achievement (Covington & Omelich, 1987). Anxiety can be a reason for a student to lose focus, become irritable or act out, withdraw, not try, or even be physically ill. Anxiety can be a reason for students to perform poorly in school, with their resulting poor performance only serving to increase their anxiety.

The concept of equilibrium was introduced earlier in this chapter with reference to the human desire to achieve balance in life. If they are not too extreme, out-of-balance situations, or situations of disequilibrium, can represent situations that motivate students to do things in an effort to get back into balance. Some situations of anxiety, however, can be so great that students are not able to discover the balance that they need. Anxiety in a small amount (i.e., a situation of mild disequilibrium) can help to improve performance by motivating students to positive action. This is referred to as **facilitating anxiety** or *anxiety in such a small amount that it actually helps to improve performance.* Too much anxiety, however, can have the opposite effect of being not motivational and interfering with student performance in a way that diminishes the performance. This anxiety is referred to as **debilitating anxiety** or *anxiety so extreme that it gets in the way of successful performance.*

This point reinforces the importance of teachers understanding their students and their various learning and personal needs and characteristics. What may seem to create an anxious moment for one student may not for another. Something that would seem to not be anxiety producing to an internalizing student with a history of success might be quite debilitating to another who has a history of failure. Students frequently become anxious before taking a test that they perceive as being difficult. Most people get nervous when they have to give a prepared speech in front of others. This condition is referred to as **state anxiety** or *temporary feelings of anxiety brought about by certain situations.* For students, such anxiety is typically the result of a sense of fear, concern, or threat, especially when they feel that their performance will not be seen as positive (Deci & Ryan, 1992). Some students, though, appear to be anxious even where there is no particular cause or state to link their anxiety to, such as in working on less complex assignments or assignments that do not appear as though they should bring about any reason for fear of failure. **Trait anxiety** is the term used *when students are anxious in circumstances that should not be seen as threatening.* Students characterized by trait anxiety by far are the more difficult for teachers to motivate.

Ormrod (2000) identifies seven common circumstances under which students may experience anxiety, even debilitating anxiety (Figure 2.5). Being aware of and having the opportunity to prepare for these circumstances represents a chance for the teacher to be proactive in working to decrease student anxiety and therefore increase student motivation in the classroom.

Figure 2.5
Sources of Anxiety in Students

Type	Definition
Physical Appearance:	Students are often concerned about their appearance. They might see themselves as too thin, too heavy, too tall, or too short. Teachers must not take these concerns lightly, because they can have significant impact on some students and their motivation and performance.
New Situations:	Students frequently experience uneasiness when encountering new situations and individuals such as schools, classes, teachers, and peers.
Judgment/Evaluation by Others:	Most students experience worry over being judged by others. This includes being evaluated by teachers on assignments and activities, as well as being accepted by classmates and friends.
Tests:	Test anxiety is often not taken seriously enough by teachers. Comments such as "Just relax," "Don't worry," or "You will get it if you study harder next time," generally have little positive impact on students who are truly anxious or experiencing debilitating anxiety in testing situations.
Excessive Classroom Demands:	What may not seem excessive to teachers may seem extremely excessive to students, especially students with high levels of anxiety. Students normally feel anxious when confronted with expectations that they feel are beyond their ability to respond to successfully.
The future:	Although some current research suggests that young people have more positive than negative outlooks for the future, this does not mean all young people. Concerns over the future, especially for students at the middle and secondary level, can be significant and effect their motivation in the classroom.

| Situations Where Self is Threatened: | Fear of failure anywhere can be powerful and debilitating. Fear of failure in public can be especially so. Many students experience levels of anxiety that are virtually paralyzing in terms of affecting their motivation and performance when the concern includes a dimension of public criticism. |

Presented by Ormrod (2000).

High anxiety brought about by intense motivational situations can have a significant negative effect on student performance. Moderate motivation is a more desirable condition for increasing student success on learning complex tasks. Ideal motivation decreases in intensity with increasing task difficulty. As tasks become more challenging and complex, the level of student motivation, likely also driven by the student's level of confidence to be successful, tends to diminish. Increasing intensity improves performance but only to a certain level. From that point at which the performance is no longer improving, continued intensity results in a lessening of the level of motivation along with the quality of the performance. This point illustrates that an understanding of the individual level of student confidence to complete a given task, as this pertains to motivation and performance, is important knowledge for the teacher to have.

Environment

Maslow's Hierarchy of Needs (Maslow, 1970) introduced earlier communicates a great deal to the discussion of the impact of environment on student motivation. Environments in which students feel safe, both physically and emotionally, that they are desired and cared for and where they "fit in" or belong contribute significantly to their motivational levels. Popular phrases seen in educational literature today refer to the preferred classroom environment or climate as needing to be inviting, warm, student-centered, safe and secure, learner-oriented, nurturing, etc. Although phrases such as these may only represent trendy language to some, they say a great deal with respect to student motivation. Perhaps the phrases would mean more if one were to think of a classroom environment that reflected the opposite of these characteristics.

The concept of *membership* is important when discussing motivation and the learning environment. When students are assigned to a teacher and a class, they become physical members of the class. But, do they also become psychological members? This is a critical question. Goodenow (1993) explains **psychological membership** in the classroom as being *the degree to which students feel personally accepted, respected, included, and supported.* The greater the level to which this is achieved, the greater the level of student motivation will be found. When students feel a sense of belonging in the classroom, through this positive psychological membership they are more likely to adopt those goals held to be valuable there. When students do not feel as though they belong or have psychological membership, goals will be perceived simply as the teacher's goals, not really applying or relevant to them and not be readily adopted by them. The social and psychological bonding that comes when students feel that they are true members of the classroom group influences the level or degree to which motivation will occur and academic engagement and learning will take place.

Higher levels of motivation as influenced by membership are seen when student needs are met for belonging/social connectedness, autonomy/self-direction, and competence (Battistich, Solomon, Kim, Watson, & Schaps, 1995). An environment perceived by students as being caring represents the type of environment in which higher levels of student motivation can be both achieved and maintained. Three characteristics (Alderman, 1999) considered essential for providing such an environment are:

1. A classroom structured for autonomy and responsibility.
2. Social support through cooperative learning activities.
3. Teacher support.

Student motivation is higher when students have a sense of freedom and responsibility, have opportunities to work with others in support of their own learning and the learning of others, and see their teachers as providing ongoing and enduring support. Even when they are not always successful, students in caring environments perceive their teachers as "being there for them," and this contributes to their ability to maintain their motivation.

CONCLUSION

Chapter 2 has introduced the concept of motivation as it applies to student learning and the role of the classroom teacher. Three important theories of motivation, behaviorist, cognitive, and humanist, were introduced and reviewed. Critical questions of what affects student motivation were also raised and explored.

The need for teachers to be informed, reflective educators with respect to achieving student motivation cannot be overstated. Teachers in classrooms throughout the country can define the term "motivation" and can even see it when it occurs. Many of these same teachers, however, cannot take what they know about motivation and apply it effectively in their classrooms. It is often stated that teachers should teach for transfer of learning in that they should assist their students to not only have the ability to "know and do" in the classroom but to be able to apply this knowledge and ability to novel situations. As with the students themselves, teachers must also be able to transfer what they know about student motivation to the active environments of their classrooms. They must be able to effectively apply what they know about motivation as it relates to student learning to energize their teaching and engage their students in their learning activities. Motivated students are happier, feel better about themselves, and learn more. These three outcomes are each desirable and attainable, providing teachers understand and can apply what is known about motivating students in learning environments.

QUESTIONS/ACTIVITIES FOR REFLECTION

1. Describe how you might motivate a student who has average ability but who does not regularly work up to his potential. The student comes from a home where neither parent is educated beyond the sixth grade and little English is spoken; Spanish is the language spoken in the home. The parents, however, are very supportive and want their child to learn and do well in school.

2. What might be some problems found in classrooms taught by teachers who lack high teacher efficacy? How might teachers come to a point where their teacher efficacy is low?

3. Why might poor performance on a test motivate some students but not others to work harder in school? Is there any type of student that might be positively motivated by poor test results? Explain.

4. A father wanted his son to excel in baseball and practiced with him from the time he was five years old. He attended all youth league games and even served as a volunteer coach on his son's teams. Although the son progressed well and seemed to be headed toward high school stardom, he refused to play baseball when he reached high school. What do you think might be some possible explanations for this dramatic change in direction? How do you think that this situation applies to the role of the teacher in the classroom?

5. If a student seems to be a victim of learned helplessness, how might the teacher be able to address the student's need to be a successful learner and not lower his or her classroom teaching standards at the same time? Is it possible to successfully address this problem in the traditional American education system today? Explain.

REFERENCES

Alderman, M. (1999). *Motivation for Achievement: Possibilities for Teaching and Learning.* Mahwah, NJ: Lawrence Erlbaum Associates, Inc.

Ames, R., & Lau, S. (1982). An attributional analysis of student help-seeking in academic settings. *Journal of Educational Psychology,* 84, 261–271.

Atkinson, J. (1964). *An Introduction to Motivation.* Princeton, NJ: Van Nostrand.

Bandura, A. (1986). *Social Foundations of Thought and Action: A Social Cognitive Theory.* Upper Saddle River, NJ: Prentice-Hall.

Bandura, A. (1993). Perceived self-efficacy in cognitive development and functioning. *Educational Psychologist,* 28(2), 117–148.

Battistich, V., Solomon, D., Kim, D., Watson, M., & Schaps, E. (1995). Schools as communities, poverty levels of student populations, and student attitudes, motives, and performances: A multilevel analysis. *American Educational Research Journal,* 32(2), 627–658.

Bernhard, J., & Siegel, L. (1994). Increasing internal locus of controls for a disadvantaged group: A computer intervention. *Computers in the Schools,* 11(1), 59–77.

Brophy, J. (1983). Conceptualizing student motivation. *Educational Psychologist,* 18, 200–215.

Brophy, J. (1998). *Motivating Students to Learn.* New York: McGraw-Hill

Covington, M., & Omelich, C. (1987). "I knew it cold before the exam": A test of the anxiety-blockage hypothesis. *Journal of Educational Psychology,* 79, 393–400.

Dacey, J. (1989). *Fundamentals of Creativity.* Lexington, MA: D.C. Heath/Lexington Books.

Deci, E., & Ryan, R. (1992). The initiation and regulation of intrinsically motivated learning and achievement. In A.K. Boggiano & T.S. Pittman (Eds.), *Achievement and Motivation: A Social-Developmental Perspective.* Cambridge, England: Cambridge University Press.

Eggen, P., & Kauchak, D. (2001). *Educational Psychology: Windows on Classroom* (5th ed.). Upper Saddle River, NJ: Merrill Prentice Hall.

Elliott, S., Kratochwill, T., Cook, J., & Travers, J. (2000). *Educational Psychology: Effective Teaching, Effective Learning* (3rd ed.). Boston: The McGraw Hill Companies.

Feather, N. (Ed.). (1982). *Expectations and Actions.* Hillsdale, NJ: Erlbaum.

Garcia, E. (1994). *Understanding and Meeting the Challenge of Student Cultural Diversity.* Boston: Houghton Mifflin.

Good, T., & Brophy, J. (2000). *Looking in Classrooms* (8th ed.). New York: Addison Wesley Longman, Inc.

Goodenow, C. (1993). The psychological sense of school membership among adolescents: Scale development and educational correlates. *Psychology in the Schools,* 30, 79–90.

Greeno, J., Collins, A., & Resnick, L. (1996). Cognition and learning. In D. Berliner & R. Calfee (Eds.), *Handbook of Educational Psychology* (pp. 15-46). New York: Macmillan.

Hamachek, D. (1987). Humanistic psychology: Theory, postulates, and implications for educational processes. In J. Glover & R. Ronning (Eds.). *Historical Foundations of Educational Psychology* (pp. 159–182). New York: Plenum Press.

Hansen, R. (1977). Anxiety. In S. Ball (Ed.), *Motivation in Education*. New York: Academic Press.

Harter, S., & Jackson, B. (1992). Trait versus nontrait conceptualizations of intrinsic/extrinsic motivational orientation. Special issues: Perspectives on intrinsic motivation. *Motivation and Emotion*, 16, 209–230.

Heider, F. (1958). *The Psychology of Interpersonal Relationships*. New York: Wiley.

Henson, K., & Eller, B. (1999). *Educational Psychology for Effective Teaching*. Belmont, CA: Wadsworth/Thompson Learning.

Knapp, M., & Woolverton, S. (1995). Social class and schooling. In J.A. Banks & C.A.M. Banks (Eds.). *Handbook of Research on Multicultural Education*. New York: Macmillan.

Kohn, A. (1992). *No Contest: The Case Against Competition*. Boston: Houghton Mifflin Company.

Lefrancois, G. (2000). *Psychology for Teaching* (10th ed.). Belmont, CA: Wadsworth/Thompson Learning.

Locke, E., & Latham, G. (1990). *A Theory of Goal Setting and Task Performance*. Englewood Cliffs, NJ: Prentice-Hall.

Maslow, A. (1970). *Motivation and Personality* (2nd ed.). New York: Harper & Row.

Ormrod, J. (2000). *Educational Psychology: Developing Learners* (3rd ed.). Upper Saddle River, NJ: Prentice-Hall, Inc.

Piaget, J. (1952). *Origins of Intelligence*. New York: International Universities Press.

Pintrich, P., & Schunk, D. (1996). *Motivation in Education: Theory, Research, and Applications*. Columbus, OH: Merrill.

Rosenthal, R., & Jacobson, L. (1968). *Pygmalion in the Classroom: Teacher Expectation and Pupils' Intellectual Development*. New York: Holt, Rinehart & Winston.

Schunk, D. (1994, April). *Goal and Self-Evaluative Influences During Children's Mathematical Skill Acquisition*. Paper presented at the Annual Meeting of the American Educational Research Association, New Orleans.

Seligman, M. (1975). *Helplessness*. San Francisco: Freeman.

Snowman, J., & Biehler, R. (2000). *Psychology Applied to Teaching* (9th ed.). Boston: Houghton Mifflin Company.

Stipek, D. (1996). Motivation and Instruction. In D. Berliner & R. Calfee (Eds.), *Handbook of Educational Psychology* (pp. 85-109). New York: Macmillan.

Strother, D. (Ed.). (1991). *Learning to Fail: Case Studies of Students at Risk*. Bloomington, IN: Phi Delta Kappa.

Weiner, B. (1990). History of motivational research in education. *Journal of Educational Psychology*, 82, 612–622.

Weiner, B. (1992). *Human Motivation: Metaphors, Theories, and Research*. Newbury Park, CA: Sage.

Weiner, B. (1994a). Ability versus effort revisited: The moral determinants of achievement evaluation and achievement as a moral system. *Educational Psychologist*, 29, 163–172.

Weiner, B. (1994b). Integrating social and personal theories of achievement striving. *Review of Educational Research,* 64, 557–573.

Wigfield, A. (1994). Expectancy-value theory of achievement motivation. A developmental perspective. *Educational Psychology,* 6, 49–78

Woolfolk, A. (2001). *Educational Psychology* (8th ed.). Needham Heights, MA: Allyn & Bacon.

Chapter 3

CREATING A MANAGED ENVIRONMENT: MODELS AND THEORIES OF MANAGEMENT

The fundamental theme of this book is the important relationship that exists between motivating students to learn and managing student behavior in the classroom. Good classroom management, as well as motivation, is essential as it relates to student learning. In the context of promoting learning in the classroom, management has been defined as follows:

> **Management:** *a system of organization that addresses all elements of the classroom (i.e., students, space, time, materials, and behavioral rules and procedures) in order to reach optimum levels of instruction and learning.*

As with the definition of motivation presented in Chapter 2, three key elements comprise this definition. Management is reflected by a specific system of organization, a focus on many elements of the classroom to include physical and personal elements, and the purpose of reaching optimum levels of instruction and learning.

The major purpose of Chapter 3 is to provide an overview of some of the major and most influential models that have been developed to manage student behavior in classroom environments. Some of these models rely less on the motivation of students in their learning than might be thought of as appropriate, given the primary theme of this text. However, a lack of understanding of these basic models in terms of their underlying theses will limit the readers of this book as they endeavor to construct what will eventually be their own best models for classroom management appropriate for their individual classrooms. To be effective, teachers must be well grounded in best practice information that relates to student motivation, classroom management, and instruction. A gap in knowledge in any of these three areas will severely lessen the potential for optimum student learning in the classroom.

A number of important management models have been developed over the years and used by educators to create positive learning environments and to manage student behavior in the classroom. A central thread running through most of these models is the emphasis on creating environments that are conducive to *preventing* student misbehavior and not just *reacting* to misbehavior once it occurs. Nevertheless, even with the best prevention measures, times will occur when students disobey their teachers or violate stated school rules. When this takes place, teachers must know how to react appropriately to such situations to maintain a desirable, safe, and productive learning environment. As noted in Chapter 1, teachers must have a discipline plan and know how to use it when problems arise. Although it is important for the teacher to know how to respond to student misbehavior so that the misconduct is ended, knowing how to establish a classroom environment that is preventive in nature is considered an even more significant teaching skill. Little learning is likely to occur in a classroom in which students feel unsafe or teachers and students face constant distractions and interruptions (Borman & Levine, 1997; Lezotte, 1997).

An initial step in learning how to establish a well-managed classroom/learning environment is to study and develop an understanding of a number of models designed for this purpose. Following this study and gaining this understanding, the next important step is to adopt a model, or features of a number of models, to the classroom. Because it is difficult to see that any one model can satisfy all situations, most teachers develop an eclectic, self-stylized approach to classroom management that borrows from the best ideas presented by one or more models or recommended behaviors. The approach that is then developed is one that is compatible with the teacher's own teaching style and philosophy of education.

Some management models actually are best used when the entire faculty and administration of a school participate in their implementation. Because many teachers discover theories and procedures they would like to implement in their own classrooms even though other teachers and administrators in their schools may not be participating in their use, a personalized approach to management generally has more appeal and can be more effective. This chapter will present the major ideas found in ten different management models and the theorists who are associated with their development, with an emphasis on their most important characteristics as applied to classroom practice. Figure 3.1 provides an overview of the models that will be considered and the theorists who are credited for their development.

Figure 3.1
Management Theorists and Management Models

Theorists	Focus of Management Models
Jacob Kounin	Focus is on teachers learning behaviors that will allow them to become better leaders in the classroom.
Rudolph Dreikurs	Focus is on analyzing behavior problems to determine their source of origin.
William Glasser	Focus is on empowering students to become better group members.
Hiam Ginott	Focus is on improving communication to avoid alienating students inhumanely.
Fred Jones	Focus is on keeping students engaged in academically appropriate activities.
Thomas Gordon	Focus is on teachers using counseling techniques to improve communication with their students.
Lee & Marlene Canter	Focus is on teachers asserting their right to teach and their students right to learn.
B.F. Skinner	Focus is on shaping student behavior with positive reinforcement.
David & Roger Johnson	Focus is on students resolving their own conflicts.
Alfie Kohn	Focus is on students becoming intrinsically motivated to value good behavior.

JACOB KOUNIN'S THEORIES

Jacob Kounin's theories have had great impact on the way many educators view the learning environment (Eggen & Kauchak, 2001). An interesting characteristic of Kounin's theories is that they tend to focus on constructs more often associated with a sociological study of small groups. Many of the other management theories that have been developed are grounded in what are more traditionally thought of as psychological constructs (Hunt, Touzel, & Wiseman, 1999). Central to the work of Kounin is the position that the classroom should be looked on as a small community, where interactions with any member of the community may affect the rest of its members. For the classroom community to function well and reach its goals (i.e., for optimum levels of academic progress to be realized), the teacher must be able to exhibit the characteristics of a successful group leader.

Five factors characterize the classrooms of teachers who adopt the theories described by Kounin (1970).

1. Student boredom is avoided.
2. Transitions between tasks and momentum within tasks flow smoothly.
3. All students remain alert and focused.
4. Teachers are aware of what is taking place in all parts of the classroom.
5. Teachers understand that interaction with any one student may have an effect on the total group.

It is recommended that teachers use a variety of different methods and materials to maintain high levels of student interest and participation to avoid student boredom. When students are aware that they are making progress toward their learning goals and are involved in a variety of interesting and meaningful activities, they are much less likely to become involved in misconduct and pose management problems for their teachers. It is also important that smooth transitions exist between learning activities and that *momentum* within lessons moves consistently toward closure. When instruction is characterized by such *thrust*, or positive momentum, the group tends to function better, and individual students are more likely to stay on task. Educational research suggests that there is a greater value in the teacher establishing a quicker paced compared with a slower paced delivery of instruction (Hunt, Touzel, & Wiseman, 1999).

Keeping students alert and focused on assigned activities also lessens the probability of classroom disturbances. Most misconduct occurs during "down times" or idle times when students are not on task, often because they either do not understand what they are supposed to do or how to do it. Kounin referred to this as **group focus** or *on-task behavior in which all students in the classroom attend to the teacher or activities that the teacher has assigned at the same time.* Teachers who are able to create functional, effective learning environments have what Kounin called *withitness*. **Withitness** occurs *when a teacher displays the ability to have an ongoing awareness of events throughout the entire classroom, not just one area of the setting.* This awareness, sometimes referred to as "eyes in the back of the head," allows teachers to preempt many disturbances and distractions before they become serious problems.

When teachers reinforce students or correct their misbehaviors, these interactions will have an effect on other students in the classroom creating what Kounin identified as the *ripple effect*. The **ripple effect** is *the effect on other students in the classroom when the teacher reinforces or corrects students for their behavior.* It is critical that teachers recognize the impact that their actions may have on all students when they correct the behavior of only one or two. Kounin believed that there is a positive effect on all students in the entire class when one student's misconduct is handled firmly. The ripple effect also can have a positive impact when one student is praised or encouraged in front of classmates, because the entire class has the opportunity to observe and learn which behaviors are desired and rewarded (Borman & Levine, 1997). Conversely, a negative ripple effect can occur if the teacher handles a management problem inappropriately, thus sending the wrong or undesired message to students about unacceptable behavior.

RUDOLF DREIKURS' THEORIES

Rudolf Dreikurs' theoretical position was founded on his experience with psychoanalytic psychology (Dreikurs & Cassell, 1972; Dreikurs, 1968). Dreikurs believed that students often misbehave because they desire recognition from the teacher and/or classmates. It was also Dreikurs' belief that students develop certain defense mechanisms that are designed to protect their self-esteem. He theorized that student misbehavior was goal directed, perhaps to get recognition or to otherwise protect self-esteem. Goals that misdirect student behavior, listed from least to most severe, are (1) *attention-seeking*, (2) *power-seeking*, (3) *revenge-seeking*, and (4) *overtly displaying inadequacy to receive special treatment.*

Attention-seeking is *a student behavior problem often exhibited by tattling and showing off or class-clowning.* **Power-seeking** *is a student behavior problem in which the student seeks to control the teacher instead of being directed by the teacher.* Students who seek revenge do things to hurt other students either physically or emotionally. **Revenge-seeking** is *a student behavior problem in which a student may do something to cause other students to be punished to "get back at them."* It was Dreikurs' opinion that students who pretend they lack the ability to do assigned work, *overtly displaying inadequacy to receive special treatment,* are exhibiting the most serious misconduct. Students may exhibit different behaviors to reach any of these four goals, and teachers should work to create learning environments with distinct characteristics designed to prevent these problem situations before they occur. Some of these distinct characteristics of the environment are:

1. Students are not reinforced when they exhibit behaviors leading to undesirable goals.
2. When students exhibit undesirable behavior, they receive preannounced logical consequences that will be unpleasant to them.
3. Students should be involved in helping the teacher set logical consequences for misconduct.
4. Teachers should not merely treat symptoms when dealing with misconduct but seek to determine the motivation behind the student's action.

5. Students should feel a responsibility to influence their peers' conduct,
6. Students must understand that, ultimately, they are responsible for their own behavior.
7. Students should be encouraged to develop self-respect while learning to respect others.

To fully use Dreikurs' theories, teachers must be able to analyze their students' misbehaviors, focusing on the cause(s) of the behaviors to determine the goals motivating the misconduct. They must also develop and be able to use the necessary interpersonal guidance skills needed to help them understand and change their misdirected behaviors in the future (Hunt, Touzel, & Wiseman, 1999).

WILLIAM GLASSER'S THEORIES

William Glasser's theoretical model is known as Reality Therapy, more recently referred to as Choice Theory, and has been used and discussed for decades (Glasser, 1965; 1969). Over the years, Glasser has refined his theories, and his work is widely endorsed by many educators today (Glasser, 1993; 1992). In developing his theories, Glasser drew on the work of Dreikurs (Zabel & Zabel, 1996) and believes that students often display misbehavior or apathy because they feel powerless in the adult world. Central to Glasser's concept of an effective learning environment is the strong belief that students must play an active role in the decision-making process.

An important tenet of Glasser's theory is that, when dealing with specific misconduct, the teacher should help students become aware of and responsible for the consequences of their own behaviors. One way that this can be done is by developing behavior contracts that result in the use of logical consequences when student misbehavior occurs. The behavior contract should be designed to clearly identify (1) the expectations that the teacher has for the student, (2) the consequences that have been identified if the behavior is exhibited or if it is not exhibited, and (3) a system for recording or monitoring the student's behavior over time. In this approach, the teacher uses behavior modification techniques to reinforce positive behavior and end unwanted conduct. If these reinforcements do not bring about the desired results, the student is removed from the group through a series of steps beginning with simple isolation and moving to in-school suspension (ISS), out-of-school suspension (OSS), and, finally, expulsion (Bennett, 1997). Research indicates that positive effects can be expected when Glasser's theories are applied correctly (Good & Brophy, 1986).

Glasser's approach to management includes the use of **class meetings** as *a process to involve students in the establishing of guidelines for acceptable behavior* *and as a forum for collaborative problem solving.* When rules and regulations must be adjusted or unique situations arise, the class meets to discuss and make decisions about the situation. Class meetings are regularly recurring events that are used to enable students to be an ongoing part of the decision-making process in the classroom and help prevent possible behavior problems, not just react to an unwanted problem occurrence. When students believe their interests and ideas are considered important and are valued in the decision-making process, they become stakeholders in the group. They then are more likely to assume responsibility and ownership for their behavior (Zabel & Zabel, 1996).

Glasser believes that the learning environment should feature at least five distinct characteristics:

1. The teacher as a democratic leader.
2. Students take part in the decision making process.
3. Students have an opportunity for cooperative or team activities.
4. Being part of the group is a privilege and source of satisfaction and enjoyment.
5. Guidelines are established and problems are solved through collaborative *class meetings.*

Glasser has long been recognized as a leader in the field of classroom management and student motivation. Like Dreikurs, he recognizes that students taking responsibility for their own behavior and helping in the establishment of the guidelines for acceptable conduct are critical elements in establishing and maintaining a well-managed learning environment.

HIAM GINOTT'S THEORIES

Hiam Ginott (1965, 1969, & 1971) was a very popular child psychologist whose books, weekly syndicated newspaper column, and television appearances (he was a regular guest on the "Today Show") influenced many parents and teachers in terms of how they interacted with children and teenagers. Ginott stressed the importance of what he called *sane messages.* **Sane messages** are *messages that focus on the undesired behavior of a student, not on the student as a person.* They never represent an attack on a student on a personal level. When teachers use sane messages they lessen the chance of alienating students while, at the same time, providing an important model for the type of behavior students should demonstrate. Because positive modeling is a significantly important aspect of any teacher's approach to classroom management, Ginott stressed that teachers should endeavor to maintain self-discipline, thus serving as models for their students of disciplined individuals.

Ginott believed that a system of effective management evolved over time through what he called "a series of little victories." To achieve these "little victories," teachers should:

1. Avoid labeling students.
2. Avoid using sarcasm.
3. Avoid praising personalities instead of behaviors.
4. Send *sane* messages.
5. Model desired behaviors.
6. Accept student apologies.
7. Help students build their self-esteem.

Ginott encouraged teachers to create learning environments in which students can realize a genuine feeling of satisfaction. He believed that students are much more satisfied in classrooms when team or cooperative learning activities are used. Teachers should make a conscious effort to encourage or invite this type of cooperation, thus giving students an opportunity to make choices and behave independently. Rather than try to boss and force students to comply through positions of power, teachers should give students the opportunity to decide on their own which alternative to take. "Do we want to work together quietly on the floor or do we want to get back in our desks? It is up to you," is a better way to address students than, "Be quiet or I will make you get in your desks." When teachers avoid ordering, bossing, and commanding, students are much more willing to cooperate and less likely to become negative and hostile.

Ginott believed that teachers should be compassionate, understanding models who communicate to students in such a way as to confirm positive expectations. A teacher who demonstrates polite, respectful behavior toward students creates an atmosphere in which students learn to communicate their own feelings in a similarly acceptable fashion. This is best accomplished when teachers are aware of students' feelings and communicate with them through the use of sane messages.

FRED JONES' THEORIES

Fred Jones (1987) supports the theory that most classroom management problems occur because students are not on task. It is Jones' position that most of classroom management problems occur when students are not focused and wasting their time. Students exhibit unwanted behaviors because they are allowed to be idle or waste time, not because they are naturally unruly, defiant, or aggressive. If teachers can control the learning environment so that "down time" is minimized, management problems will be greatly reduced (Borman & Levine, 1997).

To provide an environment where time is not wasted, teachers must learn to send messages to students through clear non-verbal communication, develop reward systems for students who are on task, arrange the physical environment to facilitate communication, and use teaching methods that keep all students focused and on task.

When the teacher does not have to interrupt the lesson to address unwanted behavior problems, the flow of the lesson is maintained, and instructional time is not wasted. Facial expressions, gestures, and movement toward students (an element of what is sometimes called proximity control) can stop unwanted behavior problems without interrupting the lesson. The overuse of corrective verbiage should be avoided. Students whose behavior is task oriented should be rewarded, with this reward then becoming an incentive for the entire class. A student who finishes his work appropriately and in a timely manner, for example, might be allowed to spend extra time on favorite activities.

The physical environment of the classroom should be arranged in such a way so that the teacher can efficiently help students who are having difficulty. Jones recognizes that students are sometimes seated in seating arrangements that make it difficult for teachers to easily get to them or near them without interrupting the flow of instruction. Semicircles, for example, may be preferable to straight rows.

In addition, students often waste time for the following reasons:

1. They cannot do what has been assigned to them.
2. They do not understand what is expected of an assignment.
3. They finish their work and have nothing else to do.
4. They see the task as boring, too difficult, or unchallenging.

Teachers must provide activities that are interesting, challenging, and that keep students moving toward a desired and meaningful goal. Jones recommends that teachers use models, charts, and examples and illustrations to provide clear directions to the students. He further emphasizes that most students in the class should not be kept waiting for extended periods of time while the teacher is explaining something to one or only a few individuals. This type of situation creates unnecessary "down time" or idle time for most of the class. Jones' theory stresses the importance of the teacher's role in managing the classroom to prevent student behavior problems from occurring. The environment that is structured to foster consistent student time on task behavior limits wasted time and minimizes student misconduct.

THOMAS GORDON'S THEORIES

Thomas Gordon (1974) developed the highly popular Teacher Effectiveness Training (TET) model for classroom management that is based on a Gestalt psychology point of view similar to the position taken by Carl Rogers (Rogers & Freiberg, 1994). Gordon emphasizes the necessity of effective communication between teacher and student if productive relationships are to exist (Woolfolk, 2001). Through the use of this model, the teacher is encouraged to take on certain counseling behaviors to create an effective, well-managed learning environment. In this environment:

1. Teachers should diagnose problems to determine problem ownership.
2. Teachers should not send accusatory messages when correcting student behavior.
3. Teachers should practice active listening when communicating with students.
4. Students are encouraged to resolve their own conflicts through a no-lose process.

Diagnosis of problem ownership is a key aspect of the successful functioning of TET. When unacceptable student behavior occurs, teachers should first determine whether the problem that is being experienced is actually theirs or their students. Student-owned problems may be associated with fears or anxiety. Teacher-owned problems, on the other hand, often involve student misconduct that frustrates the teacher, because it interrupts the flow of instruction. The owner of the problem needs to be the one initially who talks or moves ahead to solve the problem. If the problem belongs to the student, the teacher needs to use appropriate questioning and listening techniques to counsel the student through the problem or otherwise guide the student to a positive resolution to the problem. If the problem belongs to the teacher, a clear, nonaccusatory message should be sent by the teacher to the student creating the frustration, letting the student know the impact that his or her behavior is having on what the teacher is trying to accomplish in the classroom.

When the teacher owns the problem, Gordon recommends that the teacher send what he calls an *I message* to the student. The *I message* (as opposed to a *you message*) explains how a specific behavior affects the teacher without making an accusatory assault on the person or persons who exhibited the unwanted behavior. The **I message** is *a three-part communication that (1) delineates the deviant behavior, (2) describes the effect the behavior has on the teacher,* and (3) *lets the student know how the teacher feels when such behavior occurs. I messages* focus on behaviors, not students. For example, the teacher might say to a misbehaving student "When you talk out loud when I am teaching, I am unable to finish the activity that I have underway. This frustrates me and makes it difficult for me to complete the lesson that I had planned." This approach does not criticize the student personally but makes it clear that the student's behavior, talking out loud during the lesson, creates problems for the teacher and the learning of the other students. A *you message*, such as "You are really creating problems for me today with your constant talking and I am tired of it," comes across as being more directed at the student personally than to the student's behavior. The **you message** is generally seen as *a statement to the student interpreted as a personal attack or put down of the student*. Such a message is counterproductive in terms of helping to develop the desired positive atmosphere in the classroom.

Active listening, an important aspect of TET, is *a specific approach to listening in which the teacher gives full attention to both the emotional and intellectual content of what the student is saying* (Sokolove, Garrett, Sadker, & Sadker, 1990). Active listening is especially important when the student owns the problem and needs to talk about emotions and feelings. The teacher's aim in using the active listening strategy is to show students that the teacher takes their problems seriously, wants to hear what they have to say, and is willing to help them arrive at their own solutions. Through this process teachers are encouraged to:

1. Maintain eye contact with the student who is talking.
2. Paraphrase what was said by the student back to the student to give assurance that the message is both understood and important to the teacher.
3. Project an open, nonjudgmental demeanor communicating to the student that what is being said by the student is genuinely important.

Gordon encourages students when possible to resolve their own conflicts through a process he calls the *no-lose approach*. The **no-lose approach** is *an approach to helping students resolve their own conflicts or problems in such a way that all students involved feel positive about the resolution, and no one is considered a loser.* In using this approach, students first define their problem. Next, each student suggests a possible solution to the conflict. The concerned parties then work together to try to establish a solution through consensus building that is satisfactory to all involved. The solution is then implemented on a trial basis. If it is found to be unsatisfactory, another solution is similarly developed and tried. This process, recommended as following the steps of the Model for Reflection and Inquiry introduced in Chapter 1, is designed to teach students how to solve their own conflicts in a logical and reasoned way without the need for teacher intervention. Gordon's model is based on effective communication among students and teachers. When students believe their teachers listen to them when they share their feelings, they are more likely to trust their teachers and respond more openly to them (Woolfolk, 2001).

LEE AND MARLENE CANTER'S THEORIES

Lee and Marlene Canter developed a model for classroom management known as *Assertive Discipline*. **Assertive Discipline** is *a management model based on the fundamental position that teachers have the right to teach and students have the right to learn, and no one has the right to disrupt the learning environment* (Canter & Canter, 1976; 1992). The Canter model encourages teachers to make their expectations clear to their students and to follow through with established consequences for those students who choose to break established rules. Clarity and consistency must be evident if Assertive Discipline is to be successful. Important features of the model include:

1. Students must face the consequences for their own misconduct.
2. Teachers are neither hostile nor passive when dealing with misconduct.
3. Teachers do not debate or argue about the fairness of rules with students.
4. Teachers rely heavily on the use of proper nonverbal communication strategies when managing specific student misconduct.

In a well-managed classroom, students understand what is expected of them and the consequences for violating or not fulfilling these expectations. The Canters stress that teachers must communicate their expectations to students firmly and clearly and then follow these communications with appropriate actions responding in ways that increase student compliance.

Effective teachers are firm but not hostile to students and always avoid making attacks on a student's character. Such comments as "You are acting like a baby!" or "You should be ashamed of yourself!" are ineffective and alienating. Comments such as "You might get away with that when you are home, but you will not do it at school!" actually can be seen as attacking the character of the student's parents and also should be avoided. The passive teacher ignores misbehavior and fails to assert needed leadership in the classroom, where the hostile teacher alienates students with a "me against you" attitude. Teachers must assert themselves and become firm managers of student behavior. This firm approach to management, however, must never conflict with the best interests of the students for whom they are responsible.

The Canters also stress the importance of avoiding arguments with students, especially arguments in public. Because everyone should know and be clear about the rules of the classroom, teachers should avoid nagging, fussing, and debating the rules with a misbehaving student. The overuse of such verbiage is a waste of valuable instructional time and will only serve to lessen the teacher's stature in the eyes of the students and weaken the teacher's position.

To avoid superfluous talking while correcting student misbehaviors, teachers are advised to learn to use appropriate nonverbal communications. Eye contact, gestures, touches, and proximity are all effective means to help teachers assert that they are serious and in charge. Gestures, as the Canters instruct, can give added impact to verbal messages along with factors such as tone of voice and facial expression. Such nonverbal communications will help the total communication of the teacher be clearer to the student and minimize the necessity for the teacher to repeat directions and use longer and, at times, protracted verbal interactions.

The public's concern, along with the fact that many teachers fail in the profession as a result of not being able to manage the behavior of their students, has led advocates of Assertive Discipline to believe that effective teaching depends on the teacher's ability to exhibit the firmness needed to control behavior in the learning environment. However, some educators have questioned the use of Assertive Discipline. Render, Padilla, and Krank (1989) report that they could find little research supporting the effectiveness of Assertive Discipline that had been conducted by researchers other than the Canters' associates. Although evidence exists that Assertive Discipline may work in severe cases with highly disruptive students, there is no evidence to recommend or support the approach for schoolwide or districtwide adoption. Curwin and Mendler (1988) and Covaleski (1992) voice concerns that go beyond whether Assertive Discipline works or does not work to control student behavior. These educators note a concern that models of management such as Assertive Discipline do little to teach children self-control or bolster their self-worth or value systems. The Canters and their associates have answered their critics with logical arguments related to the research base for Assertive Discipline (McCormack, 1989) and the issues surrounding the model's impact on students (Canter, 1988). It is clear that teachers should thoroughly examine as many theories and models of management as possible to determine what may be best for them to use in their own individual classrooms to bring the greatest benefit to their students and themselves.

B. F. SKINNER'S THEORIES

B.F. Skinner's theories have been widely applied to behavior management, and his work goes beyond what one might consider as representing only theories for behavior management in the classroom. The application of operant conditioning principles in everyday (i.e., not laboratory) settings has been common practice since the late 1950s (Kauffman, 1989). Originally called Behavior Modification, the techniques were typically used with the severely retarded, the autistic, and the emotionally disturbed. Because positive outcomes were documented, the techniques were used more broadly with nondisabled populations (Zirpoli & Melloy, 1997). Since the late 1980s, Behavior Modification has been replaced by Applied Behavior Analysis because Behavior Modification to many has taken on a negative connotation (Alberto & Troutman, 1990; Woolfolk, 2001).

Early in the 20th century, E. L. Thorndike (1905; 1911) established the fact that people repeat behaviors that bring pleasant feelings and that the more a behavior is repeated the better one's performance becomes. These findings lay the foundation for today's Applied Behavior Analysis. **Applied Behavior Analysis** is *an approach to management that focuses on the positive, rewarding appropriate behaviors, as opposed to concentrating on the negative, punishing unwanted or inappropriate behaviors* (McCaslin & Good, 1992).

Teachers who manage their classrooms using Applied Behavior Analysis exhibit characteristics derived from behaviorist principles. Examples of these principles are:

1. Students receive positive reinforcements after exhibiting desired behaviors.
2. Teachers do not punish students who exhibit unwanted behaviors.
3. Teachers shape students' behaviors to become more desirable over time.

The concept is simple. Students are reinforced (i.e., given positive reinforcement or rewards) when they behave in a fashion the teacher desires. On the basis of behavioristic theory, the student who receives a reward will repeat the desired behavior, because the reward brings pleasure. If the teacher wants a student to stay seated, for example, the student will be rewarded in some way for being seated. Applied Behavior Analysis has been referred to as a remunerative strategy, because students receive a payoff for doing what the teacher wants done.

Not only does this model emphasize reinforcing or rewarding good behavior, teachers practicing Applied Behavior Analysis are advised to avoid the use of punishments. The positive aspect of this approach is that teachers focus on the students who are behaving in an acceptable manner, not the ones who are not. Teachers are encouraged to spend more time rewarding and praising their students, not punishing or giving them verbal retributions for misdeeds. Many behaviorists have warned against a "praise good behavior while ignoring bad behavior" philosophy (Pfiffner, Rosen, & O'Leary, 1985). In some cases, especially those of a more serious nature, disruptive behavior will persist and may even escalate if ignored. Teachers are advised to channel students to positive behavior and then reinforce this conduct. Obviously, no teacher can be positive and complimentary all of the time. In general, however, it is strongly recommended that emphasis be placed on what students are doing correctly as opposed to what they may be doing incorrectly.

Shaping behavior is important in Applied Behavior Analysis. **Shaping** refers to *the practice of gradually changing a student's unwanted actions to more acceptable behavior over time through the use of reinforcements.* There are several ways by which this shaping can take place varying from an informal approach in which the teacher simply waits for a student to exhibit desired behavior and then rewards it, to a more structured system in which the teacher elicits desired behavior through the use of tangible rewards. To shape an individual student's behavior, the teacher must first carefully measure the degree to which the behavior occurs (i.e., establish baseline data) and then analyze the environment to determine what precedes the behavior and what may be reinforcing the behavior after it occurs. After this careful analysis, a schedule can be developed to intervene with offering appropriate reinforcers when desired behaviors occur to change the unwanted behavior to more acceptable conduct. Finally, the changed behavior must be measured to determine whether the new behavior is greatly different from the previous, baseline behavior.

The unwanted behavior of a student could be the student's failing to complete any of the teacher's assigned homework. Using Applied Behavior Analysis, the teacher would first observe the student for some period of time (e.g., one week) to determine the degree to which the student failed to complete the work that had been assigned. After the completion of the observation, the teacher then would institute a reward system to motivate the student to complete the homework assignments (e.g., some tangible reinforcer could be given every time the student satisfactorily completed a set amount of work). After a period of time (perhaps two to three weeks), the teacher would then measure the student's level of homework completion again to determine whether progress had been made. The teacher should maintain assessment over time and make modifications in the reinforcement schedule as needed.

The use of behaviorist principles to shape student behavior is a somewhat controversial topic (Kohn, 1993). Although supported by many (Alberto & Troutman, 1995; Zirpoli & Melloy, 1997), questions have been raised about its use (Travers, 1977). Woolfolk (2001) notes that ethical questions may exist in that some students may be reinforced for actions that might be viewed as negative by others. The question has also been raised as to whether the wrong message is being sent when some students receive rewards for doing what they are normally expected to do anyway. Although evidence exists that behavior can be changed through the use of Applied Behavior Analysis, questions remain concerning which students benefit most from such techniques and the impact the techniques have on the entire class (Hunt, Touzel, & Wiseman, 1999). As with most highly systematic models for classroom management, Applied Behavior Analysis techniques can only be used successfully with maximum benefit after professional training has been received.

DAVID AND ROGER JOHNSON'S THEORIES

David and Roger Johnson and their associates developed the *Conflict Resolution* model to student behavior management in which students receive formal training so that they might be able to better deal with their own problems (Johnson & Johnson, 1995; Johnson & Johnson, 1997; Stevahn, Johnson, Johnson, Green, & Laginski, 1997). **Conflict Resolution** is *a management model used in school settings where students are trained to use creative problem solving in such a way as to increase the probability that students involved in a conflict can get what they want in terms of a problem solution.* This is not unlike Gordon's no-lose approach. To use Conflict Resolution, students complete a designed training program to learn how to negotiate and engage in peer mediation with their classmates when conflicts arise. The goal of Conflict Resolution is to involve students in the decision-making process to develop a workable solution to a problem that will allow all parties involved in the conflict to feel satisfied about the resolution that has been developed. The program is most commonly used on a schoolwide basis where students take part in specialized training before using the approach to ensure that their negotiations and problem-solving actions can be successful and conducted in a consistent manner. The traditional role of the teacher is somewhat minimized in Conflict Resolution in that the model emphasizes the role of students in the management of their own conflicts.

Many claims have been made supporting this integrative approach to mediation of conflicts as a model, which helps decrease management problems in schools (Tolson, McDonald, & Moriarty, 1992). Johnson and Johnson (1995), however, believe that much more research needs to be done on the process before all questions can be answered. For example, it has been argued that the model requires specialized training that must take place in ways that are not cost-effective and that take students away from their academic studies (Webster, 1993). The Johnsons and their associates are currently compiling data that they believe will demonstrate that the approach is cost-effective and can provide positive results when students receive proper training.

Conflicts among students have become all too common in school environments across the nation. Some of these conflicts have been manifested in violent acts in which students and teachers have experienced serious injury or lost their lives for little or no understandable reason. Although these extreme acts of violence account for a very small percentage of the total number of student conflicts that actually take place in schools, they are extensively covered by the media and are widely publicized. Many school conflicts result in arguments and verbal taunting, and some even culminate in physical fights; too many end when one or more students has been seriously injured. As a result of the serious and frequent nature of these problems, many educators suggest that students themselves should be involved in and learn how to find solutions to their own conflicts in a constructive manner. Conflict Resolution has promise as a model that educators can use to ease management problems on a schoolwide basis. Further research, especially in middle and high schools, is needed to determine how it can best be instituted.

ALFIE KOHN'S THEORIES

Alfie Kohn, unlike some of the other theorists that have been mentioned, has discussed and written on a wide variety of topics in education. Many who are familiar with his work may not associate him as much with behavior management as with other current topics of interest in the profession. Kohn is considered one of the leading opponents of the national movement toward a greater emphasis on test scores; his *The Case Against Standardized Testing* (Kohn, 2000) is a short but powerful argument that the testing movement is hurting, not helping education. His *No Contest: The Case Against Competition* (Kohn, 1992) is seen as an important critique of the impact of competition on American life.

Kohn (1993) takes the position that rewards and punishments represent "opposite sides of the same coin," and both should be avoided. Kohn describes himself as a person who has long been an opponent of the principles of behaviorism, which he believes are flawed and lead to many educational problems. Some of the problems directly affect the way teachers motivate and manage students. His position is that rewards (often referred to by Kohn as "bribes") and punishments can change behaviors but that the change will be short-lived, because rewards and punishments function only to change specific behaviors in specific situations. Rewards and punishments do not function to change value systems and individual character. Although they may be used to produce temporary compliance, they tend not to help bring about long-term worthwhile goals such as increased student self-reliance, creative thinking, or self-confidence. The essence of Kohn's theory is that, for long-term positive change to occur, students must internalize prosocial values and become a part of a caring community. Rewards and punishments merely train students much the way animals are trained. As opposed to being trained like animals, students must be inculturated into a learning community where they can think about and act on basic human values such as kindness, fairness, and personal responsibility. Central to the functioning of this community are the teachers' abilities to communicate with students while allowing students to communicate with them and each other (Powell, McLaughlin, Savage, & Zehm, 2001).

When one sets out to not only change observable behavior but to transform a student's core being, the task seems almost Herculean in nature. Kohn (1993) has provided a set of guidelines for teachers to follow that can serve as a framework for developing what he sees as the proper learning environment. The following elements are included in the formation of this framework.

COLLABORATION. As children mature, they should be brought into the decision-making process more and more and be given input into deciding. what is and is not acceptable. Mutual problem solving is at the heart of this type of collaboration. Teacher and student should plan together how best a problem can be faced and prevented in the future. Kohn suggests that students will often make restitution and prevent future problems when they do not fear punishment for their mistakes.

CHOICE. Children should be given the opportunity to participate in meaningful decision making concerning what will happen to them as a result of bad behavior. Students need to have real autonomy to make choices after giving their input.

CARING. Children will care for other people more if they believe other people care for them. A caring, supportive environment is at the heart of Kohn's theory.

MODELING. Adults teach by example. If students are to be intrinsically motivated to do good deeds and care for one another, they need to have teachers who are well respected to model desired conduct (e.g., listen respectfully, care for students, and treat all students honestly and fairly).

EXPLAINING. It is not enough to model desired traits. Explanations of what is desired and why certain things should or should not be done must be given in language that is understood by the students. Such clear explaining behavior leads to reasoning with students instead of demanding simple obedience. Explanations are not lectures but are explorations of why things should be done in certain ways.

ATTRIBUTING POSITION MOTIVES. A basic belief that children are born good, not bad, and a desire to accept a reasonable excuse for undesired activity is at the core of providing the type of learning environment that students need. Teachers who believe that students are basically good, and attribute to them the best possible motive for behavior consistent with the facts, are more likely to help students develop good values.

OFFERING OPPORTUNITIES TO CARE. Teachers who want caring students must give their students opportunities to demonstrate caring behavior. Students who tutor other students, care for pets, and help classmates solve problems, for example, will more readily become caring individuals themselves.

EMPHASIZING PERSPECTIVE TAKING. If a goal is to produce students who perform good deeds from a desire to do good and to help others, as opposed to seeking rewards, teachers must help students view the world from the eyes of those who are less fortunate or in some way weaker. Students must empathize or perform what is called "perspective taking." "How does it feel to be called names?" "How does it feel to be bullied?" "How does it feel to be laughed at by others?" These are questions students must reflect on in order to appreciate the effect such negative behavior can have on others. Failure to take on other people's points of view accounts for much of the behavior seen as troublesome in schools today.

Beyond this framework for developing the proper learning environment that focuses on the teacher as a stimulus for creating a positive classroom atmosphere, Kohn (1993) notes that entire schools can be organized to help students develop prosocial behaviors. Activities should be adopted across the entire school that will assist educators in developing the type of caring environment that children need and deserve.

CLASS MEETINGS. Kohn believes that students at all ages benefit from opportunities to take time to plan together, make decisions, solve problems, and reflect on the happenings of the day. These types of activities will create a feeling of community in the school and classroom and an opportunity to take on the perspectives of other students. This approach is consistent with the theories of other educators such as William Glasser.

UNITY-BUILDING ACTIVITIES. Activities designed to build a feeling of community and a belonging to the group or team are important. Such activities help students communicate better and develop understanding and empathy for one another. Some groups or teams create logos, develop newsletters, put on plays, participate in intramural activities, and arrange for many other unity-building activities that strengthen the ability of students to communicate with and understand their fellow students.

SCHOOLWIDE PROGRAMS. Schoolwide community service programs serve to develop a feeling of community within students. Programs that foster older students mentoring or tutoring younger students have great value when trying to develop feelings of caring.

PROSOCIAL LITERATURE. The stories teachers use in their classrooms serve a similar function as modeling. For example, a schoolwide literature program can stress the use of materials that emphasize desired values such as fairness, kindness, tolerance, and honesty.

Kohn has a theory of behavior that emphasizes the education of students to value goodness and respect for others. Students must want and desire to be good. It is not enough to just avoid negative behavior or to act acceptably. Students do not look for rewards or seek to avoid punishment but learn to become good human beings. Although it is hard to argue with this theory, the question seems to be one of usefulness. Can teachers show the patience that is needed for such a long, slow process of personal development to take place? Kohn would ask whether teachers can afford not to show such patience.

SELECTING MANAGEMENT MODELS

The information presented in the first part of this chapter has provided an overview of some key theories and models for managing students in school and classroom settings. Teachers are asked to analyze this information to determine which theory or collection of theories would be best suited to their individual personalities and classrooms. Before making the decision to adopt any management model, it is suggested that teachers undertake more in-depth study to include, when possible, site visitations to where different programs are being successfully used.

Curwin and Mendler (1988) provide a list of key questions to ask to guide teachers in their analysis of theories and models of classroom management. Figure 3.2 provides a list of these questions. The remainder of the chapter offers a brief analysis of each theory and model that has been presented.

Figure 3.2
Guidelines to Help Teachers Select Management Models

1. What happens to students who break rules? Punishments or consequences?
2. Is it realistically possible to reinforce the program consistently?
3. What do students learn as a result of the program?
4. Are the principles of behavior as visible and as important as the rules?
5. Do students have a say in what happens to them?
6. Do teachers have discretion in implementing consequences?
7. Is adequate time given for professional development of teachers and administrators? Is the training completed in only a day or two? Is there continuous follow-up and administrative support?
8. Does the plan account for the special relationship between teaching and discipline style, or does it focus exclusively on student behavior? Does it encourage

teachers to examine their own potential contributions to discipline problems?
9. Is the dignity of the students preserved? Are students protected from embarrassment?
10. Is the program consistent with the stated goals of the school?

From Curwin & Mendler, 1988.

1. What happens to students who break rules?

Kounin: The teacher handles the misconduct firmly to positively impact the entire class.

Dreikurs: Students receive logical consequences that they perceive as being unpleasant.

Glasser: Behavior contracts make students aware of and responsible for the consequences of their misconduct. If a student's behavior cannot be modified, the student is removed from the group.

Ginott: Students are given the choice of conducting themselves correctly or losing certain freedoms. The teacher's focus is on the behavior, not the person.

Jones: Emphasis is placed on keeping students on task to prevent misconduct.

Gordon: The teacher sends an *I message* to the student that identifies the infraction, why it is unacceptable, and how it effects the teacher's work or makes the teacher feel.

Canter and Canter: Students are given consequences when rules are broken.

Skinnerians: The focus is placed on channeling students in the correct direction so that positive reinforcements can be given for good conduct. As a result, the misdirected student is shaped into a student behaving acceptably. Serious misconduct is not ignored.

Johnson and Johnson: Emphasis is directed toward student-to-student conflict. Students should resolve these conflicts in ways that all parties see as acceptable.

Kohn: The teacher talks to the student about the misbehavior and tries to induce the student to reflect on ways to improve the situation. The teacher is certain to seek input from the student concerning what should happen while avoiding the use of rewards and punishments.

2. Is it realistically possible to reinforce the program consistently?

Kounin: The model focuses on individual teacher behavior in the classroom. When the suggested behaviors become part of the teacher's everyday conduct, consistency should be maintained.

Dreikurs: Yes. The model focuses on individual teacher behavior. Consistency will come as teachers master the behavior.

Glasser: Yes. However, consistency becomes a bit more difficult; with In-School Suspension (ISS), for example, teachers and administrators must work with all teachers. High levels of coordination are needed to maintain consistency.

Ginott: Yes. The model focuses on the interaction between a teacher and a group of students. There will be the challenge to make certain that *sane messages* are provided equitably to all students.

Jones: Yes. Nonverbal communication, reward systems, and time on task are emphasized. The challenge is to maintain the same level of effectiveness with students of varying ability and motivation.

Gordon: Yes. Like Ginott's theory, TET is based on interaction between teacher and student. As students increase in number and diversity, consistency will be a greater challenge and concern.

Canter and Canter: Yes. When teachers learn the procedures involved, they will be able to consistently reinforce the program.

Skinnerians: The behaviorist principles guiding Applied Behavior Analysis are designed to provide consistency in the reinforcement of the program.

Johnson and Johnson: The model relies on the support of trainers, counselors, administrators, and teachers to produce the desired results and focuses on the peer mediation skills of individual students. Consistently reinforcing such a program is a challenge. Further evidence is needed to answer this question.

Kohn: Yes. As was true with Ginott and Gordon, effectiveness of this model is based on the teacher's ability to communicate with students. Some students are more likely to respond to this type of reasoning than others.

3. What do students learn as a result of the use of the program?

Kounin: Students learn to stay on task and remain focused. An emphasis on reducing student boredom may lead to learning to enjoy school more.

Dreikurs: Students learn to feel responsible for their own behavior and the behaviors of classmates. Students develop more self-respect and more respect for others.

Glasser: Students learn to feel more empowered to make decisions, control their own environment, and improve their ability to work and communicate in groups.

Ginott: Through cooperative activities, students learn self-respect, self-esteem, and to develop greater satisfaction with themselves.

Jones: Students learn the importance of staying on task and making academic progress.

Gordon: Students learn to better communicate their own feelings, relate to the feelings of others, and resolve problems.

Canter and Canter: Students learn that there are consequences for interfering with the rights of others and that it is not necessary for teachers to debate and defend their positions of authority.

Skinnerians: This is an important point for debate. Critics of behaviorist principles often maintain that students learn to think they should be rewarded for doing what they should be doing as a matter of fact. Behaviorists believe students learn whatever adults want them to learn by shaping the students' behaviors. Some critics fear that student creativity is hampered.

Johnson and Johnson: Students learn to resolve conflicts in mutually satisfying ways that are fair to all concerned parties.

Kohn: Students learn to develop and use their critical thinking skills as they reflect on their own behavior as it relates to specific situations. Perhaps, most importantly, students learn to be caring, responsible, empathetic human beings who value good conduct.

4. Are the principles of behavior as visible and as important as the rules?

Kounin: Yes. The principles of good leadership by the teacher and appropriate conduct by students are not lost to any rigid set of rules and procedures.

Dreikurs: The answer is yes as in the case of Kounin's theories.

Glasser: The principles of behavior are explained clearly. The rules for conduct and consequences for misconduct are evident; if the teacher understands Glasser's theory, the principles for behavior at the theory's foundation should not be lost.

Ginott: Although Ginott dedicated much time to explaining the rules (i.e., the *do's* and *don'ts*) for teacher and student behavior, he also carefully explained the principles guiding these rules.

Jones: The basic principle guiding this theory is that most problems occur because students are allowed to waste time. This principle does not get lost in the discussion of rules and procedures.

Gordon: Although TET was developed on the principles of Gestaltist psychology similar to those of Carl Rogers, teacher techniques and student rules often seem to dominate when educators discuss the model.

Canter and Canter: Teachers often focus on the rules for behavior and techniques of administering Assertive Discipline instead of the principles on which it is based.

Skinnerians: The principles of operant conditioning go hand in hand with techniques and rules for behavior. The principles upon which the system is based are not lost.

Johnson and Johnson: The principle that students should learn to resolve their own conflicts in an amiable fashion is reinforced in the process.

Kohn: The principle that students should become caring, empathetic people is central. There is no reliance on a long list of rules.

5. Do students have a say in what happens to them?

Kounin: The emphasis is on teacher behaviors. A concern about student input is not paramount.

Dreikurs: Yes. Dreikurs suggests that students should take part in setting logical consequences for their misconduct.

Glasser: The teacher uses *class meetings* to ensure student input concerning the setting of logical consequences. Students are encouraged to develop their own plans for correcting behavior throughout the process.

Ginott: Emphasis is placed on students making choices, not on forced compliance. The teacher is asked to remain sensitive to students' feelings.

Jones: The emphasis is on the prevention of problems. Student input into what will happen when rules are broken is not a major concern.

Gordon: Much emphasis is placed on student input as teachers are encouraged to use *active listening* techniques.

Canter and Canter: The theory is based on the need for students to comply to established, non-debatable rules.

Skinnerians: Students have little control over what happens to them as their behavior is shaped. This has been an issue with the critics of behaviorism.

Johnson and Johnson: Conflict Resolution stresses the importance of training students so that they determine what happens to them when conflicts arise.

Kohn: For Kohn's theory to be actualized, students must always be involved in deciding what happens to them.

6. Do teachers have discretion in implementing consequences?

Kounin: Yes. Teachers are encouraged to be leaders and decision makers.

Dreikurs: Yes. Teachers provide logical consequences to students who exhibit misconduct. However, teachers use their own discretion in determining, along with students, the actual consequences.

Glasser: Teachers can use their discretion to a point. When student misconduct reaches a level where isolation is necessary, consequences are prescribed.

Ginott: Teachers are asked not to order, boss, or force students to comply. Teachers are given guidelines by these directions and do not lose their freedom in making judgments concerning the implementation of consequences for misbehavior.

Jones: Teachers should limit verbal corrections while using nonverbal expressions and gestures to communicate with students. The emphasis is on avoiding problems by keeping students active and engaged. Consequences for misbehavior are not a central issue. Teachers have freedom to make judgments as needed.

Gordon: TET is a structured, systematic program emphasizing clear communication between teacher and student. The structure does limit teacher discretion in the use of consequences.

Canter and Canter: Teachers have discretion to set consequences for misconduct. After the consequences are set, teachers are expected to consistently adhere to the system.

Skinnerians: Although consequences are sometimes used, especially when misbehavior is severe, the model specifically emphasizes rewarding good behaviors. Teachers have freedom to set rewards and consequences as judged appropriate.

Johnson and Johnson: Conflict Resolution does not focus on teachers setting consequences for misconduct. Students resolve problems without teacher intervention.

Kohn: Teachers have discretion because the emphasis is on individual problem solving and growth, not on consequences. Punishments (consequences) and rewards are to be replaced by reasoning, reflection, and support.

7. Is adequate time given for professional development of teachers and administrators? Is there continuous follow-up and administrative support?

These questions must be answered in the context of a specific school environment. The successful use of any model requires adequate training and administrative support over an extended period of time if maximum results are to be realized. Some models, for example TET, Reality Therapy, Conflict Resolution, and Applied Behavior Analysis, require extensive and long-term specialized training and support.

8. Does the plan account for the special relationship between teaching and discipline style, or does it focus exclusively on student behavior? Does it encourage teachers to examine their own potential contributions to discipline problems?

Kounin: The relationship between teaching style and management style is apparent in the discussion of concepts such as *withitness, thrust,* and *ripple effect.*

Dreikurs: The plan allows teachers to make their personal contribution to solving problems as they analyze student behavior and react accordingly. The relationship between teaching style and discipline style is not as obvious.

Glasser: The group and cooperative activities link the management and teaching styles of teachers. Teachers have a great potential to contribute in leading *class meetings.*

Ginott: Sending *sane messages,* modeling desired behaviors, and eliminating sarcasm toward and labeling of students are all avenues to link teaching and discipline styles.

Jones: The theory is built on the relationship between teaching and discipline styles. Methods of instruction to be used to diminish discipline problems by keeping students on task are emphasized.

Gordon: *Active listening* techniques can be used in management and instruction; yet, the focus is more on management styles. Teachers using TET should feel they are making an important contribution to the solution of problems.

Canter and Canter: Management of student behavior is the main focus. The model is also designed to empower teachers to help them realize their potential to contribute to the successful management of discipline problems.

Skinnerians: The behaviorist principles of Applied Behavior Analysis can be used for instructional practices in a method similar to the ones used to manage behavior; however, there is a definite focus on isolated behaviors as opposed to an interaction of management and instructional style.

Johnson and Johnson: Conflict Resolution focuses on student behavior, not the relationship between teaching and discipline styles. The potential contribution that teachers make is limited.

Kohn: The theory focuses on the special relationship between teaching style and discipline style. In the tradition of the early Progressive Educators, reflection in a democratic classroom permeates Kohn's ideal for managing and teaching students.

9. Is the dignity of the students preserved? Are students protected from embarrassment?

Kounin: Yes. The importance of maintaining student interest and participation is stressed. Any incident that embarrasses a student would have a definite negative *ripple effect* on the entire class.

Dreikurs: Students must develop self-respect to adjust to the environment of the classroom. Any action that negatively impacts the student's self-image is inappropriate.

Glasser: The teacher is a democratic leader who involves students in group discussion and decision-making processes. The type of relationship encouraged between teacher and student could not exist if students were not treated with dignity.

Ginott: Central to the theory is the position that teachers avoid sarcasm and labeling when interacting with students. Teachers should treat students with dignity to foster growth in their self-esteem.

Jones: Yes. Students are rewarded for productivity. There is nothing to suggest that students should be treated in an undignified fashion.

Gordon: Teachers are encouraged to avoid being accusatory and to treat students with dignity.

Canter and Canter: Yes. It is important to remember that, although teachers should avoid passive behaviors, Assertive Discipline opposes teacher hostility. When being assertive, teachers must guard against crossing the line that would result in students being treated in an embarrassing, undignified manner.

Skinnerians: The behaviorist focus is on rewarding desired behavior; the purpose is to encourage students to behave well so that they can be rewarded. Although Behaviorism is often discussed vis-à-vis humanism, this in no way implies that behaviorists are inhumane in their treatment of students.

Johnson and Johnson: Yes. Conflict Resolution is designed to empower students to solve their own problems in ways that are fair to all parties concerned.

Kohn: Fundamental to this model is the belief that no student's self-worth should ever be compromised. The teacher models a caring, empathetic attitude so students will learn to treat each other with dignity.

10. Is the program consistent with the stated goals of the school?

This question can only be answered in the context of a specific school environment. It can be said, however, that it is important to match the school's goals and philosophies with any management model to be used by the faculty in order to ensure maximum consistency and support from administrators and parents. For example, if the school has the goal of increasing time spent on academic activities, Kounin's and Jones' theories may be more of a match with the school's needs than would be the theories of Johnson and Johnson.

CONCLUSION

Chapter 3 has provided an overview of ten popular models for classroom management and identified the theorists associated with their development. An extensive amount of material (e.g., books, journal articles, tapes, and training kits) can be found on each of the models and theories that have been discussed. Teachers should review the information presented here, find ideas that appeal to their personal style and philosophy, and do further research before making a final decision about what would work best in their schools or classrooms.

Questions developed to assist teachers in the selection of management models were used as a way to systematically analyze and examine the models and guide decisions about their use in particular settings. The last section of the chapter provided preliminary answers to each question from the perspective of each of the ten models presented. Teachers are encouraged to answer each of these questions in greater detail for themselves based on further analysis of the models and a comparison with their own educational settings.

Without a theoretical basis to guide their actions, teachers run the risk of becoming inconsistent in their behaviors and, perhaps worse, making managerial decisions without understanding the full ramifications for the students involved. The information presented here can serve as a starting point to the development of this needed theoretical foundation.

QUESTIONS/ACTIVITIES FOR REFLECTION

1. Why should a teacher be aware of such a large number of models or theories for management when he or she is not likely to use most of them? What are important points to consider in adopting any model or part of a model for classroom use?

2. Take the side of a teacher who does not agree with the principles on which Applied Behavior Analysis are based and develop an argument against its use. Now, take the opposite point of view and argue for the use of Applied Behavior Analysis.

3. Create a scenario illustrating how a teacher might apply Alphie Kohn's principles of management to a classroom management problem.

4. Of all of the models discussed, which one do you think is the most sound? Explain why you chose this one. Which one do you think is the least sound? Why?

5. In what way or ways is the theory of William Glasser (Reality Therapy and the use of cl*ass meetings*) more or less applicable to teachers who teach in the upper grades (grades 7–12) as opposed to the lower grades (grades PreK–6)?

REFERENCES

Alberto, P., & Troutman, A. (1990). *Applied Behavior Analysis for Teachers: Influencing Student Performance* (3rd ed.). Columbus, OH: Merrill.

Bennett, B. (1997). Middle level discipline and young adolescents: Making the connection. In J.L. Irvin (Ed.), *What Current Research Says to the Middle Level Practitioner*. Columbus, OH: National Middle School Association.

Borman, S., & Levine, J. (1997). *A Practical Guide to Elementary Instruction: From Plan to Delivery*. Boston: Allyn & Bacon.

Canter, L. (1988). Let the educator beware: A response to Curwin and Mendler. *Educational Leadership, 46*(2), 71–73.

Canter, L., & Canter, M. (1976). *Assertive Discipline: A Take-Charge Approach for Today's Educator*. Seal Beach, CA: Canter and Associates.

Canter, L., & Canter, M. (1992). *Lee Canter's Assertive Discipline: Positive Behavior Management for Today's Classroom*. Santa Monica, CA: Canter and Associates.

Covaleski, J. (1992). Discipline and morality: Beyond rules and consequences. *The Educational Forum, 56*(2), 56–60.

Curwin, R., & Mendler, A. (1988). Packaged discipline programs: Let the buyer beware. *Educational Leadership, 46*(2), 68–71.

Dreikurs, R. (1968). *Psychology in the Classroom* (2nd ed.). New York: Harper & Row.

Dreikurs, R., & Cassell, P. (1972). *Discipline Without Tears*. New York: Hawthorn Books.

Eggen, P., & Kauchak, D. (2001). *Educational Psychology: Windows on Classrooms* (5th ed.). Upper Saddle River, NJ: Merrill Prentice Hall.

Ginott, H. (1965). *Between Parent and Child*. New York: Avon.

Ginott, H. (1969). *Between Parent and Teenager*. New York: Macmillan.

Ginott, H. (1971). *Teacher and Child*. New York: Macmillan.

Glasser, W. (1965). *Reality Therapy: A New Approach to Psychiatry*. New York: Harper & Row.

Glasser, W. (1969). *Schools without Failure*. New York: Harper & Row.

Glasser, W. (1992). *The Quality School: Managing Students Without Coercion* (2nd ed.). New York: Harper-Perennial.

Glasser, W. (1993). *The Quality School Teacher*. New York: Harper-Perennial.

Good, T., & Brophy, J. (1986). *Educational Psychology: A Realistic Approach* (3rd ed.). New York: Holt, Rhinehart, & Winston.

Gordon, T. (1974). *Teacher Effectiveness Training.* New York: Wyden.

Hunt, G., Touzel, T., & Wiseman, D. (1999). *Effective Teaching: Preparation and Implementation* (3rd ed.). Springfield, IL: Charles C. Thomas Publisher.

Johnson, D., & Johnson, R. (1995). *Teaching Students to be Peacemakers* (3rd ed.). Edina, MN: Interaction Book Company.

Johnson, D., & Johnson, R. (1997). *Joining together: Group Theory and Group Skills* (6th ed.). Boston: Allyn & Bacon.

Jones, F. (1987). *Positive Classroom Discipline.* New York: McGraw-Hill.

Kauffman, J. (1989). *Characteristics of Behavior Disorders of Children and Youth* (4th ed.). Upper Saddle River, NJ: Merrill/Prentice Hall.

Kohn, A. (1992). *No Contest: The Case Against Competition.* Rev. ed. Boston: Houghton Mifflin.

Kohn, A. (1993). Punished by Rewards: *The Trouble with Gold Stars, Incentive Plans, A's, Praise, and Other Bribes.* New York: Houghton Mifflin Company.

Kohn, A. (2000). *The Case Against Standardized Testing: Raising the Scores, Ruining the Schools.* Portsmouth, NH: Heinemann.

Kounin, J. (1970). *Discipline and Group Management in Classrooms.* New York: Holt, Rhinehart, & Winston.

Lezotte, L. (1997). *Learning for All.* Okemos, MI: Effective Schools Products, Ltd.

McCaslin, M., & Good, T. (1992). Compliant cognition: The misalliance of management and instructional goals in current school reform. *Educational Research,* 21(3), 4–17.

McCormack, S. (1989). Response to Render, Padilla and Krank: But practitioners say it works! *Educational Leadership,* 46(6), 77–79.

Pfiffner, L., Rosen, L., & O'Leary, S. (1985). The efficacy of an all-positive approach to classroom management. *Journal of Applied Behavior Analysis, 18,* 257–261.

Powell, R., McLaughlin, H., Savage, T., & Zehm, S. (2001). *Classroom Management: Perspectives on the Social Curriculum.* Upper Saddle River, NJ: Merrill/Prentice Hall.

Render, G., Padilla, J., & Krank, H. (1989). What research really shows about assertive discipline. *Educational Leadership,* 46(6), 72–75.

Rogers, C., & Freiberg, H. (1994). *Freedom to Learn* (3rd ed.). Columbus, OH: Charles E. Merrill.

Sokolove, S., Garrett, S., Sadker, M., & Sadker, D. (1990). Interpersonal communication skills. In J. Cooper (Ed.), *Classroom Teaching Skills.* Lexington, MA: D.C. Heath.

Stevahn, L., Johnson, D., Johnson, R., Green, K., & Laginski, M. (1997). Effects on high school students of conflict resolution training integrated into English literature. *The Journal of Social Psychology,* 137(3), 302–313.

Thorndike, E.L. (1905). *The Elements of Psychology.* New York: Seiler.

Thorndike, E.L. (1911). *Animal Intelligence: Experimental Studies.* New York: Macmillan.

Tolson, E., McDonald, S., & Moriarty, A. (1992). Peer mediation among high school students: A test of effectiveness. *Social Work in Education,* 14, 86–93.

Travers, R. (1977). *Essentials of Learning.* New York: Macmillan Publishing.

Webster, D. (1993). The unconvincing case for school-based conflict resolution programs for adolescents. *Health Affairs,* Winter, 127–141.

Woolfolk, A. (2001). *Educational Psychology* (8th ed.). Needham Heights, MA: Allyn
& Bacon.

Zabel, R., & Zabel, M. (1996). *Classroom Management in Context: Orchestrating Positive
Learning Environments.* Boston: Houghton Mifflin.

Zirpoli, T., & Melloy, K. (1997). *Behavior Management: Applications for Teachers and
Parents* (2nd ed.). Upper Saddle River, NJ: Merrill/Prentice Hall.

Chapter 4

BEST PRACTICE IN TEACHING FOR BEST PRACTICE IN STUDENT MOTIVATION AND CLASSROOM MANAGEMENT

No study of motivation and management in the classroom would be complete without addressing the topic of best practice in teaching. The relationship between best practice in teaching and best practice in motivation and management is well documented. When motivation and management problems arise, problems in teaching practice generally will also be found. Educational research reinforces the fact that higher levels of student motivation and fewer instances of student management problems are evident when teachers use effective teaching practices.

Tauber (1999) notes that no classroom management technique will be effective for long if effective teaching is absent. Classroom management models and their accompanying theories and recommended strategies that go with them are not substitutes for good teaching. Effective teaching may well be the most difficult job in our society and, in effect, actually represents a preventive discipline measure that keeps students so involved and interested that they are not inclined to cause problems (Glasser, 1990). But, as identified here, understanding effective teaching is not all that is needed either. It is the teacher's ability to understand and implement sound practices in student motivation and classroom management, coupled with similarly sound practices in teaching, that pull the entire learning enterprise together and make the most optimum levels of learning possible for students and comparable levels of teaching possible for teachers.

It is easy to sometimes forget or underestimate the ongoing challenges of the learning environment and not recognize the power of their ultimate impact on both teachers and students. William Chandler Bagley of the University of Illinois wrote in 1907 that, "Absolute fearlessness is the first essential for the teacher on whom rests the responsibility for governing an elementary or secondary school. This fearlessness is not alone or chiefly the expression of physical courage, although this must not be lacking. It is rather an expression of moral courage...standing firm in one's convictions even though the community may not approve...it is this sort of courage that is the rarest and, at the same time, the most essential" (Curwin & Mendler, p. 1, 1999). Courage must always be an important part of the learning process, and for many the greatest challenge is in the courage to establish, manage, and teach in the type of learning environment that will produce the best for all involved. The following statement of a high school senior reflects the power of this environment:

Silent Defiance

I'm the one who watched,
as you laughed;
I'm the one who listened patiently,
while you talked unceasingly;
I'm the one who sat silent,
as your shouts grew louder;
I'm the one who always came,
while your chair sat empty;
I'm the one whose dreams were hidden,
as yours were fulfilled;
I'm the one who cared,
while you butchered knowledge;
I'm the one who reasoned,
as you discussed;
I'm the one who will remember
when all of you will forget.

(by Heather Osborn, high school senior, from
Curwin and Mendler, pp. 1–2, 1999)

With the recognition that effective student motivation and classroom management rests on a solid foundation of effective teaching, Chapter 4 provides an overview of best teaching practices that have been identified through educational research. The relationship between quality teaching, quality student motivation, and quality classroom management will be evident.

In establishing the overall framework for this text, Chapter 1 presented the Model for Reflection and Inquiry, and it was identified that, to be effective, teachers must be good reflective practitioners. Three case studies of beginning teachers who had experienced problems of motivation and management in their classrooms were also presented. Of the three teachers featured in these case studies, Jenn (in the case study *Jenn's Planning and Analysis*) was the only teacher of the three who really dealt with the problems that she encountered as a reflective practitioner. Jenn systematically reflected on the events of her difficult day and how these events contributed to her problems in student motivation and classroom management. With Jenn's reflections being presented as an example of the use of the Model for Reflection and Inquiry, Jenn's behaviors were consistent with those of a reflective educator. She identified the problems that she had encountered, reviewed specific events of the day related to them, analyzed the events with respect to their impact on her classroom management and ability to motivate her students, and, on the basis of this information, made decisions as to how she should move forward in making adjustments for the next day. Jenn was engaged in guided problem solving and reflective thinking. Of special importance, Jenn accepted the responsibility for her student motivation and classroom management difficulties and did not lay blame for her problems on her students, her administrative support, the "types" of students she was working with, or anything else. Although they involved others, the problems were hers to solve.

Jenn's situation and the process of reflection that she went through should be considered as they relate to the information on best practice in teaching that is developed throughout the remainder of this chapter. A formal model such as the Model for Reflection and Inquiry can be used to bring logical reasoning to problems associated with student behavior and combat what is often the emotionally charged environment that accompanies problems of student motivation and classroom management. It can also guide the development of well-grounded decision making with respect to identifying solutions to these problems. Such an approach will systematically lead to higher quality in instruction, motivation, and management.

The search for best practice in teaching, and, therefore, in student motivation and classroom management, will always be ongoing and may at times seem to be an intellectually exhausting endeavor. A mistake made by many teachers occurs when it is believed that what needs to be known about best teaching practices is fully understood. This level of understanding will never be reached, because the knowledge base related to best practice in teaching continues to develop and expand. The application of this knowledge base is often quite situational in its use resulting in the need to not only know "what works" in teaching but also to know when, where, and with whom it works best. Henson and Eller (1999, p. 10) state that

> Effective teachers are always looking for better ways to teach . . . are willing to explore different approaches . . . This is why curiosity, experimentation, and risk-taking are so important to teachers. Throughout their careers, suc-

cessful teachers improve their ability to reflect on their behavior and use their reflective judgment to improve their teaching.

Educational research has identified and continues to reinforce certain teacher characteristics related to effective teaching resulting in higher student achievement. These characteristics are often referred to as best practice teaching characteristics.

ESTABLISHING A FOUNDATION FOR BEST PRACTICE IN TEACHING

Much of what is known about best practice in teaching includes information related to classroom *planning and organization, goal setting and communication, teacher instructional strategies, time management, teacher-to-student interactions, relationships with students, and classroom management rules and procedures.* Armstrong, Henson, and Savage (1997) identify the following six characteristics of effective teachers. Effective teachers:

1. **Play a central, dominant role in the classroom but involve students in planning and organization:** Effective teachers accept their important responsibility in classroom leadership but also that students who are personally invested in their own learning will develop a greater sense of ownership for their learning and achieve at higher levels.
2. **Set high goals and communicate these goals to their students:** It is important that teacher expectations be high though realistic; it is critical that teachers make their goals for their students clear not only in terms of the learning experiences that will be undertaken but also in terms of how students will be evaluated.
3. **Work mostly with the entire class and less often with small groups, sometimes providing independent work for students:** Teachers who are able to coordinate the learning of all students at the same time through larger group instructional experiences will develop a greater sense of community in the classroom and allow students to more clearly perceive their own progress but also the work and activities of others at the same time.
4. **Maintain a brisk lesson pace, requiring public and overt student participation:** Lessons that are seen moving too slowly by students, essentially only dragging along, allow for greater opportunities for students to drift away from the lesson experience; students who move forward with the lesson at a quicker pace and who are overtly involved in the instruction typically learn at higher levels and enjoy their learning more.

5. **Use little criticism, shape student responses so that they are correct, hold students responsible for their work, and attend to students equitably:** Treating students fairly, providing uplifting rather than negative comments, and letting students know that they have responsibilities as learners just as the teacher has responsibilities as a teacher result in a more wholesome and positive learning environment; students who feel safe in the learning environment and who are meaningfully involved in it are more successful in their work.

6. **Set and maintain clear rules for students' academic and social behavior:** Although not thought to be the case by some, students actually do desire and need clear boundaries in the classroom; students work better in environments that are well defined in terms of the *do's* and *don'ts*, the *right's* and *wrong's*, than they do in settings in which there is ambiguity and inconsistency as to what is acceptable and not acceptable behavior.

Borich (1992) reports on four teacher characteristics related to teaching effectiveness. These characteristics are broken down into the categories of *lesson clarity, instructional variety, task orientation and engagement,* and *student success rate.*

Lesson Clarity

Lesson clarity refers to how clearly students understand the lessons of their teachers. It is not just important that teachers believe that they are clear, what is more important is whether their students truly understand them. Teachers who are vague, use vocabulary that students do not understand or who are generally not well organized, typically are not considered as being clear in their teaching. When students do not understand the various communications of their teachers, there is little reason to think that they will be able to perform at the highest level of their potentials. Students need to understand what their teachers are saying and expect of them to benefit the most from their learning experiences.

Instructional Variety

Instructional variety refers to the general teaching repertoire of the teacher. Does the teacher use a number of different teaching strategies or only a very few? Does the teacher use many different resources in his or her teaching or use the same resources over and over? Having variety in instruction contributes to the perceived "energy" of the teacher and offers students different stimuli during lesson activities to which they may respond. The use of different instructional approaches makes the teacher seem more interesting and intriguing to students, piques students' natural curiosity to learn, and varies the stimuli in the classroom. Most students learn best through their encounters with a variety of different stimuli. The teacher with variability in the use of instructional techniques is better able to offer students more connecting points as lessons are delivered. The teacher who is skilled in using a number of different types of strategies is more effective than the teacher who is limited to only a few approaches.

Task Orientation and Engagement

Time on task is a powerful concept when analyzing the teaching-learning process. When one considers that there are only a limited number of hours in the day in which students are in school and that a good portion of the typical school day is given over to non instructional activities (e.g., moving from class to class, recess in the lower grades, lunch, traveling to and from the restroom), the question of time available for learning becomes even more critical. Teachers who have greater levels of **Academic Learning Time**, *time when students are actively and successfully involved in the lesson's activities*, will have students who learn at higher levels. Having a high level of meaningful and successful time on task communicates to students that the teacher is well prepared and "in charge." It also communicates in clear terms where the teacher's instruction is headed and what the students will be expected to know or be able to do when the end of the instructional period is reached. Students who are on task are much less likely to present behavioral problems for their teachers.

Student Success Rate

Not only is wise use of time an important characteristic of effective teachers, effective teachers also have higher rates of student success in their teaching. **Student success rate** is defined as *the rate at which students understand and correctly complete their work.* Students should not be involved in just "doing things" in the classroom. What they do should be meaningful, learning related as to what the teacher has planned for instruction, and result in successful achievement and productivity. Teachers must know the abilities and interests of their students and plan their instruction accordingly based on this knowledge. Instruction in which few students can be successful falls far short of what needs to be accomplished in the classroom. This type of situation serves no one well. Success breeds success, and students who are successful one day will be better able to see themselves as being successful on another day. (See the discussion of Attribution Theory and Locus of Control in Chapter 2 as related to reasons given for student success.) Likewise, students who experience little or no success have far greater difficulty in seeing themselves as being successful and, in the end, in actually being successful. If teachers desire for their students to be successful in their learning, they must plan, teach, and evaluate in such a way that ensures success for them.

The prevailing societal view is one that focuses on identifying quick solutions to problems. The American society is at times even referred to by some as a "fast food" or "microwave" society. It is no wonder that in such an environment many teachers take this same outlook into the classroom with respect to finding quick solutions to the problems that they encounter there. The fact is there are no quick solutions or quick fixes to difficult problems of student motivation and classroom management. The solutions that work best may be just as readily found discussed in the research related to best practice in teaching as in studies of motivation and management.

EARLY RESEARCH ON BEST PRACTICE IN TEACHING

As motivation relates to management and management relates to motivation, so does best practice in teaching relate to both of these concepts together. One of the most significant and thorough reviews of the research in the area of teacher effectiveness was conducted more than thirty years ago by Rosenshine and Furst (1971). It is still considered important reading in the field today. Although considerable research has been conducted more recently, the work of Rosenshine and Furst serves as a sound beginning point for an investigation of effective teaching behaviors related to student achievement. The effective teaching characteristics identified by Armstrong, Henson and Savage (1997) and Borich (1992) are, to some degree, an expansion and refinement of characteristics identified through earlier research.

Of particular importance to the work of Rosenshine and Furst is the understanding given to the meaning of effective teaching. Although teachers are expected to accomplish many things in their work, perhaps the most important accomplishment is guiding students to achieve at higher levels. Defining effective teaching as teaching that results in higher levels of student achievement is not to discount the importance of students developing positive feelings about themselves and the world around them and toward learning itself. It does recognize, though, that the primary purpose of the teacher is to guide and advance students in their learning. Rosenshine and Furst (1971) report a total of eleven teacher behaviors or variables (i.e., best teaching practices) related to student achievement. They are presented here in the order of the degree to which they are so related.

- Clarity
- Variability
- Enthusiasm
- Task-oriented and/or business-like behavior
- Student opportunity to learn criterion material
- Use of student ideas and general indirectness
- Criticism
- Use of structuring comments
- Types of questions
- Probing behaviors
- Level of difficulty of instruction

Clarity

Teachers who have the ability to explain concepts clearly and who are able to answer students' questions so that their students understand the answers given to them are characterized by clarity in their instruction. When teachers are clear in their communications, their students feel more secure in their learning. They are better able to comprehend what is expected of them and, as a result of this, perform at higher achievement levels.

Variability

Variability, also referred to as instructional variety (Borich, 1992), is represented by the teacher's diversity of information-sending techniques or strategies used during the presentation of lessons. Teachers who have variability in their teaching use multiple strategies to get the main ideas of their lessons across to their students. Effective teachers have the ability to use expository lesson delivery and organize students for cooperative learning activities as appropriate to the purpose of the lesson. They are capable of exhibiting many different strategies in teaching and do so regularly. Through this variety, especially when strategies are matched to student learning styles, students remain more interested in the learning activities that their teachers have planned for them and learn more as a result.

Enthusiasm

Enthusiasm has been identified as the estimation of the amount of vigor and power displayed by the teacher. It also has been associated with the teacher's level of excitement, energy, involvement, and even interest regarding both the subject matter and teaching. Although an abstract concept, students have their own ideas about the enthusiasm of their teachers. Students feel they know when teachers are enjoying their work and are excited about being in the classroom and when they are not. Students draw from the enthusiasm shown by their teachers, or at least from what they perceive as their teachers' enthusiasm, and respond accordingly. Teacher enthusiasm is related to the concept of teacher *efficacy* discussed earlier as a part of the teacher's attitude toward teaching. Teachers who exhibit enthusiasm communicate that they are confident in what they are doing, not only in their own abilities but also in the abilities of their students.

Task-Oriented and/or Business-Like Behavior

Task-oriented teachers project that they know what they expect concerning student performance and the lessons that they teach and how to attain the student performance that they seek. They are seen by their students as knowing what they are doing, organized, and focused on what needs to be accomplished. Being task oriented and business like does not mean being impersonal or aloof when working with students. It does, however, communicate that the teacher knows that something important needs to be done and that the teacher and students together will be successful in completing the task that has been or is to be undertaken.

Student Opportunity to Learn Criterion Material

Teachers who are criterion focused in their teaching communicate to students their expected instructional outcomes before beginning their instruction and then teach specifically toward the students' successful attainment of these desired outcomes. What is desired is not kept secret; there is no mystery. Students know what is expected of them and how they will be evaluated (the criteria used) as to their level of success in achieving the identified instructional outcomes. This security of direction and understanding of the evaluation process is important to students as they engage in the teacher's planned learning activities. It is also important to the teacher in that it offers the teacher additional focus and direction with respect to addressing stated objectives.

Use of Student Ideas and General Indirectness

The use of student ideas by teachers during instruction and, in so doing, communicating to students that their ideas and input are important enhances student achievement. The use of student ideas is an important part of *indi-*

rect teaching. Students have higher levels of meaningful participation and interest in their learning when their ideas are regularly incorporated into the learning process. They are more academically successful, because they perceive their teachers as valuing both them as individuals and their ideas.

Criticism

Negative relationships exist between the use of teacher criticism and student achievement. This point was identified earlier with the work of Armstrong, Henson, and Savage (1997). Teachers who are characterized by using criticism in their teaching, often seen by students as an attempt to justify their authority, typically have students who achieve less in most subject areas. Teachers who use frequent criticism are seen by their students as being less prepared for their work and less sure of themselves. The use of criticism can create a threatening environment for students and detract from the learning process, resulting in lower student achievement.

Use of Structuring Comments

The teacher's use of structuring comments or statements in communicating with students (i.e., alerting students to the more important instructional events that are about to follow in the teacher's lesson), is highly recommended. The use of structuring comments is appropriate at the start of lessons and at the start of different sections of lessons. Such comments help students focus on and attend to what will be taking place during the instruction that is to follow. The use of structuring comments also projects to students that the teacher is well planned and has a clear understanding of where the learning activity is headed.

Types of Questions

Effective teachers are skilled at asking both higher and lower level questions of cognition; the use of both types is related to student achievement. The classic system of question categorization identified by Gallagher and Aschner (1963) is helpful in understanding levels and types of questions. This system places questions into four categories: *cognitive memory, convergent, divergent,* and *evaluative.* It serves as a guide for the teacher as to the different levels of cognition of questions that they may choose to use and the intellectual processing on the part of students that they invoke. The use of different types of questions helps to maintain student interest and projects a greater variability in teaching. Hunt, Touzel, and Wiseman (1999) explain the basic characteristics of the questions used in this categorizing system.

Cognitive Memory Questions: questions that ask students to recall previously learned and memorized information; single-word answers are often used in answering questions, answers tend to sound alike and are predictable; even though more lengthy answers may be provided, they do not require creative thought and are classified clearly as right or wrong; behaviors such as recalling, recognizing, and reporting are typically involved.

Convergent Questions: questions that ask students to put facts or concepts together to obtain the single correct answer; answers to convergent questions are more complex than answers to cognitive memory questions but are still classified as either right or wrong; questions may require students to make comparisons, explain facts or concepts, state or describe relationships, or solve problems using learned procedures.

Divergent Questions: questions that ask students to engage in divergence of thought and produce responses that are original for that student; student thinking is much more creative at this level of questioning; questions may require students to predict, hypothesize, or infer; expressions such as "what if" are common to questions in this category.

Evaluative Questions: questions that ask students to make judgments or evaluations based on logically derived evidence; evidence is derived from the use of the levels of thought identified in the previous three categories; students must defend or explain their judgments based on criteria that they designate or that have been established by others.

Probing Behaviors

Probing behaviors occur when the teacher requests students to go deeper into their thinking or to elaborate on comments made or positions taken. The use of probing behaviors, typically through the use of probing questions, communicates to students that the teacher is interested in knowing more about their ideas. Probing behaviors cause students to review their ideas and explore them more thoroughly. They also help the teacher in creating a classroom atmosphere that involves student ideas and general indirectness that was identified earlier. Because by its very purpose probing for student ideas does not involve looking at what students say as being either right or wrong, probing behaviors offer natural opportunities for teachers to praise students for their thinking. Probing behaviors should be carried out in a way that is seen by students as being nonthreatening and nonjudgmental.

Level of Difficulty of Instruction

Teachers who create learning environments in which students feel appropriately challenged, but not over challenged, have established environments in which students achieve at higher levels. Teachers should offer instruction that is neither too hard nor too easy for students. Much has been said in recent years about the importance of increasing academic rigor in schools and holding students to higher standards. Although important, this should not be done at the expense of students who are simply unable to reach the higher standards that may be established. If students perceive that the difficulty of instruction offered by the teacher is beyond their ability, they may either withdraw from the instruction or act out against it. It is important for teachers, in knowing the abilities and interests of their students, to establish levels of instruction that are out of the immediate reach of their students (therefore not too easy) but that are reachable with effort and teacher assistance (therefore appropriately challenging). In terms of fully knowing their students and using this knowledge in planning and delivering their instruction, it is helpful for teachers to apply the concept of the *zone of proximal development* to their teaching. The **zone of proximal development** is defined as *a range of tasks that a student cannot yet do alone but can accomplish when assisted by a more skilled partner* (Eggen & Kauchak, 2001). To continually challenge students in appropriate ways, it is important for learning tasks to be presented at the outer reaches of this range or zone. Presenting tasks beyond this zone will cause student interest to diminish in the tasks as students will see the tasks, as being too difficult for them to be successful. Working toward them will seem to be not worth their effort for this reason. Likewise, if the teacher too regularly presents tasks at the lower end of this range or zone, students will then lose interest, because the tasks will be viewed as too simplistic and unimportant.

MORE CURRENT RESEARCH ON BEST PRACTICE IN TEACHING

Additional research has been conducted since the work of Rosenshine and Furst was published in the early 1970s. Although more current research has expanded the knowledge base related to best practice in teaching, it has not contradicted earlier findings. Eggen and Kauchak (2001) identify eight teacher characteristics associated with student achievement and refer to these characteristics as essential teaching skills.

- Attitudes
- Use of time
- Organization
- Communication
- Focus
- Feedback
- Questioning
- Review and Closure

Attitudes

The consideration of teacher attitude goes beyond seeing the teacher as merely having a "good" or "bad" attitude. Were it this simple, the influence of attitude on teaching and learning would have been fully understood long before now. Teachers have studied attitude, researchers have studied attitude, and students have responded to teacher attitude since the beginning of formal education. Woolfolk (2001) notes that teachers have a responsibility for the attitudes of their students, both positive and negative. When students have negative attitudes toward themselves or their learning, teachers must · identify the causes of these negative attitudes so that they may help them become more positive for their learning to advance. An important aspect of this process relates to teachers and their own attitudes. As presented earlier, teachers who hold the belief that they and their schools can have a positive effect on their students and their learning are said to have high *teacher efficacy* (Bruning, Schraw, & Ronning, 1995). Classrooms and schools with such teachers have increased student achievement. Teachers with high efficacy work well with low-achieving students and use praise rather than criticism to motivate and reward them. They use their time effectively and are more accepting of the unique, individual qualities of their students. High-efficacy teachers do not give up on students and more readily change their strategies and adopt and adapt instructional materials as needed to meet student needs (Poole, Okeafor, & Sloan, 1989). Low-efficacy teachers are more critical of their students and persevere less when seeking solutions to their students' learning and motivational problems. Such teachers do not hold strong beliefs that they really can make a difference in the lives of their students (Kagan, 1992). Ashton and Webb (1986) report that teachers with low efficacy tend to stratify their classes more by student ability, or what they perceive to be student ability, and then give more effort, attention, and affection to their students believed to have higher ability. Low-efficacy teachers also perceive their students' behaviors, particularly those of their low-achieving students, in terms of their potential threats to the orderliness of their classrooms. Teachers with high efficacy are not as likely to feel threatened by the misbehavior or potential misbehavior of their students.

Use of Time

Effective teachers use their time wisely. Jones' theory of management was presented in Chapter 3, with the foundation of the theory being identified that problems of student management are frequently brought about by poor or inappropriate use of time in the classroom. Wasted time or idle time leads to problems in management that could otherwise have been avoided. Time in schools and classrooms is often broken down into the following four dimensions:

1. **Allocated time:** the amount of time a particular teacher or school designates to an identified course topic or activity.
2. **Instructional time:** the portion of allocated time that is actually devoted to learning activities.
3. **Engaged time:** often referred to as time-on-task, engaged time is the portion of Instructional Time that students actually spend directly involved in learning activities.
4. **Academic learning time:** Academic learning time takes all other forms of time into account and is recognized by students not only paying attention during instructional activities but also interacting successfully with the content that is being taught; this time is that portion of the classroom time during which students are successfully engaged in meaningful learning experiences.

Given the multifaceted nature of any school, many events take place on a regular basis that compete for time that otherwise could be available for instruction. Instructional time is lost through different disruptions, interruptions, late starts, and less than smooth transitions (Karweit, 1989). Weinstein and Mignano (1993) observe that out of a typical school year only thirty to forty percent of the time is given over to quality Academic Learning Time. Research also suggests that the greater the amount of Academic Learning Time found in the classroom, the greater the level of student achievement. The best use of time in the classroom is determined by the degree to which the teacher is fully planned for instruction. The better planned the teacher is for instruction that is relevant to the interests of the students in the classroom and responsive to their learning styles and abilities, the greater the levels of student achievement that can be reached.

Organization

Being well organized does not mean being overly restrictive. Teachers who are better organized have higher achieving students than teachers who are not well organized. Students can tell whether a teacher is organized or not.

Teachers who are organized, or at least perceived by their students as being organized, have higher achieving students than those who do not have or project this quality.

Organization involves management of the classroom in terms of its physical elements and rules and procedures, as well as academic concerns, with respect to the teaching process. **Management organization** in the classroom refers to *the general organizational structure and procedures that the teacher has developed to keep the classroom running smoothly.* Organized teachers have their materials ready when it is time to begin the lesson, start on time, and have established learning routines (e.g., certain ways of taking roll and collecting papers to minimize the time these activities take and making transitions from one activity to another quickly and smoothly). Established routines in the classroom enable teachers and their students to know what to anticipate as the teacher's instruction moves forward. Effective management organization allows for classroom time to be used more productively. Although the ability to be spontaneous as the situation dictates is important, teachers who have well-established routines and procedures bring a positive predictability to their teaching, giving their students a greater sense of order and balance. This order and balance, or equilibrium in the environment that results from it, contribute to student learning. **Academic organization** in the classroom is reflected by *the teacher's means of ordering and arranging information for instruction so that students will be better able to understand the information communicated.* Effective teachers have specific organization schemes to assist students in ordering and arranging information. Being well organized academically does not mean teachers lack spontaneity or the ability to teach to the moment. Academic organization refers to the teacher being well prepared to carry out instruction in a way that assists the students as they learn and remember what is being taught. The use of diagrams, outlines, hierarchies, and schematics can be significant in not only helping teachers in presenting organized lessons but also in assisting students in making better organization of and use of the information being presented. The teacher's ability to be clear in communications with students is in many ways related to the teacher's ability to be academically organized. Good teacher organization is founded on the routines and rules the teacher has developed for both student motivation and classroom management that effectively use time wisely, thus enabling the classroom to run in an efficient manner.

Communication

Cruickshank (1985) and Snyder and colleagues (1991) identify a positive correlation between language clarity and student achievement, reinforcing the importance of teachers being clear in the use of their verbal communication. Four aspects of language clarity have been identified related to best practice in teaching:

1. **Precise terminology:**   the teacher eliminates vague and ambiguous words and phrases from presentations and interactions with students.
2. **Connected discourse:**   the teacher's presentation is thematically well connected and leads to a goal, going point by point; the absence of this type of discourse results in communication that may seem rambling to the student, being disjointed and not appropriately linked.
3. **Transition signals:**   transition signals assist in blending one topic area with the next that follows; without such signals, the teacher may be seen as merely, and abruptly, moving from topic to topic or point to point
4. **Emphasis:**   emphasis denotes the teacher specifically identifying information that is to be remembered; phrases such as, "This is important," and "Be sure to remember this," are examples of the use of emphasis; if something is of special importance, tell the students.

Students cannot be expected to learn at their maximum potentials when their teachers are not clear. Although a teacher may comment that a particular student does not pay attention and does not understand something, this is often more the teacher's problem than the student's. It is the teacher who must be expert in communication and reaching students with the language used in the classroom. Teacher clarity was first on the list of best teaching practices or teacher characteristics identified by Rosenshine and Furst (1971).

Focus

Focus is an important aspect of the teacher's ability to communicate and attend to ideas in the classroom. Focus represents bringing student attention to the lesson at the very beginning of the instructional experience and then maintaining this attention throughout the remainder of the lesson. Hunter (1984) identifies this as establishing an *anticipatory set*. **Anticipatory set** is *the mental or attitudinal foundation established by the teacher for the students at the beginning of the instructional experience that helps students to understand what they may anticipate in the instruction that will follow.* When students are focused at the beginning of the lesson, they are better connected to the body of the lesson that follows. Teachers who have good introductory focus are able to more easily gain and maintain student attention and provide a stronger connection for the students with the material being taught as the lesson progresses. Focus serves to motivate students, increase their curiosity, and make the lesson seem more interesting and intriguing. Teachers can often gain student attention successfully through the use of certain visual or auditory sensory techniques such as pictures, models, concrete objects, riddles, the overhead projector, the chalkboard, and computer technology. The importance of using such influences, classically referred to as **advance organizers** in *the use of introductory statements or activities to frame new content as a part of the lesson focus*, was developed in detail by Ausubel (1978). The use of focus techniques brings students more into the overall mainstream of the lesson than into any specific part of it. This helps students avoid difficulties in understanding the main intent of the teacher's instruction but also assists them in attending to the important individual components that make it up.

Feedback

Few individuals function well in environments characterized by ambiguity and uncertainty. Such environments bring about unnecessary stress and pressure for students. Teachers who regularly provide feedback to their students regarding the accuracy or appropriateness of their responses and their work have higher achieving students. The best feedback provides constructive information, praise, and encouragement as appropriate and is immediate and specific. Elawar and Corno (1985) observe that pertinent individual feedback that is aimed at correcting errors made during learning positively affects student performance and attitude. Such feedback not only results in increased achievement but also in increased motivation. It contributes to a greater sense of balance, because students are able to monitor their own progress. It also helps students create associations that result in more meaningful learning and advancement toward stated goals.

Feedback generally comes in one of two forms: written or oral. Providing written feedback poses a challenge for some teachers, because it is more time consuming. Because of its time-consuming nature, many teachers often provide only sketchy written feedback for their students or information that is not constructive in quality. Although it may take more time, written feedback that is specific to the nature of the students' performance is an important part of effective teaching and is positively related to student achievement. Oral feedback is more easily given, because it can be used in ongoing discussions and question-and-answer periods. The constructive value of oral feedback also is critical to enhancing student achievement. Quick, one-word responses, or responses that merely inform the student that he or she is correct or not correct, are not as effective as more elaborate responses. More elaborate or extended responses let the student know that he or she was correct or incorrect but also why this was the case.

Praise is one of the most common and adaptable forms of teacher feedback. Some interesting and not especially positive patterns in teacher use of praise have been identified through educational research (Brophy, 1981).

• Praise is not used nearly as often as most teachers believe, being used less than five times per class.

- Praise for good behavior is actually quite rare and occurs only once every two or more hours in the elementary grades and less than that as students get older.
- Praise is influenced by the type of student, such as on the quality of the responses that students give. High-achieving, well-behaved, and attentive students receive greater amounts of praise than do low-achieving and inattentive students.
- Praise is often given by teachers on the basis of the responses that they expect to receive as much as it is on the answers that the students actually give.

Considering the potential positive impact of the use of praise in the classroom, it is recommended that teachers (1) praise genuinely, (2) praise immediately, (3) praise accomplishments that students may not be aware of, (4) praise strategically with different types of students, (5) praise the effort as well as the answer, (6) praise specifically, and (7) praise judiciously. Understanding these elements of effective use of praise are important to the teaching process, because they impact the student's motivation to stay or become involved in the teacher's lesson.

Questioning

Research on teacher questioning strategies has increased considerably over the last twenty years. Gall and Artero-Boname (1995) note that the Educational Resource Information Center (ERIC) database referenced more than 100 research reports and professional papers on questioning techniques annually for the decade from 1982. Although it is important that teachers have well-developed questioning skills, such skills do not develop naturally. The development of good questioning skills comes only through specific question-asking applications that are consistently analyzed in terms of whether the questions and the way they were asked elicited the desired outcomes. Research continues to reinforce the relationship between the quality of a teacher's questioning skills and student achievement.

Although some might think that certain questions are preferred over others, such as low cognitive over high cognitive or vice versa, this is not the case. Different types of questions serve different learning purposes. The teacher should select questions as they relate to the learning outcomes desired. If the objective of the lesson is to focus on the development of certain basic skills, low cognitive questions are of better value. If the purpose is to place students in situations in which they will be expected to analyze or evaluate information or share their personal ideas, high cognitive questions should be used (Bloom, et al., 1956; Good & Brophy, 2000). Both high and low cognitive questions correlate positively with student achievement.

Eggen and Kauchak (2001), O'Flahavan, Hartman, and Pearson (1988), and Tobin (1987) report the following as characteristics of effective questioning strategies:

FREQUENCY. Generally, the more questions the better; greater numbers of questions allow for more students to be involved in the dynamics of a lesson and more opportunities for the teacher to monitor the students' and the lesson's progress.

EQUITABLE DISTRIBUTION. Teachers should strive for a pattern of questioning in which all students are called on as equally as possible; more questioning with equal distribution across the class increases the opportunity for providing more feedback and helps students stay motivated and connected to the lesson; this reduces the likelihood that students will drift away from the instruction and become involved in misconduct behaviors.

PROMPTING. The technique of prompting is one of helping students respond to questions by providing cues after an incorrect or incomplete answer or silence.

WAIT-TIME. Wait-time is the period of silence before or after a student is asked a question and when the teacher speaks again; the use of wait-time increases student learning by giving students time to think; in most classrooms, regardless of grade or ability level, wait-times are very short, frequently less than one second (Rowe, 1986); research suggests that increasing wait-time to at least three seconds will have a positive impact on student learning.

Review and Closure

Clear *review* and *closure* consistently serve as aids to learning and enhancing academic achievement. **Review** *may occur at different points of the lesson, either close to the beginning, midpoint during the body of the lesson, or at the end, when the teacher summarizes important points from previous work in helping students to link what has been learned to what will be taught in the future.* Dempster (1991) observes that when review is used effectively, teachers are able to guide students beyond a focus on only the specific information presented in the lesson into more substantive conceptual understandings. **Closure** is *a type of review that occurs at the end of the instructional period that enables the student to end the lesson with a better understanding of the topic and a place to build on in the future.* This can be accomplished through a number of techniques such as the use of questions, short written assignments, or classroom discussion. The use of each technique normally provides the teacher with valuable information related to identifying the most important place, or perhaps way, to begin the next lesson. An effective use of closure is to ask students to state in their own words important points of information covered in the lesson. This enables students to end the lesson with a better understanding of the lesson's content and a place to build on in the future. It also serves to inform the teacher. If teachers are uncertain as to what level of understanding their students have at the end of one lesson, they will not be well prepared to begin the next lesson that will follow. They will be unable to build on what their students know, because they will not really have a good understanding of what they know. Teachers may know what they taught, but this does not mean that they know what the students understand.

The last five to ten years have produced a special focus on teaching practices as related to student learning styles, brain research, and teaching and learning standards. Tiletson (2000) identifies ten teaching practices believed to have tremendous power for teachers when paired with the best research linked to their implementation. The practices are based on research in the field and on actual classroom experiences of teachers. Most teachers today are especially interested in guidance that is as real-world oriented and as practical as it can be. The following ten best teaching practices are believed to meet these criteria.

1. Create an enriched and emotionally supportive environment.
2. Use a variety of teaching strategies that address different learning styles.
3. Use strategies that help students make connections from prior learning and experiences to new learning and across disciplines.
4. Teach for long-term memory as a primary goal.
5. Integrate higher-level thinking skills into learning.
6. Use collaborative learning as an integral part of the classroom.
7. Bridge the gap between all learners, regardless of race, socioeconomic status, gender, or creed.
8. Evaluate learning through a variety for authentic assessments.
9. Promote real-world applications of learning.
10. Provide a seamless integration of technology for high-quality instruction.

ANALYZING CLASSROOMS FOR BEST PRACTICE IN TEACHING

Although it is critical that teachers have a solid knowledge base of information related to student motivation, classroom management, and best practice in teaching, having this knowledge base alone is not sufficient for teachers to consistently establish and maintain well-managed classrooms where motivated students achieve at high levels. Given the availability of so much information related to effective teaching, if this were the case, many teachers should be experiencing far fewer student motivation and classroom management problems than they presently do. Having information on best practices in teaching does not guarantee the appropriate application of this information to the teacher's behavior in the classroom.

Cangelosi (2000) identifies that teachers must take charge of their own individual classrooms and act in informed and deliberate ways for those classrooms to reflect the best practice that they desire. The role of the teacher in instruction is integrally involved in the teacher's role in student motivation and classroom management. Cangelosi recommends that teachers use The Teaching Process Model as a system for approaching classroom instruction in such a way that the instruction will be responsive to issues of motivation and management. The model is composed of six steps:

1. Determine needs of students.
2. Determine learning goal.
3. Design learning activities.
4. Prepare for the learning activities.
5. Conduct the learning activities.
6. Determine how well students have achieved the learning goal.

The Teaching Process Model is offered here, because it provides an advance organizer for systematically teaching students to replace uncooperative behaviors or misbehaviors with cooperative, positive ones. Through the teacher's instruction, in particular through the first step in determining and understanding student needs, followed by clearly identified learning goals and activities, the teacher will be able to proactively approach the teaching process in a way that will lessen the occurrences of unwanted student behaviors.

It is the ability of the teacher to reflect on and use this information that makes the greatest difference between a teacher who is a poor manager and motivator and one who is skilled in these areas. Recall Jenn's case study (*Jenn's Planning and Analysis*) presented in Chapter 1. Jenn reflected on her problems and made plans to deal with them. The Model for Reflection and Inquiry introduced earlier is recommended as being useful in guiding this reflection.

Reflection in and of itself, however, may produce little positive change. The key to the most effective reflection also includes the appropriate use of relevant information. The third step of the Model for Reflection and Inquiry is Collection of Relevant Data. It is in this step that relevant information should be sought and/or observations made as a part of the inquiry process.

What teachers know about student motivation, classroom management, and best teaching practices greatly influences the benefits that will come from this step. The depth of information collected and the appropriate use made of it will, ultimately, determine the level of the quality of the teacher's problem solving.

The *System for the Analysis of Teaching Practices* has been developed to assist teachers as they review their teaching behaviors. The *System* is built on the knowledge base of best practices in teaching and can serve as a helpful tool for teachers for self-review and making decisions to strengthen the instructional process. Return to either the *Seth's Confidence, Susan's Problem Ownership,* or *Jenn's Planning and Analysis* case study from Chapter 1 and use the instrument as though you were one of these three teachers.

SYSTEM FOR THE ANALYSIS OF TEACHING PRACTICES

Circle the appropriate number on the scale provided as you reflect on your teaching in each teacher characteristic area. Before making your selection, consider the accompanying statement(s) associated with each item as to how well the statement describes your professional behavior.

	Seldom			*Always*	
1. Clarity	1	2	3	4	5

My students understand the words that I use in my teaching; I get my ideas across clearly without the need to repeat myself.

2. Variability	1	2	3	4	5

My teaching reflects the regular use of many different teaching strategies and resources rather than only a few.

3. Enthusiasm	1	2	3	4	5

I am energetic, and my teaching reflects this energy; my enthusiasm shows in my teaching, my preparation, and the classroom environment that I establish.

4. Task-oriented   1   2   3   4   5

I conduct my classroom in a positive yet businesslike manner. Students know where they are headed in their learning activities; my teaching is focused on the desired learning outcomes at all times.

5. Students Learning Criterion Material   1   2   3   4   5

My students know in advance of the learning activities what is important and how they will be evaluated. My assessments do not include "extras" that my students were not aware of.

6. Use of Student Ideas   1   2   3   4   5

My teaching is characterized by a heavy involvement of student ideas. Students know from the way I teach that their ideas are important.

7. Structuring Comments   1   2   3   4   5

I use structuring comments at the beginning of my lessons and as I move through my lessons to help my students stay focused on my objectives and know what is expected of them.

8. Level of Difficulty   1   2   3   4   5

My expectations are challenging but not beyond the reach of my students. Students are not "left behind" in my class; they know that they can be successful.

9. Success Rates   1   2   3   4   5

My students are consistently successful; no student considers himself or herself a failure, because my approach to teaching ensures success for all.

10. Attitude   1   2   3   4   5

I know that if I plan my lessons thoroughly and select learning activities appropriately all of my students can succeed. It may take extra effort, but I can make a difference with all of my students.

11. Use of Time   1   2   3   4   5

Students do not have idle time in my classroom but stay actively and successfully engaged in meaningful experiences.

12. Organization   1   2   3   4   5

My classroom and teaching are organized, and my students recognize this. I am well prepared, and my teaching transitions are smooth and controlled.

13. Communication   1   2   3   4   5

I communicate clearly to my students. This includes both verbal and nonverbal messages. I seldom need to repeat myself.

14. Focus   1   2   3   4   5

Students understand the purpose of my lessons and my lessons stay focused. Spontaneous events do take place, but my students know where my lessons are headed and the outcomes that are desired.

15. Feedback   1   2   3   4   5

Students receive ample feedback related to their progress during my lessons and through my assessments. They regularly receive oral and written feedback that explains their progress to them.

16. Questioning   1   2   3   4   5

I regularly use both higher and lower order questioning. Students are asked many questions to develop their thinking and so I can know what they understand.

17. Probing Behaviors   1   2   3   4   5

My teaching includes probing students so that they may go deeper into and expand on their ideas, especially as their ideas relate to what I am teaching.

18. Pacing   1   2   3   4   5

My lesson pace is normally quicker as opposed to slower.

19. Review and Closure   1   2   3   4   5

I review at the beginning of my lessons what has just been previously taught. I review again through closure at the end of each lesson.

20. Criticism   1   2   3   4   5

My classroom environment is positive, open and inviting. I seldom use criticism with my students.

Scoring Your Analysis

Twenty items make up the *System for the Analysis of Teaching Practices* with a maximum possible rating of 5 on each item. The instrument is not intended for evaluation purposes but as a guide for reflection and determining instructional directions for the future. It offers a way to analyze individual teacher behaviors and a teacher's performance in its entirety by combining individual ratings together. Each behavior is treated as having the same level of importance.

The following rating scheme may be used when seeking a combined rating of all items.

Points	*Self-Rating*
93–100	Excellent
86–92	Above average
79–85	Average
70–78	Below average
Below 70	Unsatisfactory

CONCLUSION

Chapter 4 has included a detailed overview of educational research related to what is popularly referred to as best practice in teaching. In so doing, information provided reinforces two important points. First, for teachers to be effective they need to have a strong knowledge base of information on what is known about best practice in teaching, student motivation, and classroom management. The body of knowledge in these areas has continued to grow steadily since early studies were conducted. Second, teachers need to be able to use what they know to make sound decisions in the classroom. Knowing important information and not being able to use it leaves the teacher at a level of being less than optimally effective and students at a level at which they are not learning at their greatest potentials.

The *System for the Analysis of Teaching Practices* was introduced as a way to systematically analyze teaching performance in twenty teacher behavior areas. The *System* is built on the best teaching practices introduced throughout the chapter and is research based in its makeup. Teachers, and those who desire to be teachers, are encouraged to study and then use the instrument in real or hypothetical situations as it represents the most current thinking on characteristics and behaviors of effective teachers as related to student achievement.

The knowledge base related to best practice in teaching, student motivation, and classroom management will never be complete, because educators who are formal researchers and those who are practicing teachers continually search for those instructional strategies and teacher behaviors that will enhance learning in the classroom. This is a critically important dynamic of the teaching profession. Just as students in the classroom have expectations placed on them for what they need to know, so to do their teachers. Teachers cannot afford to be complacent with respect to their own need to remain active learners themselves. This learning must include the knowledge of teaching, motivation, and management and the skills in how to best use this knowledge.

QUESTIONS/ACTIVITIES FOR REFLECTION

1. Evaluate Susan's teaching in the case study *Susan's Problem Ownership* as completely as you can using the *System for the Analysis of Teaching Practices*. Rate each item of the *System* and then total the scores. Discuss your ratings with another student in the class.

2. What are some strategies that a teacher might use to improve his or her questioning technique? Explain what it means to match questioning practices to the purpose of a lesson.

3. What can a teacher do to maintain high efficacy when working with students who are working below grade level?

4. All of the items on the instrument *System for the Analysis of Teaching Practices* have been given equal value. If it is the case that they all are not equal, which do you consider to be the five most important of the twenty included in the instrument? Why have you selected these five?

5. Many teachers strive for higher levels of Engaged Time in their teaching, but this is actually different from Academic Learning Time. What are the main differences between Engaged Time and Academic Learning Time, and what can a teacher do to increase the amount of Academic Learning Time in the classroom?

REFERENCES

Armstrong, D., Henson, K., & Savage, T. (1997). *Teaching Today: An Introduction to Education* (5th ed.). New York: Macmillan.

Ashton, P., & Webb, R. (1986). *Making a Difference: Teachers' Sense of Efficacy and Student Achievement*. White Plains, NY: Longman.

Ausubel, D. (1978). In defense of advance organizers: A reply to the critics. *Review of Educational Research, 48,* 251–159.

Bloom, B., Englehart, M., Furst, E., Hill, W., & Krathwohl, D. (1956). *Taxonomy of Educational Objectives. Handbook I: Cognitive Domain.* New York: David McKay.

Borich, G. (1992). *Effective Teaching Methods.* New York: Merrill.

Brophy, J. (1981). Teacher praise. A functional analysis. *Review of Educational Research, 51(1),* 5–32.

Bruning, R., Schraw, G., & Ronning, R. (1995). *Cognitive Psychology and Instruction* (2nd ed.). Upper Saddle River, NJ: Prentice Hall.

Cangelosi, J. (2000). *Classroom Management Strategies: Gaining and Maintaining Students' Cooperation.* New York: John Wiley & Sons, Inc.

Cruickshank, D. (1985). Applying research on teacher clarity. *Journal of Teacher Education, 35(2)*, 44–48.

Curwin, R., & Mendler, A. (1999). *Discipline with Dignity.* Alexandria, VA: Association for Supervision and Curriculum Development.

Dempster, F. (1991). Synthesis of research on reviews and tests. *Educational Leadership, 48(7)*, 71–76.

Eggen, P., & Kauchak, D. (2001). *Educational Psychology: Windows on Classrooms* (5th ed.). Upper Saddle River, NJ: Merrill Prentice Hall.

Elawar, M., & Corno, L. (1985). A factorial experiment in teachers' written feedback on student homework. *Journal of Educational Psychology, 77(2)*, 162–173.

Elliott, S., Kratochwill, T., Cook, J., & Travers, J. (2000). *Educational Psychology: Effective Teaching, Effective Learning* (3rd ed.). New York: McGraw Hill.

Gall, M., & Artero-Boname, M. (1995) Questioning. In L. Anderson (Ed.), *International Encyclopedia of Teaching and Teacher Education* (2nd ed.). Tarrytown, NY: Elsevier Science Inc.

Gallagher, J., & Aschner, M. (1963). A Preliminary Report of the Analysis of Classroom Interaction. *Merrill-Palmer Quarterly, 9*, 183–194.

Glasser, W. (1990). *The Quality School: Managing Students Without Coercion.* New York: Harper & Row.

Good, T., & Brophy, J. (2000). *Looking in Classrooms* (8th ed.). New York: Addison Wesley Longman, Inc.

Henson, K., & Eller, B. (1999). *Educational Psychology for Effective Teaching.* Belmont, CA: Wadsworth Publishing Company.

Hunt, G., Touzel, & Wiseman, D. (1999). *Effective Teaching: Preparation and Implementation* (3rd ed.). Springfield, IL: Charles C. Thomas Publisher.

Hunter, M. (1984). Knowing, teaching and supervising. In P. Hosford, (Ed.), *Using What We Know About Teaching.* Alexandria, VA: Association for Supervision and Curriculum Development.

Kagan, D. (1992). Implications of Research on Teacher Belief. *Educational Psychologist, 27*, 65–90.

Karweit, N. (1989). Time and learning: A review. In R.E. Slavin (Ed.), *School and Classroom Organization.* Hillsdale, NJ: Erlbaum.

O'Flahavan, J., Hartman, D., & Pearson, D. (1988). Teacher Questioning and Feedback Practices: A Twenty-Year Retrospective. In J. Readence, R. Baldwin, J. Konopak, & P. O'Keefe (Eds.), *Dialogues in Literacy Research* (pp. 183-208). Chicago: National Reading Conference.

O'Keefe, P., & Johnson, M. (1987, April). *Teacher's Abilities to Understand the Perspectives of Students: A Case Study of Two Teachers.* Paper presented at the Annual Meeting of the American Educational Research Association, Washington, DC.

Poole, M., Okeafor, K., & Sloan, E. (1989, April). *Teachers' Interactions, Personal Efficacy, and Change Implementation.* Paper presented at the Annual Meeting of the American Educational Research Association, San Francisco.

Rosenshine, B., & Furst, N. (1971). Research in teacher performance criteria. In B.O. Smith (Ed.), *Research in Teacher Education.* Englewood Cliffs, NJ: Prentice-Hall.

Rowe, M. (1986). Wait-time: Slowing down may be a way of speeding up. *Journal of Teacher Education, 37(1)*, 43–50.

Snyder, S., Bushur, L., Hoeksema, P., Olson, M., Clark, S., & Snyder, J. (1991, April). *The Effect of Instructional Clarity and Concept Structure on Students' Achievement and Perception.* Paper presented at the Annual Meeting of the American Educational Research Association, Chicago.

Tauber, R. (1999). *Classroom Management: Sound Theory and Effective Practice* (3rd ed.). Westport, CN: Bergin & Garvey.

Tiletson, D. (2000). *10 Best Teaching Practices: How Brain Research, Learning Styles, and Standards Define Teaching Competencies.* Thousand Oaks, CA: Corwin Press, Inc.

Tobin, K. (1987). Role of wait-time in higher cognitive level learning. *Review of Educational Research, 57(1),* 69–95.

Weinstein, C., & Mignano, A., Jr. (1993). *Elementary Classroom Management.* New York: McGraw-Hill.

Woolfolk, A. (2001). *Educational Psychology* (8th ed.). Needham Heights, MA: Allyn & Bacon.

Chapter 5

SPECIAL PROBLEMS AND CONCERNS IN
STUDENT MOTIVATION AND
CLASSROOM MANAGEMENT

Many concepts related to student motivation and classroom management have been discussed in previous chapters in this text that are applicable to a wide variety of classroom settings across the entire PreK–12 continuum. Although a wealth of important information is available that addresses issues of student motivation and classroom management in a broad and general way, parents and teachers many times have their own specific questions concerning behavior management and student motivation. These questions frequently arise as a result of concerns that must be addressed in their local schools and communities. Some questions represent concerns that are so situationally unique that it is difficult to address them out of the context of the schools and communities in which they arise. Others are broad and widespread enough that they can and should be discussed in a forum such as this that allows for greater applicability to their study and to their possible answers. The problems and concerns chosen for discussion here were selected because of their relevancy to many teachers and parents in individual schools, classrooms, and school districts across the country.

ZERO TOLERANCE

During the decade of the 1990s, many school districts adopted what have come to be referred to as zero tolerance policies related to student behavioral management. **Zero tolerance** is *a policy for managing student behavior, usually adopted on a school district-wide basis, represented by the use of certain predetermined consequences when particular rules are broken; the consequences are applied*

118

automatically regardless of the circumstances surrounding the rule being broken. Zero tolerance policies actually grew out of national drug enforcement efforts and later were used by public schools to address an array of unwanted student behavior problems that were frequently dangerous in nature (Skiba & Peterson, 1999). School systems began adopting tough codes regarding student behavior after Congress passed the 1994 Gun-Free Schools Act, which required one-year expulsions for any child bringing a firearm or bomb to school. Zero-tolerance policies in many states, however, also are written to address such areas as fighting, drug or alcohol use, and gang activity, as well as less dangerous offenses like possessing over-the-counter medications, disrespect of authority, sexual harassment, threats, and vandalism. In 1997 more than 90 percent of the public schools across the country had zero-tolerance policies for firearms or other weapons and more than 85 percent had the policies for drugs and alcohol (Koch, 2000).

Although there are those who oppose zero-tolerance policies in schools, as well as many who favor their use, most of the respondents to the 31st Annual Phi Delta Kappa/Gallup Poll of the Public's Attitudes Toward the Public Schools supported the use of policies of zero tolerance as they relate to drug and alcohol use by students (Rose & Gallup, 1999). Few adults have any tolerance at all when considering such behaviors as young people using drugs or drinking alcohol. All instances of student misbehavior, however, are not assessed this easily. For example, a zero-tolerance policy becomes much less clear if the word "using" is replaced with "possessing." Consider the following all-to-common scenario: a *student in the elementary school was suspended from school because her mother put a butter knife in her lunchbox so that she could spread jelly on her sandwich.* The suspension took place because the school district had a zero-tolerance policy against the possession of weapons (in this case knives) on any school campus. The student brought a knife to school in her lunchbox, and, therefore, the policy was applicable to her. Although many people argue that the little girl should not be suspended, they still are in agreement that knives should not be allowed on school property. Just this one simple illustration points to the complexity of the issue.

One of the major complaints voiced about zero-tolerance policies is that minor, sometimes seemingly innocent, infractions receive the same punishments as more serious violations as was seen here in the example with the butter knife. Curwin and Mendler (1999b), two well-known educators who have written a great deal about behavior management and student motivation, strongly support the validity of this complaint. They argue that the major problem with zero-tolerance policies is that they treat all behaviors the same without allowing for a close examination of the motivation behind each individual behavior. Essentially, they are broadly as opposed to situationally applied. This, in turn, creates an unfair system, they aver, which treats a student whose behavior may reflect only a minor problem with the same consequences of a student whose behavior is clearly antisocial.

Many educators also find fault with the type of atmosphere believed to be created in a school in which a zero-tolerance policy is practiced. Hyman and Snook (2000) take the position that schools characterized by behavior controls such as zero-tolerance policies are not as likely to develop attitudes and behaviors in students that are supportive of a productive democratic society. They argue that the philosophy of zero tolerance, with its strong foundation on external rules and harsh punishments, tends to exacerbate youth violence, not abate it. Dwyer, Osher, and Hoffman (2000) explain that their research indicates that educators should avoid using techniques that label students or try to oversimplify complex management and motivational issues. They caution that harsh penalties and zero-tolerance policies are not the answer to problems of school violence. Instead of focusing on student behaviors in isolation, the critics of zero-tolerance policies recommend that schools should promote management policies that focus on the individual differences among students and the motivation behind given student behaviors. Management models that do this tend to include input from a variety of individuals, including students, steps to correct unwanted behaviors through reflection, and interaction in a democratic, student-centered atmosphere (Curwin & Mendler, 1999b; Dwyer, Osher, & Hoffman, 2000; Skiba & Peterson, 1999; Wagner, Knudsen, & Harper, 1999/2000). Opponents of zero-tolerance systems also find the approach to student behavioral management offensive to the philosophy of student-centered schooling and democratic ideals. Skiba and Peterson (2000) identify that even though they enjoy a certain level of popularity, there presently is a lack of empirical evidence supporting the use of zero-tolerance programs, and their use may, in fact, be counterproductive. Although supporters of zero-tolerance policies credit recent declines in crime and school weapons cases to the implementation of the policies, there are little data to support this claim. In spite of the lack of compelling statistics, however, 85 percent of principals, 79 percent of teachers, and 82 percent of students credit zero-tolerance policies with keeping drugs out of schools (Koch, 2000).

There is no question that certain types of student behaviors cannot be tolerated in school settings. There likewise are important issues that must be addressed concerning the severity of the consequences associated with certain student misbehaviors, the motivation behind certain behaviors, and the developmental characteristics of students exhibiting the behaviors. Essex (2000), for example, makes a strong statement for the development of zero tolerance policies in cases of sexual harassment. And yet, there must be differences between how such policies are applied across the PreK–12 continuum such as in kindergarten versus high school settings. Taylor (2000) notes that zero tolerance policies should exist to protect middle level gay and lesbian students from being subjected to name calling and similar harassment. In selecting any system of behavior management or consequences for these types of unwanted student behaviors, at what point do students benefit most from sensitivity training and education to heighten social awareness as opposed to experiencing punishment for their behaviors? Is it possible that punishment will make the harassing students even more aggressive toward gays and lesbians? Many believe that it will.

Zero-tolerance policies have been only moderately effective at best. Blair (1999) cautions that four conditions must be present if the policies have any chance of making a positive difference in controlling student behavior:

1. Clear consequences for misbehavior must be developed and applied consistently.
2. All stakeholders (e.g., educators, parents, students) must collaborate in developing the policies.
3. Those developing the policies must have a knowledge base of what has worked and failed in other school districts.
4. There must be an integration of a comprehensive health and education program to help individual students with their problems.

Today's world is one in which some students bring guns to school and threaten or actually do harm to other students and teachers. Drugs are often found and sold within the walls of elementary, middle, and high schools. There are schools in which young female students are frightened to walk down hallways, because they are often touched and talked to in ways that are grossly unacceptable, and in which both young female and young male students alike are afraid when they go into school restrooms. Parents and educators worry about the safety of young people on and off of school grounds, because they cannot tolerate bad things happening to the children and adolescents they hold dear.

The challenge is how best to establish an atmosphere within all schools that is safe, healthy, and educationally productive. A major question that must be dealt with when considering zero-tolerance policies is, "how far should school policies go to protect students at the expense of certain democratic principles and rights that should permeate society?"

EXPULSION

Tied closely to the concept of zero tolerance is the practice of expulsion. **Expulsion** is *a process exercised by a school district's governing authority, generally the school board, of banning a student from attending school for the remainder of the* *school year or the remainder of the school year plus an additional period of time carried into the next school year.* An example of this might be when a student is expelled in May for the remainder of the school year plus all or a portion of the next school year. The enforcement of an expulsion and the determination of the length of the expulsion are made by the school board in a session at which the student is allowed to have legal representation. Zero-tolerance rules often result in either suspension in which the student is not allowed to return to school for a short period of time (e.g., three or four days) or expulsion.

Expulsion is the most serious strategy used in student behavior management. When expulsion is used, the student's right to a public education is forfeited. In expelling a student from school, the position has been taken that the negative impact of having the student in the school setting outweighs or is greater than the negative impact on the student's life when the student is removed from school. Although some students have the financial means to attend a private school or pay tuition to attend school in another school district, many expelled students do not have such options and spend their time out of school in unsupervised activities. This type of situation often leads to even greater problems. The decision to manage behavior through expulsion can have a profound negative impact on the lives of students and their families and should never be approached lightly.

Expulsion and Exceptional Students

The management and motivation of exceptional students raises unique questions in the minds of many educators and parents regarding expulsion. The expulsion of exceptional or special students is an issue that creates its own set of complex concerns. King (1996) suggests that there is a double standard with respect to the management of exceptional students vis-a-vis other students and presents a number of court cases to support the point that current laws place an inordinate burden on educators when questions of the management of exceptional students arise. Some believe that current laws may actually encourage exceptional students to demonstrate a lack of responsibility for their behavior and a lack of respect for the system. Before they are suspended or expelled, educators must offer proof that the unacceptable behavior of exceptional students is not a manifestation of the student's condition of exceptionality. Morrison and D'Incau (2000) studied special education students in California who had been referred for expulsion and identified that the causes of the unwanted behaviors were often triggered by events outside of the school. Even though they were performing poorly in school, it was often determined that the school system was not providing the needed services to help them deal with their deep-seated, lingering problems. King (1996) identifies that some educators actually believe that it should be easier to remove students with exceptionalities from the school setting when their behavior seriously interferes with the learning or safety of others. Others (Morrison & D'Incau, 2000) argue that schools need to do more to help exceptional students and support them within the regular school environment. Decisions regarding expulsion, in particular when they involve students with exceptionalities, are extremely difficult to make and typically require legal guidance.

There are obvious concerns about the rights of all students with special attention being given to the rights of students with exceptionalities under Public Law 94-142, the Individuals with Disabilities Education Act (IDEA) of 1975. The courts have, for the most part, supported school districts when their rights to expel individual students have been challenged. Even in cases in which due process questions have arisen, the courts have consistently backed school district decisions (Zirkel, 1997; Zirkel & Gluckman, 1997). One reason given for the courts having supported school districts is that expulsion frequently takes place as a result of extreme circumstances such as violence, drug-related behavior, and general antisocial behavior, which often impacts on the learning and safety of other students and which society strongly condemns. Little tolerance is shown for such behaviors when they are school related.

Townsend (2000) raises a serious concern with the results of expulsion policies in observing that African-Americans as a group are the recipients of a disproportionate amount of suspensions and expulsions. A recent survey of twelve large school districts showed that in some districts black students are three to five times more likely to be expelled or receive suspensions than white students. In Phoenix, Arizona, for example, blacks made up only four percent of the high school population but received 21 percent of the expulsions and suspensions. White students made up only 18 percent of the expulsions or suspensions but made up 74 percent of the population. Figures from the U. S. Department of Education identified that in 1997 black students represented 17 percent of the public school enrollment nationwide while also making up 32 percent of those suspended (Koch, 2000). Expulsions add to the problems already experienced by many African-American youths, resulting in poorer educational opportunities and, ultimately, a greater rate of dropping out of school. Townsend observes that the high rate of expulsions among African-Americans sometimes is due to or at least influenced by the cultural differences between these students and the predominantly white, middle class teaching workforce. These cultural differences often lead to misunderstandings and misinterpretations of attitudes, behavior, tone, and working styles.

The problem that Townsend (2000) addresses is, for many, at the heart of the expulsion issue. Students who are most likely to be expelled and alienated from the system are the same students who often are already having problems in school and who could benefit most from a quality public school education before entering the job market. Students who have difficulty learning and fitting into the middle-class school society become unhappy, alienated, and less likely to comply with their teachers' expectations. Middle-class children come to school to be educated and are reinforced for the values and mores of their society. Low socioeconomic status (SES) minority students come to school to be educated and to get changed. This change is frequently painful and hard to accept. In response to what is often interpreted as "forced change," many of these students rebel and threaten the safety and learning of others. They often fail, drop out, or are expelled and enter the world lacking the necessary skills to support themselves, become nurturing parents, and become productive members of the community. Such children ultimately have their own children (too often before they become adults they become parents), and these children then come to school without the necessary parental and home support to be successful. The cycle continues and repeats itself seemingly *ad infinitum*.

This is not an argument to abolish expulsion as an approach to behavior management. Schools cannot be allowed to become sites for drug deals or arenas for violence. It is an argument, however, for being careful and reflective before using expulsion as a management strategy. If used at all, expulsion should be the final, last resort to solve student management problems. Educational research shows that expelled students who don't attend alternative classes are less likely to re-enter school at a later point in their lives and more likely to get mixed up in gang activity, drug use, and otherwise run afoul of the law (Koch, 2000). Expulsion should be used only when educators are certain that the impact of a student's negative behavior on the learning environment and safety of the school and other students outweighs the fact that the behavior of the student being expelled may deteriorate beyond help in the future after the expulsion.

TEACHING EXCEPTIONAL STUDENTS

When managing students who have exceptionalities, there is more to be concerned with than just the legal, social, and educational ramifications of expulsion. Public Law 94-142 directs educators to ensure that students addressed in this legislation receive the most appropriate education possible in the least restrictive environment (LRE). Special students are diagnosed, an individualized educational plan (IEP) is developed for each student by a team of educators, usually with parent participation, and they are included as appropriate in a regular classroom setting for either the entire or part of each school day. Management and motivational problems associated with many exceptional students are related to the difficulty that they have in competing academically with other students, in receiving positive attention from their teachers and other students, and in feeling equal to and accepted by other students (Curwin & Mendler, 1999a).

If a teacher has a student with an exceptionality who is characterized by exhibiting unacceptable behaviors in a regular classroom setting, it is important that a plan or specific strategy be developed to help the student adjust to the setting in which he has been placed. If the teacher chooses to ignore the student's special needs and continues to teach as if the student were like all other students in the class, problems most definitely will occur, and the student's rights will have been violated. If ignored, the student's unacceptable behavior will likely continue and probably worsen. The teacher's behavior in not addressing the problem will be running contrary to federal law. Teachers cannot let problems go unresolved but must make adaptations in their instructional programs to accommodate the unique characteristics of exceptional students (Curwin & Mendler, 1999a).

Gottlieb and Weinberg (1999) report on four reasons that some students have difficulty fitting in the mainstream of American public education. These reasons were identified after a study to determine whether differences exist between students who are referred and those who are not referred for special education services. Gottlieb and Weinberg note that:

1. Referred students come from families that are more transient than those of nonreferred students.
2. Most of the students who were referred received a referral because they were behavior problems, weak academically, or highly unmotivated.
3. Referred students were late to school substantially more often than nonreferred students.
4. Most referrals were made by a very small number of teachers who lacked training in the use of behavior management and instructional techniques that could be used as interventions that might reduce the need for referrals.

Gottlieb and Weinberg conclude that many students are referred for special education placements for reasons of being difficult to teach, presenting management problems for their teachers, and being different from the other students. Unfortunately, when these students are included in regular classrooms, they are many times being sent back into environments where, too frequently, they already have shown a history of unacceptable behavior and poor performance. This can lead to increased management and motivation difficulties for their teachers and enhanced learning problems for the students themselves.

When principals and teachers work with special students, it is important that they have an understanding of the laws that protect their legal rights when behavior management techniques are being considered. Teachers and administrators need to be familiar with the basic features of IDEA, Section 504 of the Vocational Rehabilitation Act of 1973, the Americans with Disabilities Act of 1990, and the IDEA Amendments of 1997 (Smith & Colon, 1998). Osborne (1998) explains how the 1997 Amendments to IDEA have clarified much of the gray area that previously existed concerning the discipline of students with exceptionalities, noting that the Amendments expand the authority of school officials when such students are found to have drugs or weapons in their possession. The Amendments aid in the determination of whether a student's unacceptable conduct is related to the student's exceptionality and clarify that educational services must be continued for the student even when the student has been suspended or expelled for misconduct unrelated to the disability.

The provisions of the IDEA Amendments of 1997 also impact the behavior management responsibilities of IEP teams (Smith, 2000). The Amendments identify that a special education student can be placed in a 45-day interim placement in an alternative setting as a result of behaviors involving weapons, drugs, or dangerous activity (Dayton, 2000). When this 45-day interim placement is used, however, the IEP team must conduct an assessment of the behavior to determine wether a link exists between the misconduct and the student's exceptionality. The team must also develop an intervention program, an IEP that addresses the unwanted behavior, and designate an interim alternative educational setting for the student.

When regular classroom teachers, special educators, and school administrators manage the behavior of exceptional students, many factors must be considered related to their actions. Weatherly (2000), an attorney who specializes in case work for students with exceptionalities, recommends that school officials follow specific guidelines in such cases. These guidelines include:

- Suggesting appropriate individualized education services for each student.
- Getting all appropriate educators together with parents for IEP meetings.
- Setting all final decisions for education and placement in IEP meetings.
- Not letting cost or availability of services interfere with decisions.
- Avoiding the inclusion of unnecessary details in the IEP.
- Giving due consideration to outside private evaluations of students.
- Sending parents written notice of any proposed changes in the educational program.
- Developing a behavioral management plan for disruptive students.
- Showing care when suspending or expelling disabled students.
- Remembering that the right to a free and appropriate public education belongs to the student, not the parents.

Curwin and Mendler (1999a) acknowledge that regular classroom teachers who have included students have much to consider regarding their approaches to classroom management and student motivation. In preparation for working successfully with such students, it is recommended that teachers first address their own feelings toward the realities of working with exceptional learners. Teachers of students with exceptionalities must learn to deal with the frustrations and defeats that may come after long hours of planning and dedicated instruction. Teachers also need to be prepared to give an appropriate level of responsibility for behavior and learning to the special student himself or herself. Many teachers actually take too much responsibility for the behaviors of their students. They must recognize that they cannot accept excuses for behavior from students that are not legitimate and that they cannot solve all of their students' problems for them. Teachers can and should, however, set clear and appropriate limits and expect students to follow them. Exceptional students, as with regular students, must learn to take responsibility for their own behaviors and take an active part in their own problem solving and decision making. It is essential for teachers to be able to communicate with the special students in their classrooms even if the students themselves have communication difficulties. In so doing, teachers must be prepared to give special students honest feedback. This feedback might often include praise but may well need to also include constructive criticism. Teachers actually can, when carefully done, help an exceptional student by publicly acknowledging their own mistakes. This strategy of communication and openness tells the student that it is acceptable to try and sometimes fail. The classroom should be an inviting and structured environment. Many, if not most, students with exceptionalities perform best in environments that are highly structured and, therefore, predictable.

ADDRESSING DIVERSITY

Across the country many schools and classrooms are characterized by students of diverse socioeconomic backgrounds, skin colors, religious practices, and national origins. Although this kind of diversity can form the foundation for rich and varied educational experiences for all students, it can also contribute to problems in communication and understanding between teachers and students and teachers and parents. These problems can be manifested through instructional challenges in making the curriculum relevant, interesting, and appropriately rigorous, and through classroom management and student motivation difficulties.

Most educators in schools today reflect a white, middle-class perspective. Students who come from a different segment of society, having different cultural backgrounds and life experiences, can quickly find it difficult to communicate and feel comfortable with many of their teachers and administrators. Banks (1994) identifies the concern that some teachers have problems helping students of color for many reasons, including the fact that many teachers and administrators may even hold negative perceptions of and expectations for their students. These negative perceptions and expectations generally emerge from a lack of understanding of the students' backgrounds and a difficulty in communicating openly and honestly with them. McEwan (2000) makes an important point in noting that behavioral expectations must be high for all students. If a student comes from a difficult family situation with an impoverished background and holds values different from those held by his teacher, he or she must still be required to exhibit acceptable conduct as is expected of others. To expect less is to violate the student's right to an equal educational opportunity. If negative student behaviors are ignored by a teacher based solely on a student's background, in time the teacher will most assuredly be faced with a troublesome student discipline problem. This was discussed earlier as related to teacher expectations and teacher efficacy. One of a teacher's greatest challenges is to hold appropriately high expectations for all students while meeting the sometimes unique needs that students from diverse backgrounds bring to the school and classroom.

The term *diversity* is a term used frequently in educational literature today. It perhaps is used so often by so many people in so many different ways that even though it is commonly used, its meaning is taken for granted or even misunderstood. **Diversity,** *in the school or classroom, pertains to the variety of backgrounds or circumstances from which students come as they enter the schooling environment.* The key issue is a simple one to understand. Most teachers and administrators come from white, middle-class backgrounds while working with many students who do not. Even teachers themselves who do not come from a white, middle-class background but who come from a background of a different culture may not be prepared to deal with the challenges that they find in the classroom when called on to serve students from a different socioeconomic status or culture from their own. Many are quick to form stereotypes of their students that unfairly label and characterize them. This lack of understanding of ethnic and cultural sensitivity on the part of some teachers and administrators can quickly lead to a total misunderstanding of student behaviors. For example, students coming from some cultural backgrounds may have adopted a set of behaviors that are accepted and considered appropriate in the home but that are not considered this way at school. A situation such as this may lead these students to react in unanticipated ways to many of the traditional approaches to behavior management used by their teachers. Teacher expectations and procedures used at school in conducting classroom instruction may also be very foreign to them (Zabel &

Zabel, 1996). Inappropriate behaviors should not be ignored; however, helping students from diverse backgrounds includes having sensitivity to the customs of their backgrounds and an understanding of why they have different values and behaviors than those traditionally found in and rewarded by schools. Change can be both difficult and slow. But, it can only take place positively if educators are informed, patient, and nonjudgmental.

There is no doubt that socioeconomic factors have a major impact on the quality of education any student receives, regardless of the school. A 1994 report from the Children's Defense Fund identifies that almost one fifth of all school children live in poverty and more than forty percent of that group come from families whose income is less than one half the poverty level (Children's Defense Fund, 1994). Children from such backgrounds are at risk of failure, especially in the present-day world of high-stakes standardized testing. They also are at risk of being misunderstood, not having their personal and learning needs met, and subject to higher levels of disciplinary actions, suspensions, and expulsions from school (Townsend, 2000). Cummings and Haggerty (1997) report on a program entitled *Raising Healthy Children* that is designed to reduce the problems associated with adolescence for at-risk students. Emphasis in the program is placed on developing a bond between students, their family members, and the school. *Raising Healthy Children* offers teachers training in proactive classroom management strategies, motivation skills needed for at-risk students, and techniques for teaching social skills and reading. Through the program, parents participate in workshops designed to help their children (students) socially and academically while collaborating with their teachers. Such programs as this that offer specific skills to teachers while developing a strong parenting component represent positive approaches to dealing with problems that may result from social and cultural diversity.

Matus (1999) stresses that many disadvantaged students attend high schools in urban communities and describes many of the unique challenges that they face. Many of these adolescents from such communities hold full-time jobs, making it virtually impossible for them to complete the homework that their teachers assign. Because of their work schedules, they also are often tired and easily distracted at school. Matus urges teachers and administrators to use what he calls a "humanistic approach" to management with such students and advocates peer mediation programs and flexible scheduling of classes and assignments to help them adjust simultaneously to school and work schedules. Conflict Resolution, an example of a peer mediation program, was introduced in Chapter 3. Matus also reinforces the importance of treating students with respect, not yelling or speaking harshly to them, and rewarding them when they do well. He identifies, as have others who have conducted research in this area, that for teachers to be effective they must be sensitive to the needs of their students. They must make a direct attempt to understand the reasons for their students' behaviors when such behaviors may seem to be unacceptable.

As previously noted, public schools are institutions built on middle-class values and mores and run by a teaching workforce that comes from a predominantly white, middle-class background. Many students in the public schools, however, are neither middle class nor white, resulting in a greater chance for miscommunications and misunderstandings between teachers and students. Efforts at behavior management, which can create tension in any situation, can bring about classroom problems where miscommunications and misunderstandings in this context can prove to be especially damaging. Although all students should be held to high standards of conduct in the school setting, regardless of their personal backgrounds and circumstances, teachers and administrators need to be knowledgeable of and sensitive to the unique needs of a diverse student body and of each student in the student body. This type of sensitivity in teachers and administrators can come only from an understanding of the reasons for certain behaviors that students exhibit. Having this understanding will enable them to be more effective in helping them conduct themselves in acceptable ways. Lack of sensitivity can quickly create a "me against them" attitude or feelings of pity on the part of teachers and administrators. Either of these attitudes will lead to feelings of alienation on the part of at-risk students.

VIOLENCE

No topic has drawn greater controversy and attention to public schools in recent years than school violence and the resulting demands for safer learning environments. The public is horrified every time a story of injury, attack, or violent death in a school setting is in the news. The tragedy of Columbine High School in Littleton, Colorado, in April, 1999, where two teenagers killed 12 fellow students and a teacher before committing suicide, was brought into living rooms across the country by virtually 24-hour news coverage. More recently, the shooting deaths of two students and the wounding of 13 more by a 15 year-old boy at Santana High School in Santee, California, in March, 2001, has served as a stark reminder that school violence can still occur, and the cause for concern still remains. Such events frighten parents and students and have elicited questions about school safety across the nation. Concern for discipline in schools and school safety were well documented in Chapter 1.

Although recent and tragic school shootings have reminded the nation that violent death at school is intolerable no matter how rare an event, children are safer in schools than in the community or the home. Overall, school violence continues to drop, according to an annual report card on school crime published by the U. S. Department of Education. Since 1992, crime against students—including theft, rape, sexual assault, robbery, aggravated assault, and simple assault—has decreased by nearly a third. Research released by the U. S. Department of Education confirms that schools remain among the safest places for children and youth. This past school year, 90 percent of the nation's schools reported no serious violent crime, and 43 percent said that they experienced no crime at all (*Community Update*, 2001). Less than 1 percent of the 2,500 child homicides and suicides during the last six months of 1997 took place at school or on the way to and from school. There were also significant decreases between 1993 and 1997 in the percentages of high school students who carried a weapon on school property or were involved in a physical fight at school (*Good News*, p. 22, 2000). Even with this information, however, school violence has led many administrators and school boards to develop stronger behavior management policies in their schools, and zero-tolerance policies for violent acts and weapons of any sort have become the standard in many communities. As was discussed earlier, however, these policies do not always solve the problems they are intended to address.

Lasting solutions to problems of school violence lie in effective measures of problem prevention, in being proactive, not just in dealing with problems once they have occurred. Students who are at the point at which they are ready to commit violent acts against their classmates or teachers are not likely to be thwarted by discipline threats or zero-tolerance policies. More systemic solutions (i.e., well-planned preventive solutions) must be developed and implemented that involve the school, the family, and other support agencies found in the community.

Wallace (2000), a teacher in Jefferson County, Colorado, reacted to the reasons why two students shot and killed a number of their classmates at Columbine High School. Wallace asserts that a problem exists in society in general when high status and recognition is granted to some students (e.g., athletes), and those who excel in less glamorous activities such as band or drama are ignored by comparison. Students who do not excel in high-profile activities often feel alienated, especially if they lack popularity with those who do excel. Schools must make every effort possible to address the needs of the gifted, the introverted, and those interested in nonmainstream activities. It is important that those students who enjoy high status in the school do not malign those who do not and are seen as nonconformists.

Sprague and Walker (2000) stress the importance of early identification of students who are at risk of committing violent acts in the future. Several models exist that can be used to predict future violent behavior that focus on pathology within the student, ecological factors, and past behaviors. For example, children who have shown a number of antisocial behaviors in multiple settings are more prone to be violent in the future than students who do not display these behaviors. Such factors as living in poverty, living with adults who abuse drugs and alcohol, and being a victim of child abuse are among the factors that can interact with other characteristics to predict the probability of future dysfunctional behaviors. Sprague and Walker (2000) recommend a model for the prevention of violent behavior that has three distinct tiers.

1. All students in the school are given instruction in such fundamental skills as conflict resolution and violence prevention in an effort to create a positive learning environment throughout the school.
2. Identify those students who exhibit a pattern of factors that indicate that they are apt to be involved in future violent behavior and provide them with a specialized intervention program designed to lessen the impact of their risk factors.
3. Identify students who are already engaged in dysfunctional, antisocial behavior. These students must receive specialized, professional help designed to change their attitudes and behavior patterns.

The following listing of behaviors represent early warning signs of potential violent behavior in students. Teachers and students are advised to be observant for these behaviors and respond accordingly. Ignoring known warning signs is definitely not the appropriate course to take.

1. Social withdrawal
2. Excessive feelings of isolation and being alone
3. Excessive feelings of rejection
4. Feelings of being picked on and persecuted
5. Low school interest and poor academic performance
6. Uncontrolled anger
7. Patterns of impulsive and chronic hitting, intimidating, and bullying behaviors
8. History of discipline problems
9. Intolerance for differences and prejudicial attitudes
10. Drug use and alcohol use
11. Affiliation with gangs
12. Inappropriate access to, possession of, and use of firearms
13. Serious threats of violence
14. Being a victim of violence
15. Expression of violence in writings and drawings
16. Past history of violent and aggressive behavior

One major concern related to violence in schools is the existence of organized gangs. Dowling-Sendor (1998a), an appellate defender from North Carolina, provides important information for school administrators when reacting to the existence of gangs within their schools. First, all school policies must be comprehensive and should serve to prohibit gang activity while also working to motivate students not to engage in such activity. Second, when dealing with the prohibition of certain types of dress or symbols, a student's First and Fourteenth Amendment rights cannot be violated. Third, a student should be allowed the opportunity to deny any accusation that an item of clothing or symbol has any gang significance. Educators should seek help from students, parents, law enforcement, and community agencies to provide students with alternatives to gang activities (Dowling-Sendor, 1998b). Curwin and Mendler (1999a) stress the importance of parent involvement at the time gang behavior is suspected. School principals should appeal to parents for their assistance in finding immediate resolutions if problems are identified. Parents should be told that the school will not tolerate gang activities and that the principal is prepared to take action, to include contacting any authorities and agencies as necessary, to maintain a safe school environment. After parents have had an opportunity to react and propose solutions to the identified problems, students should join the dialogue to hear their parents say that the problems will come to an end. Violent behavior is not acceptable and will not be tolerated.

Violence in schools is a problem that parents, educators, and students alike agree cannot be allowed to occur. Although school violence is not a new phenomenon, the tragic events of recent years have aroused parents, educators, and school boards to take what are sometimes believed to be dramatic actions to prevent further violence from taking place in their communities. Although popular with some, stringent school rules for behavior and zero-tolerance policies do not always prevent radical, dysfunctional behavior. Educators have come to recognize that dealing with crime and violence requires a total community effort (Rossman & Morley, 1996). Many schools have formed effective alliances with other agencies in their communities (e.g., law enforcement and mental health), to combat crime and violence in a more comprehensive way. Because school violence is something that must be prevented and not just dealt with after the fact, it is in a school district's best interest and the best interest of all involved to have a sound prevention plan in place.

SCHOOL UNIFORMS

One possible, and in some places popular, solution to school violence, gang activity, and difficult student behavior problems that received high interest beginning in the 1990s is having students wear school uniforms. The view in support of this strategy has been that if all students are dressed alike, unique gang clothing and symbols would be easier to detect. School uniforms make it more difficult for drug pushers and other undesirable persons to come on school campuses during school hours without being spotted by authorities. It also has been argued that the wearing of school uniforms is an effective strategy to lessen the differences of socioeconomic status that are often apparent in diverse schooling situations.

Many educators and noneducators are in favor of requiring school uniforms. The 3rd Phi Delta Kappa Poll of Teachers' Attitudes Toward the Public Schools (Langdon, 1996) indicated that fifty-three percent of the general public favored school uniforms, whereas approximately two thirds of the teachers favored them. Although a strategy viewed favorably by many teachers and to a lesser degree by the general public, there is as yet no evidence that having students wear school uniforms improves the learning environment of a school.

Stanley (1996) provides an overview of the results of a mandatory uniform program in the elementary and middle schools of Long Beach, California. After one year of the program being in operation, there were significant decreases in suspensions, assault/battery, assault with a deadly weapon, fighting, sex offenses, robbery, extortion, possession of both drugs and weapons, and vandalism. There also were fewer disruptions in class, overall unacceptable student behavior, uncooperativeness, bad attitudes, and poor work ethics. Parents felt that the uniform policy had led to positive results and were in greater support of the school. The students, however, were less than enthusiastic about wearing the uniforms and denied that the uniforms had led to positive results observed by others.

Kommer (1999) uses his experiences as a former middle school principal in Los Angeles, California, to add support to the development of school uniform policies. Kommer identifies the following positive results of school uniform programs. School uniforms:

1. Help to reduce gang influence
2. Create a more positive and businesslike atmosphere
3. Increase pride in the school
4. Reduce problems for students related to choosing what to wear to school
5. Reduce strife between students and parents concerning what to wear
6. Lower the stress and expense for parents related to buying school clothes

Kommer advises those who wish to institute a uniform policy to make uniforms mandatory, not voluntary. Mandatory programs are seen as working better than those that are voluntary. It is wise, however, to provide an opt-out option for parents who are adamantly opposed to uniforms or whose child transfers into the school after the beginning of the school year. A uniform policy will work if parents and students are involved throughout the decision-making process. If it is decided that a school uniform program is to be implemented, Kommer suggests that students be given the ultimate decision as to what the uniform will look like.

Hamilton (1999), a principal of an elementary school in Plainfield, New Jersey, has had experiences similar to those of Kommer and also stresses the importance of getting parents and students involved early in the decision-making process. Parents who are in favor of the uniform policy can be encouraged to talk with those parents who are opposed to the idea. This positive support from parent peers, along with as much data as possible from the school, usually convinces those in opposition to at least try the new program. Parents who find buying uniforms a financial burden can receive assistance to ease this problem through local businesses or charitable organizations (Hamilton, 1999; Stanley, 1996).

There are those who are as strongly opposed to school uniform policies as there are those in support of them (Caruso, 1996; Evans, 1996). Arguments against uniform policies include the view that:

1. Such policies are an infringement on First Amendment rights
2. Having such a policy is a tool of power for school administrators
3. Uniforms represent an unnecessary cost burden given to parents
4. Gangs and violence still exist even with uniforms being worn
5. Uniforms do not do away with class distinctions between the "haves" and the "have nots."

All of these issues are important and must be addressed when the possibility of initiating a school uniform policy is discussed.

Black (1998) suggests that the real push behind school uniform policies has been more political than research based. A recent study done by Educational Testing Service (1998) shows no apparent relationship between the use of school uniforms and student achievement or behavior. Black concludes that there is little meaningful research evidence to support that having students wear school uniforms will improve discipline, increase student respect for teachers, promote school spirit, raise academic performance, equalize social status, or any other claims made by those promoting uniform policies. The little evidence that does exist is for elementary and middle schools; no evidence exists to support school uniforms for high school students. In spite of differing views and in an attempt to solve student management problems in schools, some educational leaders and school boards have instituted school uniform policies, and a number of the communities that have such policies report positive results. Those who oppose such policies, however, continue to note that at this time there is little empirical data, certainly no compelling data, supporting a link between the use of school uniform policies and desired student behavior outcomes. The approach clearly deserves further study.

DRUG ABUSE

Drug abuse has been seen as a major problem in and out of schools across the country for many years. Like many other societal problems, substance abuse has a powerful negative impact on young people. The 31st Annual Phi Delta Kappa/Gallup Poll of the Public's Attitudes Toward the Public Schools (Rose & Gallup, 1999) reports public concern over drug use by school-aged youth as being a significant concern, although the level of concern seems to have lessened somewhat over the past few years. The 1996 poll (Rose & Gallup, 1996) listed drug abuse as the number one concern of the public, being mentioned by sixteen percent of the respondents. The 1999 poll reported drug use being mentioned by eight percent of respondents and tied with overcrowded schools as the fourth major issue while ranking behind lack of discipline, violence, and lack of funding. This modest reduction of concern by the public should not be misinterpreted as a significant lessening of concern for student behaviors in this area. Drug use among young people remains at levels near or even above the peak years of 1979-1980 (Curwin & Mendler, 1999a).

In a major survey of more than 10,000 high school students, researchers investigated the relationship between school violence (i.e., carrying a weapon, being in a physical fight, damaging and stealing property, threatening with a weapon, and missing school because to safety concerns) and substance abuse (Lowry, Cohen, Modzeleski, Kann, Collins, & Kolbe, 1999). A little more than half of the respondents reported drinking alcohol and approximately one fourth reported using marijuana. Approximately one third reported that they had been offered, sold, or given illegal drugs on school property in the last year. Nearly 60 percent noted that they had used one or more of the substances in the previous month. The study also reported that the prevalence of school violence factors was greater for those students who had used at least one of the substances than for those who had not. Researchers with the U. S. Department of Education and the Centers for Disease Control and Prevention in Atlanta, Georgia, suggest that drug abuse and school violence are so closely related that the problems associated with each one should be approached in a coordinated fashion. Addressing these serious problems in an isolated manner or in a fashion that separates one from the other risks less than optimum attention being given to either one.

Another related study was conducted to determine knowledge levels, feelings, and attitudes of kindergarten students regarding alcohol, tobacco, and other drugs. The sample for this study was drawn from high-risk elementary schools in Lexington, Kentucky (Hahn, Hall, Rayens, Burt, Corley, & Sheffel, 2000). Results indicate that approximately one in six kindergartners were able to identify marijuana, crack cocaine, LSD, injectable drugs, or other illegal substances. Although most of the children in the study voiced negative attitudes toward drug use, some of the kindergarten students viewed drug use positively. The recognition of cigarettes and alcohol were not related to demographic factors. Minority children, however, were much more likely to be knowledgeable about illicit drugs than nonminority children. How do such young children know so much about illegal substances? Curwin and Mendler (1999a) report that young people are highly influenced by their close friends and their parents as this relates to their knowledge and their likelihood of becoming involved in drug use.

Many substance abuse programs have been developed in recent years in an effort to help control the drug use problem among young people. Jones (1997) describes an evaluation of forty-seven such programs with only six earning high marks. The six rated most favorably were Alcohol Misuse Prevention Study (AMPS), Life Skills Training, the Michigan Model, Project ALERT, Project Northland, and Drug Abuse Resistance Education (DARE). However, virtually all drug prevention programs get mixed reviews. Adair (2000) evaluated fifty drug prevention programs and suggested that Jones (1997) was correct only in the high rating of ALERT, believing that ALERT is especially good for middle school students. Elias, Gager, and Leon (1997), in their assessment of drug prevention programs, disagree with Jones' (1997) position on DARE. They found DARE to have only two of what they report as being the necessary characteristics of a good program and identified that QUEST was the best program with Here's Looking at You, 2000, Growing Healthy, and Social Decision Making-Social Problem Solving (SDM-SPS) also being good programs. Brown (1997) suggests that all drug abuse prevention programs fall short of meeting students' needs and argues that even the ones considered best lack complete utility, because they do not focus on student capabilities and do not provide honest information to students. Brown fears that many federal and state mandates stand in the way of best-practice alternatives. It is difficult to get agreement among the experts as to which prevention programs work best. It is clear, however, that there is obvious room for improvement in most programs. Jones (1997) outlines some factors that are important to acknowledge concerning the quality and completeness of any program. Successful programs help students with problem solving, social skills, and goal setting while providing training and support for teachers and family and community involvement. Good programs also provide students with accurate information about drug use.

Mendler and Curwin (1999a) share an important perspective on working with students who may be involved with illegal substances in noting that teachers and parents should guard against accepting excuses and empty promises. Students who use drugs typically do not complete their school-work at the level of those who do not abuse drugs, and teachers must adhere to strict consequences for such behavior. When teachers notice changes in the behavior of a student that may indicate drug use, the student should be told about this observation. This should be done without accusation of drug use but as a caring teacher sharing an observation regarding a change in student behavior with a student. If the teacher has tried to communicate this information to the student and the behavior goes unchanged, the teacher should then approach the student with the suspicion of drug use. It is important for the teacher, when taking this action, to listen to the student and interact in a caring and nonaccusatory or nonthreatening manner.

Schools today are under tremendous pressure to improve the scholastic performance of students, and much time and money are being dedicated to the academic preparation of students, teachers, and administrators. All feel accountable, and pressure, for reaching higher and higher levels of student academic achievement. Teachers must not forget, however, that many students have needs that go far beyond the academic concerns of the school, community, and even the state. It is important, as Wooley, Eberst, and Bradley (2000) observe, that a coordinated program be offered that will help to reduce the prevalence of problems such as drug use and underage drinking. The strongest coordinated program will include the school, family, and appropriate community agencies.

THE FIRST YEAR OF TEACHING

The first year of teaching is a time of great challenge, complexity, and adjustment, because beginning teachers must be able to respond to many new and different demands and respond to them effectively. In a review of a large number of studies focusing on problems faced by beginning teachers, classroom discipline heads the list of important issues that beginning teachers face and motivating students is second (Tauber, 1999; Veenman, 1986).

Martin and Baldwin (1996) studied how beginning teachers are different from experienced teachers in the way they perceive classroom management and how school counselors can help them develop better learning environments in their classrooms. They found that teachers who had taught three years or less had more controlling attitudes toward students than did those who had taught more than three years. Martin and Baldwin suggest that this controlling attitude toward students might result in less favorable learning conditions and damage to student self-esteem. They recommend that school counselors be used to coordinate mentor programs between experienced and novice teachers. School counselors could also lead support groups in which new teachers could brainstorm solutions to shared problems and provide consultation to new teachers concerning best-practice techniques for managing and motivating students.

Beginning teachers need a well-planned, extensive, and continuous induction program with a strong mentoring component with master teachers that lasts for at least the entire first year of teaching if not longer. Morgan (1997) encourages experienced teachers to assist first-year teachers by providing them with practical information, political savoir-faire, and professional support. Practical information involves important, everyday matters such as how to fill out purchase orders, the location of preferred parking places, and which copy machine to use. Political savoir-faire deals with how certain things are perceived and what may or may not be acceptable behavior in certain situations such as dealing with parents and colleagues. Professional support involves sharing lesson plans, hints on ways to motivate certain students, and methods of classroom management. When inexperienced teachers receive this type of advice from supportive, experienced teachers, they typically become less frustrated and more likely to remain in teaching longer.

Principals also must be key figures in the mentoring of new teachers. Brock and Grady (1998) report findings from a study done to gather information from principals and first-year teachers that explored the needs of beginning teachers and how principals can best assist them. The study showed that most principals offer new teachers some type of orientation program, assign mentors to new teachers, and spend time working with new teachers on an individual basis. Although the new teachers in the study believed that the orientation and mentoring programs were helpful, most indicated that they would have preferred to have had more time with the principal to get clearer perspectives on the principal's expectations for them and more immediate feedback on their performance.

There are many teacher education programs throughout the country that prepare candidates for initial certification. Across these programs, there is often a wide variance in abilities among graduates even of the same program. Tauber (1999) reports that few teacher education programs make available and even fewer programs require students to take specific courses in the area of classroom management. This is surprising given the repeatedly high rating of concern that teachers give to working with student behavior problems. Much of what teachers learn with respect to classroom management techniques comes through school district efforts in in-service training or what some more offhandedly refer to as "on-the-job training." Because programs vary in their approaches to preparing teachers and because individuals are naturally different in many ways, all first-year teachers are not equally prepared to teach, manage and motivate students. This is especially true, because the level and ultimate effectiveness of their preparation may very well be relative to the type of school in which they are teaching. A first-year teacher who might be well prepared to teach in a rural school setting may find it difficult to be successful in an inner-city setting. Likewise, teaching in a suburban school site near a large metropolitan area like Chicago or Miami would present a different set of challenges from those found on an Indian reservation in Oklahoma or in an Appalachian area in North Carolina. Teacher training institutions must continue to improve in preparing their graduates to teach in present-day, standards-driven, diverse school settings. Principals also must understand the significant role that they play in the development and success of first-year teachers and, at times, teachers-in-training. Many of the frustrations that drive young teachers out of the profession could be significantly reduced by more real-world–based initial preparation, effective instructional leadership, strong induction programs, and supportive, experienced colleagues willing to share with and support first-year teachers. Professionals already in the field should see it as their responsibility to do everything in their power to ensure the success of beginning teachers.

TEACHER STRESS

Dealing with disruptions and students who are unmotivated are constant sources of stress for classroom teachers. If this stress is sustained over long periods of time, the result can be teacher burnout. A teacher who suffers from **teacher burnout** is characterized by having reached a *point of extreme stress at which the teacher has lost his or her enthusiasm for teaching and has little energy to focus on helping students learn.* Coming to work is difficult for such teachers who often complain of headaches, exhaustion, frustration, irritability, outbursts of anger, and many other similar symptoms including depression (Curwin & Mendler, 1999a; Hendrickson, 1979). Teacher preparation programs rarely include skill development, at least in-depth skill development, to help teachers deal with overwrought individuals. But, understanding conflict and stress is the first step toward managing it. Reducing stress for all parties will allow teachers to focus on the more important aspects of their jobs. Stress undermines physical, emotional, and intellectual energies precisely when strength in these areas is needed most (Morris, 1998).

Although related, teacher burnout, and attrition (i.e., leaving the profession) are not the same thing. Some teachers leave the profession because they are experiencing symptoms of burnout but many others leave for other reasons. All teachers who burn out do not quit. Some remain in the classroom, although they have lost virtually all zest for their work (Zabel & Zabel, 1996). If the negative effects of being burned out cannot be reversed, it is in the best interest of the students and the schools and communities they are there to serve when these teachers leave the profession.

Zabel and Zabel (1996) observe that there are certain factors that exist in a teacher's world that augment the possibility of burnout. The number of students assigned to a teacher can be seen by the teacher as creating an unfair burden, although in some cases this feeling may be more a result of perception than reality. Such a feeling is important, though, if it is real to the teacher. Stronger feelings of support from parents, other teachers, and especially administrators can ease the perception of being overburdened. Curwin and Mendler (1999a) emphasize that the type of student assigned to teachers can be a determiner of teacher stress. Students with exceptionalities, especially those with emotional or behavioral problems, can behave in ways that are stressful to their teachers and classmates. Teachers can also become burned out if the expectations that they have for their jobs are greatly different than the realities of their jobs. Most teachers enter the profession for the intrinsic rewards that come with teaching, not extrinsic rewards such as salary. If a teacher does not receive intrinsic rewards from students, parents, or colleagues and teaching in general, if sufficient external rewards are not present, of if teaching in some way disappoints a perhaps overly idealistic view of the profession, job-related stress may be the end result. Disparity between expectations for teaching and the reality of teaching can be a real cause of stress. Many teachers become frustrated and develop feelings of inadequacy as a result of poor student performance. In this era of high-stakes testing and accountability, increased expectations for student achievement have placed great stress on teachers and students alike. Because of these and other complex factors, many teachers are caught in a cycle of unfulfilled expectations and negative feelings, behaviors, and reactions from students, parents, colleagues, and administrators. In the end, they become frustrated, because circumstances are not as they had expected, which, ultimately, can lead to negative behaviors in the classroom. Negative teacher behaviors in the classroom often result in increasing negative behaviors on the part of students (i.e., disruptive behaviors). Increased levels of discipline problems, in turn, bring about increased levels of stress and frustration for teachers.

If the stress cycle is to be broken, teachers need to be able to examine their own feelings and emotions as a first step toward stress reduction. In so doing, teachers must be prepared and capable of assessing how their feelings and behaviors affect their relationships with their students and colleagues (Rizzo & Zabel, 1988). Because behavior management problems are a primary cause of teacher stress and burnout, teachers must give special attention to the way their own behaviors affect their students if stress is to be reduced and brought under control. A teacher who dislikes or is feeling dissatisfied with his or her teaching quickly conveys these feelings to students who, recognizing this, often exhibit unwanted behaviors that create more stress for the teacher. For this situation to improve, teachers must confront their feelings of stress and do something proactive to be able to appropriately cope with them. Teachers who avoid holding back their emotions by finding safe ways to vent their feelings are much less likely to become overly stressed. Withheld emotions often lead to negative and depressing thoughts. Teachers who are able to think and act more positively are more likely to project an acceptable image to their students, which then improves life in the classroom for everyone concerned (Curwin & Mendler, 1999a).

A good sense of humor is a wonderful aid when combating burnout. Although easy to say yet hard to do, if a person can simply learn to laugh at himself or herself and not take too many things on a personal level, stress can be reduced. At times, however, too much stress can lead to dangerous depression or seriously aggressive acts. When serious problems of this nature are identified, it is advisable for the teacher to seek professional assistance from someone who specializes in issues dealing with job-related stress.

Administrators can and need to help teachers who are having stress-related problems (Pawlas, 1997). Principals should always take time to listen to a teacher's frustrations. A problem that may sound trivial to the principal is likely to be truly stressful to the teacher who took the first step to visit the principal to talk about the problem. Principals should be supportive and, whenever possible, make a point of looking for something good to share with a frustrated teacher. Giving reassuring advice or help to a teacher who seems to have encountered a particularly frustrating situation can be especially beneficial. The principal, for example, might speak to a disruptive student or request a meeting with the student's parents as a strategy to be of special assistance. Supportive, reassuring behavior by the principal can do a great deal to lift a teacher's morale. Some principals have created special support groups within their schools as a strategy to help teachers get help in stress reduction. Activities such as yoga, meditation, breathing exercises, and dance, to name a few, have also been used as means to make the workplace more enjoyable and reduce the stress related to the responsibilities of teaching.

CONCLUSION

A discussion of zero-tolerance policies, expulsion, managing special students, addressing diversity, violence, school uniforms, and drug abuse began this review of special problems and concerns related to student management and motivation in classrooms and schools. These topics are identified as recurring issues for discussion when teachers share their concerns about managing and motivating students in contemporary school settings. The discussion has sought to provide current information that will help teachers advance their skills and knowledge to meet the demands of a dynamic and challenging profession while encouraging further investigation and study.

The last two topics discussed in this chapter are of a slightly different nature. Special concerns of beginning teachers and the impact of stress and teacher burnout are seen as having special importance in any investigation of issues of best practice in classroom management and student motivation. Management and motivation concerns are uniquely related to both of these topics, because issues of management and motivation are tightly intertwined with many of the problems related to the first year of teaching and the ongoing pressures of working in the profession. Consequently, they are potential causes of teacher stress and burnout. This chapter has sought to extend the landscape of understanding of management and motivation in the classroom while reinforcing the important need for educators at all levels to continue their study in these critical areas.

QUESTIONS/ACTIVITIES FOR REFLECTION

1. What is your personal assessment of zero-tolerance policies related to student behavior management? Do you see them as positive or not positive? If you were a building administrator interested in adopting such a policy, how would you begin the process? What would be important questions that need to be addressed?

2. Many teachers hold the view that expelling certain chronic misbehaving students from school is needed for the greater good of helping other students who exhibit positive behaviors. Others see expulsion as an act of discarding a human being into a world of little hope or positive future. Evaluate the strategy of expulsion as a means of dealing with student misbehavior. Explain why you have made the evaluation you have made.

3. The practice of including exceptional students in regular classrooms has resulted in greater diversity in classrooms than ever before. Many regular classroom teachers are strongly in support of this practice, whereas some hold the view that the presence of exceptional learners in regular classrooms helps neither the regular students nor those that are exceptional. If you were a teacher in a regular classroom with exceptional learn-

ers, what are the important questions that you would need to ask and have answers to maintain a well-managed classroom with highly motivated students?

4. If you were a teacher new to the profession, what personal plan might you put in place to address the potential problems of stress and burnout? What would be the key elements of the plan, and how would you go about ensuring that the plan was successful?

5. A number of early warning signs related to potential student violence were introduced in the chapter. Interview three teachers working in classrooms today and review the signs on the list with them. What is their assessment of the problem of violence in schools and classrooms today and the accuracy of the warning signs on the list?

REFERENCES

Adair, J. (2000). Tackling teens' no. 1 problem. *Educational Leadership, 57*, 44–47.

Banks, J. (1994). *An Introduction to Multicultural Education.* Needham Heights, MA: Allyn & Bacon.

Black, S. (1998). Forever plaid? *American School Board Journal, 185*, 42–45.

Blair, F. (1999). Does zero tolerance work? *Principal, 79*, 36–37.

Brock, B., & Grady, M. (1998). Beginning teacher induction programs: The role of the principal. *Clearing House, 71*, 179–183.

Brown, J. (1997). Curriculum: Listen to the kids. *American School Board Journal, 184*, 38, 40, 47.

Caruso, P. (1996). Individuality vs. conformity: The issue behind school uniforms. *NASSP Bulletin, 80*, 83–88.

Children's Defense Fund. (1994). *The State of America's Children* 1994. Washington, DC: Children's Defense Fund.

Community Update. (February/March 2001). U.S. Department of Education, Issue No. 85.

Cummings, C., & Haggerty, K. (1997). Raising healthy children. *Educational Leadership, 54*, 28–30.

Curwin, R., & Mendler, A. (1999a). *Discipline With Dignity.* Alexandria, VA: American Association of Supervision and Curriculum Development.

Curwin, R., & Mendler, A. (1999b). Zero tolerance for zero tolerance. *Phi Delta Kappan, 81*, 119–120.

Dayton, J. (2000). Discipline procedures for students with disabilities. *Clearing House, 73*, 153–156.

Dowling-Sendor. B. (1998a). Watching what students wear. *American School Board Journal, 185*, 12–13.

Dowling-Sendor, B. (1998b). Gangs and rosaries. *American School Board Journal, 185,* 22, 24.

Dwyer, K., Osher, D., & Hoffman, C. (2000). Creating responsive schools: Contextualizing, early warning, timely response. *Exceptional Children, 66,* 347–365.

Educational Testing Service. (1998). Beyond assumptions. *American Educator, 22,* 32–35.

Elias, M., Gager, P., and Leon, S. (1997). Selecting a substance abuse prevention program. *Principal, 76,* 23–24, 27.

Essex, N. (2000). Classroom harassment: The principal's liability. *Principal, 79,* 52–55.

Evans, D. (1996). School uniforms: An 'unfashionable' dissent. *Phi Delta Kappan, 78,* 139.

Good News About American Education. (2000). Washington, DC: Center on Education Policy and the American Youth Policy Forum.

Gottlieb, J., & Weinberg, S. (1999). Comparison of students referred and not referred for special education. *Elementary School Journal,* 187–199, vol. 99, No. 3..

Hahn, E., Hall, L., Rayens, M., Burt, A., Corley, D., & Sheffel, K. (2000). Kindergarten children's knowledge and perceptions of alcohol, tobacco, and other drugs. *Journal of School Health, 70,* 51–55.

Hamilton, K. (1999). Implementing a school uniform policy. *Principal, 79,* 46–47.

Hendrickson, B. (1979). Teacher burnout: How to recognize it, what to do about it. *Learning, 7,* 36–38.

Hyman, I., & Snook, P. (2000). Dangerous schools and what you can do about them. *Phi Delta Kappan, 81,* 488–498; 500–501.

Jones, R. (1997). More than just no. *American School Board Journal, 184,* 30–32.

King, A. (1996). Exclusionary discipline and the forfeiture of special education rights: A survey. *NASSP Bulletin, 80,* 49–64.

Koch, K. (2000, March 10). Zero tolerance. *Congressional Quarterly Researcher.* Washington, DC: Congressional Quarterly, Inc., 187–204.

Kommer, D. (1999). Beyond fashion patrol: School uniforms for middle grades. *Middle School Journal, 30,* 23–26.

Langdon, C. (1996). The 3rd Phi Delta Kappa poll of teachers' attitudes toward the public schools. *Phi Delta Kappan, 78,* 244–250.

Lowry, R., Cohen, L., Modzeleski, W., Kann, L., Collins, J., & Kolbe, L. (1999). School violence, substance use, and availability of illegal drugs on school property among U.S. high school students. *Journal of School Health, 69,* 347–355.

McEwan, B. (2000). *The Art of Classroom Management: Effective Practices for Building Equitable Learning Communities.* Upper Saddle River, NJ: Merrill.

Martin. N., & Baldwin, B. (1996). Helping beginning teachers foster healthy classroom management: Implications for elementary school counselors. *Elementary School Guidance & Counseling, 31,* 106–113.

Matus, D. (1999). Humanism and effective urban secondary classroom management. *Clearing House, 72,* 305–307.

Morgon, M. (1997). Dear colleague: A letter from a new teacher to experienced teachers. *Clearing House, 70,* 250–252.

Morris, R. (1998). Conflict: Theory must inform reality. The Kappa Delta Pi Record, Fall, 14-17.

Morrison, G., & D'Incau, B. (2000). Developmental and services trajectories of students with disabilities recommended for expulsion from school. *Exceptional Children, 66,* 257–272.

Osborne, A. (1998). The principal and discipline with special education students. *NASSP Bulletin, 82,* 1–8.

Pawlas, G. (1997). Seven tips to reduce teacher stress. *High School Magazine, 4,* 42–43.

Rizzo, J., & Zabel, R. (1988). *Educating Children and Adolescents With Behavioral Disorders: An Integrative Approach.* Boston: Allyn & Bacon.

Rose, L., & Gallup, A. (1996). The 28th annual Phi Delta Kappa/Gallup poll of the public's attitudes toward the public schools. *Phi Delta Kappan, 78,* 41–59.

Rose, L., & Gallup, A. (1999). The 31st annual Phi Delta Kappa/Gallup poll of the public's attitudes toward the public schools. *Phi Delta Kappan, 81,* 41–56.

Rossman, S., & Morley, E. (1996). Introduction. *Education and Urban Society, 28,* 395–411.

Skiba, R., & Peterson, R. (1999). The dark side of zero tolerance-Can punishment lead to safe schools? *Phi Delta Kappan, 80,* 372-376; 381–382.

Skiba, R., & Peterson, R. (2000). School discipline at a crossroads: From zero tolerance to early response. *Exceptional Children, 66,* 335–346.

Smith, C. (2000). Behavioral and discipline provisions of IDEA '97: Implicit competencies yet to be confirmed. *Exceptional Children, 66,* 403–412.

Smith, J., & Colon. R. (1998). Legal responsibilities toward students with disabilities: What every administrator should know. *NASSP Bulletin, 82,* 40–53.

Sprague, J., & Walker. H. (2000). Early identification and intervention for youth with antisocial and violent behavior. *Exceptional Children, 66.* 367-379.

Stanley, M. (1996). School uniforms and safety. *Education and Urban Society, 28,* 424–435.

Tauber, R. (1999). *Classroom Management: Sound Theory and Effective Practice* (3rd. ed.). Westport, CN: Bergin & Garvey.

Taylor, H. (2000). Meeting the needs of lesbian and gay young adolescents. *Clearing House, 73,* 221–224.

Townsend, B. (2000). The disproportionate discipline of African American learners: Reducing suspensions and expulsions. *Exceptional Children, 66,* 381–391.

Veenman, S. (1986). Perceived problems of beginning teachers. *Review of Educational Research, 54,* 143–178.

Wagner, M., Knudsen, C., & Harper, V. (2000). The evil joker. *Educational Leadership, 57,* 47–50.

Wallace, M. (2000). Nurturing nonconformists. *Educational Leadership, 57,* 44–46.

Weatherly, J. (2000. Special rules for special ed. *American School Board Journal, 187,* 26-27

Wooley, S., Eberst, R., & Bradley, B. (1999/2000). Creative collaborations with health providers. *Educational Leadership, 57,* 25–28.

Zabel, R., & Zabel, M. (1996). *Classroom Management in Context: Orchestrating Positive Learning Environments.* Boston: Houghton Mifflin Company.

Zirkel, P. (1997). The Midol case. *Phi Delta Kappan, 78,* 803–804.

Zirkel, P., & Gluckman, I. (1997). Due process in student suspensions and expulsions. *Principal, 76,* 62–63.

Chapter 6

RESPONDING TO STUDENT MOTIVATION AND BEHAVIOR PROBLEMS

The ability to respond to specific classroom behavioral problems so that the problems are effectively addressed represents a special skill, or perhaps more accurately a set of skills, that requires refinement over time. Effective teachers as reflective practitioners must individually analyze unacceptable behaviors exhibited by students to develop appropriate ways to address each behavior and manage and motivate those students who are not conducting themselves in ways appropriate to the classroom.

This chapter will examine several instances of student conduct that are seen as motivation and behavior problems by most teachers (Charles, 1976; Hunt, Touzel, & Wiseman, 1999). The use of the Model for Reflection and Inquiry introduced in Chapter 1 to effectively address problems of classroom management and student motivation will be illustrated through the use of behavior management scenarios as practical examples of typical classroom problem situations.

TEACHER REACTIONS TO STUDENT MISCONDUCT

Teachers can and do prevent many problems from occurring through the effective use of managerial and motivational techniques that they regularly incorporate into their teaching. It has already been noted that effective teachers have to address fewer student behavior problems than teachers who are considered to be not effective. Even with well-thought-out preventive measures in place, however, the occasion will occur in virtually any classroom when a student acts in an undesirable fashion. This may be represented by a minor infraction of rules such as talking too loudly or not waiting for others to finish talking before speaking. Or, a student behavior problem could be of a more serious nature such as a student endangering the safety of other students or doing something that directly interferes with the learning of classmates. Teachers need to be prepared on a daily basis to alter (some might say correct) the behavior of some students. As introduced in Chapter 1, teachers need to be prepared to discipline those students who do not respond to the teacher's instructional, motivational, and management plans.

Schlechty (1976) suggests that any one of three different approaches to classroom leadership (i.e., management) can be used by teachers to modify student behavior. Schlechty's position, influenced by the earlier work of social psychologists such as French and Raven (1959), is that, to be effective, teachers must earn or otherwise gain a type of social power or leadership over the students in the classroom. If the teacher does not maintain leadership of the group, leadership will be gained by someone else, in this case one or more students. Teachers are believed to manage their classrooms through the use of one of the following three strategies: *normative, remunerative,* or *coercive.* **Normative strategies** are *behavior strategies used by the teacher in maintaining a well-managed classroom based on all involved doing what is traditionally expected of them because each person knows his or her expected role;* teachers are expected to ask students to do certain things, and students are expected to do what their teachers ask them to do. **Remunerative strategies** are *behavior strategies used by the teacher that are based on the power of rewards.* Rewards can take the form of special privileges, extra time to participate in enjoyable activities, or more tangible rewards such as candy or tokens (Borich, 2000; Borich & Tombari, 1997). **Coercive strategies** are *behavior strategies used by the teacher that are based on the power of punishment.* If students do not behave properly, they will be punished. Some educators believe that an over reliance on coercive strategies may alienate students to the point that they withdraw from the learning process (Borich, 2000). Many teachers, however, even with this potential concern, try to manage the learning environment through the use of coercive power. Coercive strategies can produce short-term gain coupled with long-term loss.

Normative power depends on the teacher's ability to gain respect from students. When teachers are seen as knowledgeable, trustworthy, fair, and concerned, students more readily respond to their requests (Goodlad, 1984). When teachers treat students with respect, students develop a greater sense of belonging in the classroom. Students respond more consistently to a system of management based on normative strategies when a respectful and trusting environment has been established. Glasser (1986) stresses the importance of such a relationship between students and their teachers if effective management is to be realized. Normative power is positional in that the role of *teacher* carries with it, by its very nature, a high degree of influence and authority. If teachers conduct themselves the way students believe teachers should conduct themselves, students will more frequently respond positively to their teacher's use of normative strategies and do what their teachers ask, simply because it is their teachers who are making the requests.

Operant conditioning forms the foundation of remunerative management. Chapter 4 included a discussion of the Applied Behavior Analysis management theory that is based on B.F. Skinner's theory of operant conditioning. The basic purpose that drives remunerative management is the motivation by reward of students so that they will continue to exhibit, and even intensify, acceptable conduct. The parent who gives money to a child for every "A" on the report card, the teacher who shows a special film because the students all made good grades on a mathematics test, or the principal who hosts a pizza party for all students who make the Honor Roll all represent the use of remuneration to motivate and manage students. One of the most important aspects of remunerative management is that it focuses on the positive, not the negative, aspects of students' behaviors. In spite of this, many educators criticize the management and motivation by remuneration approach, suggesting that students should not be expected to exhibit appropriate behavior only for the purpose of receiving rewards (Kohn, 1993).

Coercive management relies on the use of physical or psychological pain or discomfort, taking away belongings or privileges, or threatening either of these measures to persuade (i.e., motivate) students to discontinue unwanted behaviors. An important concern regarding the use of coercive strategies is the fear that their use may increase student antagonism and lead to students becoming alienated from the learning process (Borich, 2000). Because coercive strategies focus on the negative aspects of student behavior, it is important that teachers avoid the use of consequences that belittle, embarrass, or attack the character of a student. When consequences are given for undesirable behavior, teachers should focus on just that, the undesirable behavior, not the student. What should be emphasized in efforts to extinguish a student's unwanted behavior is that it is the behavior that is unwanted, not the student. Comments such as, "I don't know what you get away with at home, but you cannot do that in my room," or "Stop acting so immature," are attacks on the student's character or that of the student's parents. Attacks such as these result in hurt and embarrassment with the typical end result being alienated, angry students. In some cases such attacks may also produce alienated and angry parents.

If a student does something that is considered inappropriate, the teacher should deal with the misbehavior and the consequence swiftly. Identifying the consequences for undesirable behavior early in the school year emphasizes to students that they have an important responsibility for their own self-control (i.e., self-regulation) and forewarns them of the end result if they do not take this responsibility seriously (Emmer, Evertson, & Worsham, 2000; Evertson, Emmer, & Worsham, 2000; McCormick & Pressley, 1997). Early identification also helps to make clear in the communication process between the teacher and his or her students just what is considered as being unacceptable and what is not. In establishing these ground rules, the teacher will have taken an important preventive step in dealing with potential management problems in the classroom.

THE PROACTIVE TEACHER

Being characterized as proactive as opposed to reactive in teaching says a great deal about how the teacher approaches his or her responsibilities in the profession. The **proactive teacher** is *a teacher who has the ability to "head off" most management problems before they occur and respond to management problems when they do occur in such a way that sets the stage for learning to continue in the future.* Given that there will be cases of student misconduct from time to time in all classrooms to which teachers will need to respond, it is important that teachers remain focused on the purpose behind any use of their power. The teacher's primary purpose in reacting to student misconduct is to change the behavior of the student so that the school environment will be safe and conducive to learning for all students, including the student exhibiting the misbehavior. The purpose is not simply to react to a disturbance or unacceptable behavior so that the disturbance or behavior is eliminated. In reacting to student misbehaviors, the teacher's emphasis should be on eliminating the unacceptable behaviors so that students displaying these behaviors, and their classmates, will gain the greatest benefit from their schooling experiences. Effective teachers see their responses to student behavior problems as an additional opportunity to teach their students so that the learning environment will be improved. They, in effect, teach their students what proper behavior is all about and how they can exhibit proper behavior. In doing this they also teach, and reinforce, what behaviors are considered to be not proper. Their responses to student behavior problems focus specifically on the undesired student behaviors while avoiding personal attacks on students; this is a crucial aspect of effective management. Teacher responses seen as personal attacks on the students themselves will only increase the probability of future disruptive behavior. More importantly, such responses by the teacher can result in a decrease in learning. Teachers who concentrate their efforts on motivating students to do better, as opposed to focusing their attention on policing students to not misbehave, establish more productive learning environments and fruitful relationships with their students.

Cotton (1999) lists thirteen teacher behaviors that research indicates are associated with a behavior management system that will help teachers create a learning environment that encourages students to conduct themselves appropriately. When used, the system also decreases the likelihood that students will misbehave in the future. Cotton recommends that effective teachers:

1. Set behavior standards that are similar to the standards set in the building conduct code.
2. Tell students that there are high standards for conduct in the classroom and clearly explain rules and consequences for their behavior.
3. Are conscious of cultural influences on conduct.
4. Provide a written set of behavior standards to students and review the standards periodically.
5. Establish clear and specific rules at the beginning of each year or semester.
6. Allow students to help in the establishment of rules and procedures in grades 4–12.
7. Provide appropriate amounts of review and reteaching of rules in PreK–3 settings.
8. Link discipline sanctions to the students' inappropriate behavior, and avoid using or threatening to use corporal punishment.
9. Focus on teaching positive, prosocial behaviors, especially when students consistently repeat inappropriate behaviors.
10. Quickly stop students who are disruptive to avoid loss of learning time
11. Focus on inappropriate behaviors, not the students' past offenses or personalities.
12. Handle disciplinary problems themselves, with referrals to administrators only in rare situations.
13. Actively seek new methods and strategies to improve their behavior management skills.

Teachers who exhibit these behaviors are considered proactive in their approaches to student motivation and classroom management. Instead of waiting for a disruption to occur before acting, or being reactive, they use behaviors or strategies designed specifically to create an environment that decreases the potential for inappropriate conduct occurring in the first place. Hunt, Touzel, and Wiseman (1999) discuss eight behaviors that characterize teachers who create environments designed to promote positive student behavior and diminish student misbehavior. The teacher should:

1. Thoroughly prepare so that all students stay on task with activities suitable for their individual rates, styles, and abilities of learning.
2. Develop classroom routines that help students get through noninstructional times when behavior problems are most frequent.

3. Communicate with parents to develop a strong support system to better work with specific management problems.
4. Maintain a professional demeanor when carrying out their duties and responsibilities.
5. Recognize inappropriate student behaviors and deal with them rapidly while ignoring insignificant conduct.
6. Exhibit calm, confident behavior when correcting inappropriate student conduct.
7. Immediately follow up on directives when students do not respond positively.
8. Focus on preventing problems instead of reacting to problems.

These behaviors focus on the development of classroom learning environments where teachers can rely mainly on a normative management system, with the teacher and students forming a positive learning relationship founded on trust and respect. They also reinforce the need for the teacher to use effective teaching practices that will keep students focused and involved in constructive learning activities and reduce "down times" when most misbehavior occurs.

Maintaining a professional demeanor, exhibiting a calm and confident composure, and reacting only to truly inappropriate as opposed minor student misbehaviors are all ways for teachers to earn the trust and respect of students. Following through with appropriate consequences when students fail to respond to directives is an essential behavior used by effective teachers to develop consistency in their management. Schlechty (1976) and Hunt and Bedwell (1982) note that teachers who retreat (i.e., ignore students who do not respond positively to a teacher request) increase the probability of having more management problems in the future. The need to know how to prevent problems has similarity to the need for the teaching profession to become more science than art and for teachers to recognize their need to know what works specifically and in what situations (Marzano, Pickering, & Pollock, 2001). For this to happen educators must have a desire and commitment to change. Knowing how to prevent problems, for example, requires being willing and able to learn from past mistakes and accomplishments along with seeking and utilizing the assistance of other professionals. Freiberg and Driscoll (2000) use the term **advancework** in referring to *the process of preventing problems before they begin rather than reacting to problems after they have already occurred.* Advancework requires teachers to gather data to develop a better understanding of their students, the community and school, and the impact the content being taught has on the behavior of their students.

Good and Brophy (2000) include one further aspect of effective management not yet discussed to this point. Teachers who desire to minimize their management problems set as a goal the development of inner self-control in students. It is not sufficient for teachers to be satisfied merely in being able to manage their classrooms and students. A major part of the inculturation that should take place in any school is for students to learn to manage themselves to live in a supportive environment with others. Without self-control it is difficult, if not impossible, for students to resolve the various conflicts that may develop in their lives on any given day. The development of self-control was previously discussed in reference to students becoming self-regulated learners.

The first days of the school year or the beginning of a semester are critical for the teacher to develop a system (i.e., rules and procedures) for effective classroom management. Various research studies have identified that one important quality that characterizes effective teachers as managers is that they establish their expectations for student behavior during the first few weeks of the school year or semester and consistently reinforce them thereafter (Emmer, Evertson, & Worsham, 2000; Freiberg & Driscoll, 2000). Evertson, Emmer, and Worsham (2000) suggest that teachers should use the first weeks of the school year to clearly communicate their rules and procedures to their students, to observe student attitudes and work habits, and to begin instruction with a high level of energy and enthusiasm. This will greatly help to establish a solid foundation on which the teacher's academic program can be built.

Effective teachers project themselves as leaders in the classroom while creating a learning environment based on concern, trust, and respect. Students maintain a high level of productivity, because they are regularly engaged in learning activities appropriate for their learning styles, interests, and abilities. Students have a clear understanding of the rules and procedures for classroom behavior, and the consequences that accompany the breaking of rules or not following procedures. They observe that the teacher quickly and consistently takes action to ensure that all students follow established rules and procedures. Students understand that there exists a high standard for conduct and that they must assume responsibility for their own behavior.

Teachers who aspire to meet these expectations and who follow these guidelines will have students who more regularly conduct themselves in an appropriate fashion. As any experienced teacher can attest, however, it is unrealistic to believe all student misbehavior can be prohibited. Behavior management problems can still occur even in what may seem to be the best of classroom situations. As a result of their study and prior planning, however, effective teachers are prepared to handle these problems swiftly with as little interruption to the learning process as possible. Hunt, Touzel, and Wiseman (1999) organize effective teaching concerns related to motivation and management into three categories: *personal considerations, instructional considerations,* and *environmental considerations* (Figure 6-1).

Figure 6.1
Considerations for the Prevention of Management Problems

Personal Considerations	Instructional Considerations	Environmental Considerations
Conduct one's self in a calm, confident fashion.	Able students must be challenged.	The classroom must be a clean, comfortable setting.
Be prepared for unexpected events.	Low-ability students should not be placed in unduly frustrating situations.	The classroom should be void of major distractions to learning.
Praise positive behavior.		
Show respect and affection for learners.	Instruction should be both exciting and enjoyable.	A few rules for acceptable conduct should be clearly stated.
Treat students in a consistent fashion.	A variety of questioning patterns should be utilized.	Parents and administrators must offer support.
Ensure that student ideas are valued.		The atmosphere should be one of acceptance.
	All students should experience success.	

ADDRESSING SPECIFIC MANAGEMENT PROBLEMS

The teacher's role in student motivation and classroom management should be examined in the context of the ideas and recommendations presented throughout the entire body of this text and not in any one chapter. As emphasized, the most productive learning environments are those in which high levels of motivation and the absence of student misbehaviors are found. In spite of the teacher's best efforts to be well planned and motivating, and even with a sound management plan, however, the time will inevitably come when some students will behave in ways that are believed not to be acceptable and where the teacher will need to take action to correct these behaviors.

What is unacceptable behavior? It is important for teachers, and students, to have the answer to this question clearly in mind, because effective teachers don't react to just any student behavior that seems undesirable. Consider the following four definitions of unacceptable behavior:

1. Any behavior that disrupts the learning of one or more students.
2. Any behavior that threatens the safety of one or more students.
3. Any behavior that is in direct violation of written schoolwide or classroom rules.
4. Any behavior that is a violation of accepted social mores (e.g., the use of profanity, inappropriate touching).

In addition to these four definitions, teachers will likely wish to identify rules for student behavior specific to their individual classrooms as a part of their own management and discipline plans. What is unacceptable in one teacher's classroom may be acceptable in another teacher's whereas some behaviors are always unacceptable in every classroom. Some teachers may have the expectation that students may speak only after first raising their hand and being recognized. Other teachers may encourage more open discussion and actually expect spontaneous participation from their students. However, if there are schoolwide rules for certain behaviors (e.g., that no candy is to be eaten in classrooms or no hats are to be worn inside the school building), all teachers are expected to enforce these rules.

The number of rules a teacher has influences how much time the teacher will spend monitoring and managing student behaviors. The more rules there are the more time will be spent in seeing that they are followed. Teachers should only have those rules considered to be most important and that relate specifically to promoting the instructional program of the classroom. The fewer rules the better with no more than five or six being considered maximum by many teachers. Not only do greater numbers of rules create added monitoring problems for teachers, large numbers of rules create problems for students in trying to remember them and the consequences that will occur when they are not followed.

Many authors have identified and categorized various kinds of student misbehaviors found in classrooms and made suggestions concerning methods teachers can use when confronted with them. It should be recalled that student misbehavior needs to be analyzed and then addressed in a situational manner. Behaviors are contextual. What may prompt a behavior in one student may not in another. Likewise, what may prove to be an effective remedy to one problem in one situation may or may not be as effective in another (Gootman, 2001). The following section of the chapter examines eight frequently observed student misconduct behaviors and provides suggestions for teacher intervention. The suggestions are recommended as important ones to be considered when a teacher is faced with a particular student misbehavior. Even with this information, however, teachers should analyze and evaluate each situation independently and then apply the most suitable solution called for. The behaviors included here are *inattention, dis-*

ruptive talking, chronic avoidance of work, unruliness, aggression, attention-seeking, defiance, and dishonesty. Some of the behaviors are considered as being more serious than others; they are examined here from least to most serious in nature.

Inattention

Inattention behaviors are defined simply as *students not paying attention when the teacher is conducting instruction or when participation in an instructional activity is expected.* Common inattention behaviors exhibited by students are daydreaming, staring into space, doing unrelated work, doodling, or even playing with some toy or other object during instructional time. Inattention is seen as the least severe management problem, in part because the inattentive student tends not to disturb other students in the classroom. Inattention is still considered to be unacceptable behavior, however, inasmuch as when students are inattentive to the teacher or the teacher's planned activities they are not engaged in the learning process. Also, if not addressed, their inattention can be adopted by other students in the classroom if the inattention is seen by them as being acceptable.

Working with Students with Inattention Problems

If a teacher's lesson is progressing well, the teacher who has twenty-five students in a classroom is advised not to interrupt the instructional process that is being effective with twenty-four students for one student who may be inattentive. Although it is important that all students attend to the teacher's lesson, there are more subtle ways of effectively handling the problem of a student being inattentive than to disrupt the learning of the rest of the students in the class to eliminate the inattentive behavior of one or even a few students. Moving physically closer to an inattentive student, for example, will usually help bring the student's attention back to the learning task or to what the teacher is saying. This use of what is sometimes referred to as proximity control will allow the teacher to modify the student's behavior without ever having to say a word. When teachers are physically close to students, the likelihood of student misbehavior diminishes.

Teachers can do a number of things to be proactive in preventing student inattention, with the first step being to evaluate the physical arrangement of the classroom. Researchers established years ago that students sitting in certain parts of the classroom get less teacher attention than others and are, therefore, more likely to be inattentive if they are so inclined (Adams & Biddle, 1970). It is recommended that seating arrangements be developed so that those students most inclined to be inattentive sit as near the teacher as possible. The corners of the classroom farthest from the teacher are areas to avoid for students prone to inattentiveness. The distance between the student and the teacher is an important variable when determining the likelihood of a student being inattentive.

Another important physical factor affecting inattention is spacing. Students who are seated too closely to one another automatically have greater opportunities for distractions. When students are seated at tables, adequate space must be provided so that each student has a comfortable work area that does not encroach on other students. It is best when a space is provided away from the student's immediate study or work area for the storage of excess books and supplies that can become distractions. Lack of adequate space and comfort increases the probability that distractions and eventually inattentiveness will take place.

Room temperature is another physical factor that affects attention. Although comfort level as far as temperature is concerned varies from individual to individual, it is generally better to have the room temperature slightly cool rather than warm. If the room temperature gets too warm, activity may slow down, and some students are likely to become sleepy.

A final physical factor affecting inattention is the presence of distractions in the classroom. Most elementary school students sitting beside a window overlooking a playground are almost certain to be distracted. Similarly, many students at the secondary level sitting beside an open door leading to a busy hallway may also lose their focus on the lesson. Although there are some distractions over which teachers have little control (e.g., construction workers, the first snow of the year, the onset of important events), to the degree possible, distractions should be eliminated or at least minimized to help students stay on task.

The teacher's own instruction can be another factor that can impact student attentiveness. Student inattention will increase when the teacher's instruction lacks excitement and enthusiasm. Although some may say that teachers cannot be exciting every minute of the day, this is little consolation when students are inattentive or exhibiting some other form of unwanted behavior. Instruction that is not stimulating may reflect insufficient preparation on the part of the teacher in terms of preparing for instruction, motivation, and management at the same time. Effective teachers are enthusiastic and often animated. They think about their students individually when they plan their lessons in terms of how a particular activity will draw students into the center of the instructional process or leave them on the edge. Teachers who have students who are inattentive are often characterized by (1) doing the same thing over and over, (2) lacking in spontaneity and excitement, (3) teaching subject matter that students see as having little importance or meaning to them or as being too difficult for them to master, and (4) not engaging students actively in the learning process. Teachers are encouraged to use a variety of different instructional strategies, vary stimuli to encourage student interest, and use multimedia presentations and hands-on activities to add excitement to their instruction. Even though quiet, sedentary activities have a place in the classroom, many students, especially younger students, have trouble maintaining attention when involved in activities that do not require their involvement for extended periods of time. Classrooms where students are given the opportunity and even expected to actively participate in the learning activities and the actual planning of the activities as appropriate depending on their age, constitute environments that foster student attentiveness. Students who are involved in learning activities that are meaningful to them are seldom inattentive.

Beyond questions of classroom environment and instruction, certain personal characteristics of the teacher may augment student inattention. The monotonic voice that drones on has become a symbol of the stereotypical bore. Teachers who talk in this manner should not be surprised if their students become inattentive or even disruptive. Voice inflections are recommended along with complementary gestures to enliven the teacher's instructional delivery. The use of humor at the moment students are starting to let their minds wander also is an effective strategy. Never underestimate the effectiveness of an appropriate joke or humorous anecdote with students of all ages.

The source of some attention problems can be found in the students themselves as opposed to the teacher or the physical environment. Some students may be inattentive even though the teacher is doing an excellent job teaching a dynamic curriculum because of personal problems either at school or outside of school that are so severe that it is difficult, if not impossible, for them to attend to their class work. Also, students who have been allowed to be inattentive at other times in other classes or during other lessons may have developed a pattern of behavior or habit of not attending to the lessons that their teachers present. They may have developed shorter attention spans simply because they have never been encouraged or required to be attentive. To help a student become attentive, the teacher first must understand the reason why the student is not attentive. Gaining this understanding will require problem solving and analysis on the part of the teacher. If the cause of the student's inattention is a personal problem, counseling may be needed. If the student simply has poor learning habits, it is the teacher's responsibility to reinforce the student when good attention is shown and not give reinforcement when it is not.

Developing an effective questioning technique can be a very effective strategy to help students be more attentive (Good & Brophy, 2000). Teachers are encouraged to ask a variety of questions and direct these questions to a variety of students. When a teacher asks a question first and then calls on a student for an answer, this questioning approach encourages all students to listen to the question, in case they may be called on, as well as the answer. Teachers should remain aware of to whom they have directed their questions to make sure that their questions are uniformly delivered throughout the classroom. This strategy was discussed in Chapter 4 in reference to the equitable distribution of the teacher's questions. It is easy to fall into a pattern of directing questions to only a few students, typically to those who are more normally responsive and attentive. This pattern of question asking allows, or even encourages, students who are not involved in the questioning process to become inattentive as they become more and more distant and disconnected from the lesson. Asking questions can draw students actively into the instructional process or embarrass them publicly in the classroom. A teacher who calls on a student knowing that the student is being inattentive and thinking that putting the student "on the spot" in front of his or her classmates will cause the student to be more attentive in the future can be making a major mistake in judgment. Not only may the student not be attentive in the future, the student may also resent the teacher for the public embarrassment and be motivated to be involved in more serious forms of student misbehaviors than inattention.

Teachers are encouraged never to reinforce or reward student inattention; unfortunately, this is an error that is easy to commit. When a teacher gives directions and students do not pay attention, the teacher is actually reinforcing undesirable behavior when the directions are regularly repeated or when students are allowed to ignore the directions that have been given. This teacher behavior also sends the message to the other students in the class that being attentive is not necessary. Good listening habits represent learned behaviors, and students who habitually fail to be attentive will only improve their abilities to pay attention if their behaviors are shaped by the teacher to do so. This will take time. Teachers must be patient yet firm.

Disruptive Talking

Disruptive talking is *talking that interferes with the learning process by interrupting the teacher while teaching or students as they are listening to the teacher or as they are involved in completing activities that the teacher has assigned.* Different teachers set different standards for acceptable student talk in the classroom, and this fact itself can cause confusion for students who move from teacher to teacher during the school day. There may be no other standard for unacceptable student behavior that varies as much from teacher to teacher as the one that serves to define acceptable talking in the classroom.

Working with Students with Disruptive Talking Problems

Different teachers invariably have different views of what is and is not an "appropriate" level of student talk in the classroom. Individual teachers may even vary during the school day or from day-to-day as to what they consider to be a permissible level of student talk. This variance could even be determined by the type of lesson that is being conducted. A teacher normally will accept more student talk when a cooperative group activity is taking place than when students are involved in a more traditional teacher-led discussion. All students can understand and adjust to these differences when they clearly know what the teacher expects. However, problems are created for students when they do not know just what teachers expect or when teachers change what they consider to be the acceptable level of talk based on reasons unknown to the students. It is confusing to students when teachers fluctuate in the amount and level of talk that is seen as being acceptable from situation to situation for no apparent reason. Teachers need to be consistent with their standards in this area and avoid punishing a student one day for a behavior that was looked on as acceptable on another.

Students become involved in disruptive talk for many reasons. Although the need to talk with peers is a strong drive for many students, teachers can and should take steps to prevent or eliminate such unwanted interaction when it is disruptive to the instructional process. One strategy to address this type of problem is for the teacher to be certain that directions and instructions are stated clearly. Students often talk to classmates as they try to figure out what the teacher wants them to do. Teachers should observe students for nonverbal indications of confusion and ask questions to be certain that their directions are clear to everyone before having students start an activity or moving on to the next segment of a lesson. Idle talk also can be a result of unmotivating lessons. As is true with inattention, much unwanted talk will disappear if students are involved in motivating lessons that require their participation and that hold their interests.

The prevention of disruptive talk begins with the teacher. Students who are given an assignment that is stimulating and meaningful enough to hold their interest and adequate to keep them occupied for the entire instructional period are much less likely to become involved in unwanted talk. This is an important point to remember, because disruptive student talk can also occur when students have been given work that is too simple and that results in an abundance of idle time. It can also occur when they have been given work that is too difficult, which leads to frustration, because students do not perceive themselves as being successful on what the teacher wants them to do. It is critical that teachers understand the abilities and interests of their students in planning and delivering their instruction, in particular as this relates to student talk and attention.

It is not uncommon for certain special events in the school or classroom to lead to unwanted talking, and teachers must be prepared for this. For example, teachers should explain to students what they consider to be appropriate behavior when guests come to the classroom, when the class goes to an assembly, or when students go on field trips. Teachers should talk to students about these and other similar events before they occur and review with them what they may expect. These are all considered as preventive measures on the teacher's part. Students will have a natural curiosity and will want to ask questions and talk when special events such as these occur. If the teacher prepares for this beforehand, instead of waiting until the level of student excitement is at the highest, there will be less unwanted talking, confusion, and frustration on the part of the student and the teacher.

Certain instructional activities will naturally stimulate what may initially seem to be unwanted talking, especially with younger students. Teachers are encouraged to discuss the problem and its causes with the entire class if this occurs. Although it is difficult for students to objectively examine their behavior when they are excited, it is possible for them to look back at a later time and reflect on what they did that may have been considered inappropriate and discuss ways to avoid what may have been unacceptable behavior. Glasser (1998) believes that teachers who lead by example, instead of bossing students, and who develop positive relationships with their students (i.e., they are liked and respected), will have positive results from the class meetings that he recommends be used to address an issue such as this.

Although some undesired talking can be explained by unexpected events or the use of certain instructional activities, some students have problems with excessive talking regardless of what is taking place in the classroom. In many cases, these students can be better controlled through the classroom seating arrangement. There are some students who will talk excessively if they are allowed to sit together, and simply separating their seats will usually reduce if not eliminate this behavior. As with inattentiveness and the use of proximity control, nearness to the teacher in many cases can act as a preventive measure for unwanted talking.

A word of caution is important with respect to student talk. Teachers are encouraged to rethink their goals in teaching if they desire to teach in classrooms where student-to-student talk is generally discouraged or considered inappropriate. Instructional settings are also social settings, and student interaction with peers and teachers is essential if optimal levels of achievement are to be reached. Although some teachers may have strong views concerning problems of excessive student talk, the ability to communicate ideas is one of the most important life skills an individual can develop. It would be regrettable to think that any teacher's classroom was structured in such a way as to discourage the development of open communication. Conversation can be contagious, and teachers cannot allow students to talk and chatter freely to the extent that they and their peers have problems learning and the teacher has problems teaching. At the same time, it is also important not to let the classroom be represented by unrealistic desires for a level of silence that may be more appropriate for a library than for an environment in which active student exploration is to be expected and desired.

Chronic Avoidance of Work

All teachers are aware that some students habitually do not complete the assignments that they have been given (Evertson, Emmer, & Worsham, 2000). **Chronic Avoidance of Work** is *a misbehavior demonstrated by a student who consistently fails to complete his or her assigned work after repeated teacher effort to get the work completed.* This can represent a serious problem if students find that when they fail to do their assigned work that no negative consequence results. If not completing their work has no meaning, students will become less and less likely to complete their work as the school year progresses. Teachers need to have a management system in place to regularly follow up on the assignments they give to students to make sure that the assignments are being completed in the manner and time frame expected. Avoidance of work, although perhaps not openly disruptive to the class, is a serious matter, because the student involved is not taking part in important learning activities. If one student does not finish assignments as expected with no consequences, other students are apt to follow suit. This is an example of what Kounin (1970) referred to as the *ripple effect.*

Working with Students with Chronic Avoidance of Work Problems

In a situation in which assignments are not completed in a timely manner, the teacher needs to determine wether the student's ability to complete the assignment is the primary cause of the problem. The teacher should determine this before any interaction with the student takes place. This should actually be determined before the assignment is given. If a student has learning difficulties or otherwise lacks the necessary prerequisite skills or knowledge to complete assignments that the teacher has given, an adjustment in what is assigned needs to be made. Students should not be held responsible for work that they are not able to complete if the problem of completing the work is based on a basic lack of ability on their part. Assignments that teachers give should be made with an understanding of student ability in mind. In cases in which a student is overwhelmed by the totality of an assignment given, but yet has the ability to complete the work, it may be beneficial for the teacher to break the assignment up into smaller units.

When a student has the ability to do the assigned work, but is for some reason choosing not to do so, early intervention on the teacher's part is needed

(Evertson, Emmer, & Worsham, 2000). Before taking any action, however, the teacher typically will need additional data or pertinent information about the student to be able to determine why the assignments are not being regularly completed, especially in a classroom in which other students are successfully completing the same assignments. This normally requires collecting and checking student work frequently while carefully maintaining and recording the results. This activity represents an application of the third step in the Model for Reflection and Inquiry. Using these records, teachers can more easily determine to what degree a student is not completing homework and/or classroom assignments. Follow-up conversations with the student and possibly with other teachers who are familiar with the student may then be used to determine why the work assigned is not being completed.

It has already been identified that some students do not finish their work because an assignment may be too challenging for them. Personal problems may also interfere with a student's ability to do what the teacher desires. Death or illness of a loved one, divorce or separation of parents, difficult home environment where a student has neither the time nor place to complete assignments, and abuse are a few examples of the many types of problems that can interfere with a student completing his or her schoolwork. A teacher who discovers that a student has such a problem should work closely with the student, giving help and support until the situation has improved or the student is more in control of the situation. The school counselor can often help such students deal with their personal problems and become better able to meet their responsibilities at school and in the classroom.

After inquiring into the situation, the teacher may discover that neither personal problems nor learning problems are the causes of the student's incomplete work. Some students simply choose not to complete their assignments, because they are not appropriately motivated to do so. Evertson, Emmer, and Worsham (2000) suggest that a parent conference is one of the best techniques to use in intervening to change the behavior of students who choose not to finish homework and classroom assignments. When this strategy is used, it is important to be able to show parents the records that have been kept of the student's past performance. What students are telling parents at home may be different from what is actually taking place in school. A record of past homework or classroom assignments that were never completed is important evidence to show a parent who has been told by the student that no such assignments were made or that assignments were turned in. A monitoring or recording system should be developed in which the teacher can send a list of homework assignments with needed materials home on a regular (e.g., daily or weekly) basis for the parents' review.

Parents and teachers together might want to explore setting up a reward system to encourage a student to regularly complete assignments that are given. A behavior contract discussed earlier in Chapter 3 as recommended by William Glasser can be an effective tool to use in a situation such as this. Teachers need to be careful, however, not to decrease penalties or increase grades simply because the student may make a slight improvement over time. It is easy to send a message that doing half of the work is acceptable when this is not the case. To have the optimum effect, if a reward system is used it must encourage students to put forth the maximum effort.

Unruliness

Unruliness is *a state of general student misbehavior characterized by a lack of self-control that may be exhibited by such behaviors as talking loudly, running in hallways, using unacceptable language, getting out of seats without permission, and playing practical jokes.* Unruly students are not generally aggressive or defiant but habitually break school and classroom rules. One reason why this behavior syndrome is considered less severe than other behaviors is because unruly students, as a rule, typically do not desire to hurt others or be disrespectful but just lack personal self-control. They frequently seem out of control to teachers and other students alike.

Working with Students with Unruliness Problems

Some students are unruly simply because unruly behavior has been modeled around them on a regular basis. They have copied this behavior and may have even been rewarded for it. A child growing up in a family in which the adults disregard manners normally looked on as acceptable, show constant criticism of mainstream values, curse, and question authority, will often go to school and display these same types of behaviors. This unruliness over time becomes ingrained in the student and represents an adopted personality trait. Unruly students, however, also come from family backgrounds that do not model such traits. This fact reinforces that a student's home environment cannot always be looked on as the determiner of a student's behavior. Whatever the origin of a student's unruliness, if nothing is done to correct the behavior, it will augment over time. To accent the problem, unruly students can become negative role models that other students may choose to emulate if the teacher does not intervene and respond to the problem.

Many students find the social and academic adjustments in a school setting difficult and uncomfortable when they do not receive satisfaction from academic and social activities. This lack of satisfaction can trigger rebellious or unruly behaviors. When teachers react to unruliness, they may very well be dealing with the symptom, not the cause of the misconduct if they have not investigated the situation thoroughly. Students who are unruly typically need closer supervision than other students and an effective technique to use with them is close monitoring. Close monitoring is important but can be a challenge under certain conditions such as field trips, laboratory work, and other activities where consistent teacher supervision is more difficult.

Unruly students need to experience success in school as do all students. Repeated failure increases the likelihood of repeated misconduct. Although there must be consequences when students break established rules, teachers must be certain to separate their reaction to a negative behavior from a reaction to the student as a human being. Unruly students are often unpopular with many of their peers and, unfortunately, many of their teachers. It is important to build within them a sense of self-worth and belonging. Such students need to be in controlled situations where they have an opportunity for success, are reinforced when success is achieved, and are not overstimulated to a point where they will lose self-control. When encountering an unruly student, teachers should have the frame of mind that they are dealing with someone who needs support and nurturing more than discipline and control.

It is recommended that student isolation be given serious consideration when it becomes necessary to discipline an unruly student. If isolation is used, it needs to take place in a nonstimulating area. Students should see the isolation as an opportunity for them to calm down and regain their self-control rather than as punishment, and it should be clearly explained to them why they are there. Although it should not be seen as a punishment, neither should it be seen as a reward. A student who sees being isolated as a reward may be saying volumes about how he or she sees being in the teacher's regular classroom environment. After the prescribed period of isolation is over and a student who has been isolated is back in the normal classroom setting, the teacher should guide the student to exhibit desired behaviors and reward these positive actions appropriately. The behaviors of unruly students will change in positive ways when they begin to experience more success, in particular on activities that are meaningful and of value to them. This change in behavior will also result in more social acceptance by their peer group.

Aggression

Aggressive behavior is *a serious student misbehavior often represented by fighting although lesser forms of aggressive behavior are not uncommon, such as name-calling or other verbal attacks, pushing and shoving, and overly physical play.* Aggressive behavior is a serious problem in schools and classrooms, because when aggressive behaviors are displayed, there exists the possibility that one or more students may be injured. Because even nonfighting aggression can result in physical combat if allowed to escalate, the teacher must deal with aggressive behavior in a quick and decisive manner.

Working with Students with Aggression Problems

A key strategy to use in working with students who have been fighting, name calling, or pushing and shoving is to allow them to "cool down" before any interaction with them or teacher follow-up takes place. It is best to keep students who have been fighting away from one another and from their peers when possible immediately after the fight has taken place. Classmates have a tendency to fuel an already volatile situation when emotions are running high. Evertson, Emmer, and Worsham (2000) suggest that when the students are mature enough, having each student write his or her version of why the fight began is a good "cooling off," defusing activity. After the students have calmed down, the teacher then can meet with each of them individually to discuss whatever problem had precipitated the fight. The teacher should stress the inappropriateness of fighting and the need to solve problems in a more acceptable way and discuss with the students how their problem could have been resolved differently. If the teacher finds it difficult to get an accurate explanation of why the fight started from the students involved, it is acceptable to ask uninvolved students for additional information. It is best not to do this in front of the combatants, however, because this will only increase the likelihood of further emotional outbursts.

Virtually all schools and school districts have set procedures to follow when handling student fights. Teachers must clearly understand the policies and procedures that are in place in their schools and districts, and these procedures should always be followed. Typical procedures involve school administrators, parents, and guidance personnel and are designed to ensure the safety of all students on the school grounds. Conflict resolution programs, presented in Chapter 3, have been successful in dealing with this type of student behavior at the middle and high school levels.

Many teachers are concerned about whether they should actually try to physically break up a fight that is underway. Only if the teacher believes that it is safe to do so, perhaps with younger students, is it recommended to separate students who are fighting. In a situation in which a fight occurs, the first step should be to have all other students leave the immediate scene so that they will not be injured. Such an environment is not safe for spectators and may tend to spur on the combatants. If the teacher does not feel safe separating the fighting students, a loud command to stop fighting should be issued, and someone should be sent to quickly bring help (Evertson, Emmer,

& Worsham, 2000). One difficulty in dealing with aggressive behavior is the fact that aggressive behavior situations frequently escalate quickly, and the teacher often has little time to react. Nevertheless, through their own alertness and *withitness* in being aware of what is taking place throughout the classroom, the teacher can deter many problems and certainly diffuse many situations before they become violent or physical encounters. When violent outbreaks do occur, however, teachers need to remain calm in facing such situations and, through their prior planning, know just what they are going to do before such situations occur.

Although most aggression in the school setting is manifested in momentary outbursts as a consequence of frustration, some students have problems that can only be effectively addressed by professional assistance, such as would be provided by a counselor or psychologist. There are times when help beyond that which the teacher can provide may be required. Some students come from homes and communities where they see aggression modeled frequently and believe that the use of aggressive behavior is a normal way to solve problems. Other aggressive students have histories of academic failure and frustration at school and have become alienated from the mainstream of the school environment. They often display aggressive behavior as a type of defense mechanism. Finally, situations in which students have been physically or emotionally abused, or perhaps seen a parent and/or sibling abused, can represent the background of an aggressively behaving student. These students, all too frequently, become aggressive and abusive themselves as a reaction to what they have experienced at home. Regardless of the reason, teachers cannot allow aggressive behavior to exist in the classroom environment. A display of aggressive behavior that the teacher does not respond to represents a true threat to the teacher's ability to teach and to be the classroom leader.

Long-term solutions to aggressive behavior require that teachers make it clear to students that such behaviors are unacceptable. Teachers should listen patiently when discussing problems with aggressive students and refrain from verbal chastisements and emotional outbursts, because this will only further arouse their aggressiveness (Brophy & McCaslin, 1992). As with all forms of student misbehavior, it is necessary to understand the sources of the frustrations of aggressive students to be able to help them regain and then maintain their self-control.

Attention-Seeking

It is commonly understood by teachers at all grade levels that some students misbehave simply to get the attention of their classmates or the teacher. **Attention-seeking** behavior is *a student misbehavior problem often manifested in* *tattling by younger students to get their teachers' attention or by older students acting as the class clown or the show off as a way to get attention from the teacher and other students.* Tattling, caused by peer pressures and other social considerations, tends to become less frequent as students grow older.

Working with Students with Attention-Seeking Problems

Regardless of the method chosen by an attention-seeking student (i.e., tattling, clowning), attention-seeking behavior should not be reinforced by the teacher or other students in the class. As with students exhibiting any form of misconduct, attention-seeking students, for some reason important to them, need special attention in the social setting of the classroom. Teachers should not doubt or deny that it is the case that some students have a special need for attention but should provide such students an opportunity to receive the attention that they need in an appropriate manner. Instead of clowning to get attention, an attention-seeking student might be given the opportunity to receive attention by helping the teacher in some meaningful way, such as sharing ideas, stories, or reports to the class at an acceptable time.

Some attention seekers are characterized by insecurity, because they do not receive the attention that they need at home, in the peer group, or from the teacher. A teacher must avoid demeaning or publicly chastising an attention-seeking student for his or her behavior, because there is, at least for the student, an important motive behind it. Effective teachers seek to learn more about the cause of the undesired behavior and ways to satisfy the student's need appropriately. Such students, in fact, might benefit from receiving praise in front of the group when they conduct themselves properly. It is best to redirect the inappropriate behavior of an attention-seeking student through private, not public, conversations. Although it may be a temptation for some teachers when dealing with chronic attention seekers to tell them to "act their age" or "stop acting silly," these responses harm more than help the situation. The best procedure to follow in working with an attention-seeking student is to ignore unwanted attention-seeking while channeling the student to a way of getting attention in an acceptable manner. Teachers should make every effort to give attention to students when possible but only reinforce them when their behavior is appropriate (Good & Brophy, 2000).

It is important for the teacher to prepare the environment to prevent problems with attention seekers as it is with other forms of student misbehavior. This is best done by communicating the guidelines for appropriate behavior early in the school year and then consistently following those rules and procedures that have been established (Levin & Nolan, 2000). Some student tattling can be prevented simply by telling students early in the year what kinds of information they should and should not report to the teacher (Evertson, Emmer, & Worsham, 2000). This is also true for other forms of student attention-seeking. When all students know what is considered as proper behavior in the classroom, the attention-seeking student can often be quickly cut off and directed back to an appropriate activity by being reminded of what has and what has not been identified as acceptable behavior.

A part of preparing the environment to eliminate or reduce attention seeking from certain students could involve a special consideration of the teacher's instructional program. If teachers closely monitor the unwanted behaviors of their students they might well discover that some students are seeking attention when they have nothing else that seems meaningful or interesting to do. If this is the case, it provides an important message for the teacher regarding the importance of ensuring that all students are actively involved in high-interest and meaningful learning activities. If this is established, the frequency of student attention-seeking behaviors, and likely all student misbehaviors, will be reduced.

Defiance

Defiant behavior is *a serious form of student misbehavior in which a student refuses to do what the teacher asks of him or her or boldly talks back to the teacher in a hostile or threatening way.* Defiance is a serious type of misbehavior, because it threatens the leadership position of the teacher. If a student is allowed to be defiant to the teacher, with no meaningful consequence to follow, it is possible that other students also will do so, resulting in a total loss of classroom control. This is one of the worst possible things that could happen to a teacher, and the teacher must think and act quickly when faced with student defiance.

Working with Students with Defiance Problems

Teachers are encouraged to use caution when dealing with any defiant or hostile student, because such a student is not likely to comply to normal verbal commands. A student who challenges a teacher usually realizes that serious, deviant behavior has already taken place and may allow his or her emotions to intensify. Rather than take offense at what has been said or done, it is recommended that the teacher stay calm and, if possible, direct the student out of the classroom to an area where a teacher-to-student conversation can be held privately. Removing the student from the immediate classroom setting has three major advantages:

1. The student is given time to get his or her emotions under control.
2. The peer audience in the classroom will not be able to stir emotions and reinforce further defiance.
3. The need of the student to keep face in front of the rest of the students in the class will be gone.

In rare situations, some students may become so emotionally hostile that they refuse to leave the classroom. With a younger or smaller student, the teacher can simply escort the student from the classroom. If the student is larger, however, and refuses to leave the classroom, it is advisable for the teacher to send another student for an administrator or another teacher for help. It is not advisable that the teacher risk having a physical confrontation with the student.

When talking with defiant students, the teacher is encouraged to exhibit as much openness as possible. Rude remarks from students should not be taken personally and should not be followed by similar remarks from the teacher. Sarcasm is never warranted, and its use can quickly cause the situation to worsen. The teacher is advised not to participate in an argument with a defiant student and should try to separate the student as a person from the student's undesirable conduct. Given these considerations, the teacher has a responsibility to explain to the defiant student that the behavior that has been shown will result in consequences and that these consequences will be carried out in a just and timely manner (Evertson, Emmer, & Worsham, 2000).

Causes of defiance are often deep seated, and defiant behavior is frequently accompanied by a level of anger and frustration that may have reached a point that can no longer be contained. This hostility could be a result of problems at school, both academic and social, and problems found in the student's home life. In cases in which students have chronic problems with these types of outbursts, professional help may be warranted. Regardless of whether the student displays frequent defiance or has simply had a momentary loss of control, an understanding teacher who is willing to listen and help can be an important support for the student. A private teacher-to-student conference may allow the student to see the teacher as being fair and concerned when this may not have been what was initially thought. Through this building of rapport and trust, the student may be able to understand why the teacher acted the way he or she did. Because the teacher is encouraged to interact with defiant students on a one-to-one basis, the teacher also may feel freer to admit mistakes, if they were made, and discuss ways to improve the classroom climate to lessen stress and frustration. Although a teacher cannot afford to ignore a defiant act because it challenges the teacher's authority, it is important for the teacher not to react to defiant students in a confrontational way.

Dishonesty

Dishonest behaviors represent *one of the most serious forms of student misconduct often exhibited through cheating and/or stealing and telling untruths or lying.* Cheating and stealing generally have a more devastating impact on the entire classroom because they automatically affect others and are more difficult to deal with in a positive, proactive fashion. Some teachers have rated dishonesty as the most serious problem they must deal with in the management of their students (Charles, 1976; Hunt, Touzel, & Wiseman, 1999).

Working with Students with Dishonesty Problems

One problem that teachers encounter when dealing with dishonesty in the classroom is that children and adolescents, at least young adolescents, are still in the formative stages of their moral development. What is right and wrong is often very much determined by the situation for many students. They are still learning right from wrong, appropriate from inappropriate, etc. Because of this, teachers are advised to focus on the intent and the impact and results of such behavior. For example, children in the early elementary grades often do not have a clear understanding of *truth* and *ownership* as would be expected of them if they were older. Young adolescent students may decide to steal a test paper from their teacher's desk as much for the excitement of the adventure and the accomplishment as from a desire to cheat and improve their grades. Regardless of the motivation, teachers have the responsibility to guide students in their learning of acceptable standards of conduct and cannot condone dishonesty. No matter the age of the student, dishonesty should always be cast in a very unfavorable light. Nonetheless, teachers again must remember that many students do not come from backgrounds that reflect and promote middle-class standards of behavior that are typically common to teachers and school environments. Many students must learn acceptable behavior at school, in this case honesty, although the home and community should and will no doubt play an important role in this learning process as well. Such behavioral development typically is long term in nature.

When dealing with a student who has possibly been dishonest (e.g., cheating, stealing, or lying), the teacher must be cautious not to label the student when approaching the student having committed the misbehavior. If a student is labeled as a *cheat* or a *thief,* or a *liar,* the possible ill effects on the student's future behavior and self-concept is a consequence that needs to be avoided. Telling students they are bad or dishonest may cause them to think of themselves negatively and begin to consistently assume these roles. Students would then be following the teacher's prophecy for or about them as was discussed earlier in this text. As with confronting students with other forms of misbehavior, the teacher should never accuse a student of having been dishonest publicly with other students, or teachers, serving as an audience.

Because it is important to help students understand the importance of honest behavior, there needs to be consequences for dishonest behavior. For example, the student could lose valued privileges. However, beyond trying to determine appropriate consequences, it is also important to determine the cause of the misbehavior. If a student cheated because the assigned work was at too difficult a level, a new assignment should be made in the future that will allow the student to achieve success without cheating. The need for the teacher to have an accurate understanding of a student's ability and make appropriate assignments based on this understanding has been previously emphasized under the heading Chronic Avoidance of Work. One characteristic of students who have a history of failure is a reliance on getting help from others (perhaps through cheating) as opposed to relying on their own ability to study and learn. This feeling of learned helplessness and low self-concept must be overcome before a meaningful and long-lasting change in behavior can be expected (Weiner, 1985).

APPLYING THE MODEL FOR REFLECTION AND INQUIRY

As discussed in Chapter 1, the Model for Reflection and Inquiry, essentially the model of the scientific method, is a recommended process for the teacher to follow when dealing with student misbehaviors and/or motivation problems. Possible applications of this model will be examined in the following section of the chapter where teachers are confronted with some of the common problems that have been previously discussed.

Janice's Problem

Janice is a sixth-grade student in a middle school organized through the use of integrated instructional teams. During the first six weeks of school, Janice's performance was very much like what would have been expected based on the grades she received in school before this year. On her first grade report, Janice received a "B+" in mathematics and an "A" in all other subjects. However, soon after the next grading period began, Janice's behavior began to change. Her teachers all noticed she no longer completed all assignments, and, too often, failed to even attempt much of her homework. These problems were discussed at a team planning meeting, and it was determined that Janice was likely to receive a "D" in language arts and no higher than a "C" in all other courses on her next report card.

At least one problem in this case is easy to define. Janice, who in the past has been a model student, no longer completes her class and homework assignments. This has had a major negative impact on her performance in all subjects. Because there seemed to be no obvious or apparent problems in her classes at school that the team members who served as Janice's teachers could identify, they hypothesized that perhaps the change in Janice's behavior was due to a new boyfriend (not an uncommon problem with sixth-grade preteens) or to some problems at home. Ms. Greene, Janice's mathematics teacher, called Janice's mother, Ms. Barton, to share insights. Ms. Barton was certain Janice did not have a boyfriend although interest in the opposite sex was certainly increasing. Ms. Barton assured Ms. Greene that Janice was getting along fine at home. She did share that Janice often said that school didn't seem very interesting to her and that she saw little purpose in her school work. She preferred to spend her evenings on the phone or listening to music while reading magazines rather than studying or completing assignments for school.

On learning this, the teachers changed their hypothesis; Janice, it was now believed, had lost her motivation and interest in school. Perhaps school was no longer fun, purposeful, or challenging for her. Ms. Greene now talked with Janice with a broader background of information gained from the parent conference, collective teacher observations, and discussions in class. Janice admitted that she had lost interest in school and actually disliked many of her assignments. In her opinion, they took her away from more interesting thoughts and activities. With this new information allowing for a better understanding of the problem, the teachers decided to challenge Janice with more sophisticated assignments that they hoped would pique her interest while helping her to better see the importance of learning to her future. By working with Janice's mother, they were able to develop a system to motivate Janice through rewards related to her interests when she successfully completed her schoolwork.

George's Problem

George is a first-grade student who had his kindergarten experience through home schooling. Early on, Ms. Williams, his teacher, observed that George had difficulty in his relationships with other students. Even during the first weeks of school, there had been complaints from other students about George hitting and even biting other students. Ms. Williams talked with George and used isolation in the "Timeout" area as a consequence. However, during the fourth week of school George lost his temper on the playground and threw a rock that barely missed hitting another child; George was so upset he had to be physically restrained until he calmed down so that he would not hurt the other child or himself. Ms. Williams realized she had a more serious problem to deal with than she had at first thought.

Like Janice, George's problem can be identified. George has bouts of aggression that can disrupt the instructional environment and endanger the safety of others. Ms. Williams, George's teacher, has a serious problem. Because George had been home schooled up until this time, there were few if any school records that could provide helpful insight into his previous schooling experiences and behaviors. Through her observations of George, her experience with other children, and her consultations with Ms. Langston, the principal, Ms. Williams hypothesized that George had a problem with aggression and that this was not just a simple problem of adjusting to school. Ms. Williams wondered if George's staying home the previous year was actually related to this problem. Through a conference with Mr. and Ms. Cobb, George's parents, additional information was gained. Ms. Williams learned that George had shown signs of aggression early in life and that there was a history of problems at church, in daycare, and with other children in the community. George was kept home the previous year in hopes that he would "grow out" of the problem. Unfortunately, the problem did not lessen, and the Cobbs admitted that they were anxious to get help. Ms. Williams' hypothesis had been correct. Through the resources of the school system, the Cobbs were able to get professional help for George so that he could function in the least restrictive environment in his schooling. In dealing with serious problems of this nature, the parents, teachers, administrators, counselors, and psychologists all recognized that they would need to patiently but deliberately work together as a team over time to achieve the results that they desired.

Monica's Problem

Monica is a senior in high school who has always made above-average grades in her classes with the exception of French I, which was a struggle for her to achieve a "C-", her final grade last year. Monica made a very respectable score on the SAT and has been accepted to the state university where both of her parents graduated. Monica's parents, Mr. and Ms. Pepper, both teach at the high school she attends and are very proud of her. They have promised to buy Monica a new car for graduation so that she can more easily visit home from the university next year. One day, the Peppers were called by Mr. Long, the principal, to come to the office at the end of school. When they arrived, Mr. Long told them that Mr. Davis had caught Monica cheating on a French II examination.

The identified problem is that Monica has cheated on a test. This cannot be treated as a minor infraction. Neither Monica nor her classmates can be allowed to think that cheating goes without consequences. Mr. Davis, Mr. Long, and the Peppers all hypothesized that Monica cheated because she needed the two units of French to complete her admission to the university. She did not want to disappoint her parents and ruin her plans for next year but felt that she could not be successful without cheating. Mr. Davis was wise enough to also hypothesize that Monica had a low level of self-confidence and a self-efficacy problem that left her feeling helpless to pass French II through her own individual efforts. Mr. Davis realized that as long as Monica held an external locus of control she would continue to have problems with motivation and confidence and that this could also cause serious problems for her after she completed high school and began taking classes at the university. After talking with Monica's French I teacher from the previous year, Mr. Davis met with Monica and developed a program of study in which, through her own efforts, Monica would be able to pass French II. Monica did face the consequences of her serious misconduct that meant that she would have to re-take the test that she had cheated on and do additional work in the class. However, because of the practices of her teacher acting as a reflective educator, she came out of a difficult situation a stronger, better person.

In each of these cases the teachers involved, with help from others, identified the problems they were dealing with, planned workable solutions, and were able to help their students. The students were able to become more successful in school through the use of reflection and inquiry on the part of their teachers. Instead of simply reacting to misbehaviors in isolation, the teachers collected data from a variety of sources that helped them make more informed decisions to effectively address the problems that they and their students were dealing with. When faced with problems of classroom management and student motivation, reflective educators do not enter into "me against you" conflicts with their students. They seek to eliminate their students' misbehaviors with an eye on gaining needed skills and motivation so that such mistakes will not hamper their learning or adjustment in the future.

CONCLUSION

This chapter has provided information and recommended appropriate strategies when responding to specific types of student misbehaviors. Recommendations related to the teacher's role in establishing a strong management system were also included. These recommendations pertain to the teacher giving attention to identified personal, instructional, and environmental considerations. As has been the case in other areas of the text, the need for the teacher to be proactive and well planned in dealing with issues of student motivation and classroom management, as well as being able to address problems when the occur, has been emphasized.

The chapter also addressed types of student misbehaviors believed to be both common and serious to the teacher's ability to effectively teach students and manage the learning environment. These misbehaviors were inattention, disruptive talking, chronic avoidance of work, unruliness, aggression, attention-seeking, defiance, and dishonesty. All of these misbehaviors represent threats to teachers in carrying out their instructional responsibilities. The information provided defined the misbehaviors and then gave guidance as to possible ways to respond to them.

Finally, the chapter concluded with three short situations for analysis and illustrated the use of the Model for Reflection and Inquiry as a tool to guide the teacher in logical problem solving with respect to responding to student misbehaviors in the classroom. Two important aspects of dealing with problems of student motivation and classroom management are evident. First, teachers have to have an understanding of individual students and their issues in these areas, as well as a broad knowledge of motivation and management, to be able to effectively address the problems that they encounter in the classroom. Second, teachers have to have the ability to use their understanding about students and knowledge about motivation and management in a reasoned and logical way to put this information to its greatest use. Having knowledge about students, motivation, and management and not knowing how to use it will cause the teacher to fall far short of what is needed in effective teaching. Likewise, having knowledge about reasoned decision making and logical problem solving without a solid knowledge base of information on which to base problem solutions also will cause the teacher to fall short of what is needed. It is believed that the knowledge base of information presented here on student motivation and classroom management, coupled with the use of the Model for Reflection and Inquiry, together, will allow the teacher to effectively resolve most problems that will be encountered in the classroom. With this achieved, the teacher will then be able to advance the instructional program for the greatest benefit of all involved.

QUESTIONS/ACTIVITIES FOR REFLECTION

1. Analyze the statement, "teachers can frequently prevent problems before they ever occur." In your opinion, what does this statement mean? Do you agree with it? Explain.

2. Although criticized by some, coercive management strategies are used by many teachers every day. How do you assess their use in the classroom in terms of whether they should or should not have a place in a teacher's management plan?

3. How do you think that a teacher can truly prepare himself or herself to only react to a student's misbehavior as opposed to react to the student as a person?

4. How would you go about helping a student understand the difference between sharing information with the teacher to be helpful, or even prevent a problem from occurring, and tattling?

5. If you were a teacher who recognized that a colleague was having problems in getting students to complete work primarily because the work that was being assigned was simply too difficult for the students, how would you help your colleague come to realize that this was the case? How can a teacher maintain high standards in assignments that are made and still adjust to a variety of ability levels or levels of understanding in the classroom?

REFERENCES

Adams, R., & Biddle, B. (1970). *Realities of Teaching: Explorations with Video Tape.* New York: Holt.

Borich, G. (2000). *Effective Teaching Methods* (4th ed.). Upper Saddle River, NJ: Merrill/Prentice Hall.

Borich, G., & Tombari, M. (1997). *Educational Psychology: A Contemporary Approach* (2nd ed.). New York: Longman.

Brophy, J., & McCaslin, M. (1992). Teachers report of how they perceive and cope with problem students. *Elementary School Journal, 93*(1), 3–68.

Charles, C. (1976). *Educational Psychology: The Instructional Endeavor* (2nd ed.). St. Louis, MO: CV Mosby.

Cotton, K. (1999). *Research You Can Use to Improve Results.* Alexandria, VA: Association for Supervision and Curriculum Development.

Emmer, E., Evertson, C., & Worsham, M. (2000). *Classroom Management for Secondary Teachers* (5th ed.). Needham Heights, MA: Allyn & Bacon.

Evertson, C., Emmer, E., & Worsham, M. (2000). *Classroom Management for Elementary Teachers* (5th ed.). Boston: Allyn & Bacon.

Freiberg, H., & Driscoll, A. (2000). *Universal Teaching Strategies* (3rd ed.). Boston: Allyn & Bacon.

French, J., & Raven, B. (1959). The bases of social power. In D. Cartwright (Ed.), *Studies in Social Power* (pp. 150–168). Ann Arbor, MI: University of Michigan Press.

Glasser, W. (1986). *Control Theory in the Classroom.* New York: Harper & Row.

Glasser, W. (1998). *The Quality School Teacher.* New York: Harper Perennial.

Good, T., & Brophy, J. (2000). *Looking in Classrooms* (8th ed.). New York: Addison Wesley Longman.

Goodlad, J. (1984). *A Place Called School.* New York: McGraw-Hill.

Gootman, M. (2001). *The Caring Teacher's Guide to Discipline: Helping Young Students Learn Self-control, Responsibility, and Respect* (2nd ed.). Thousand Oaks, CA: Corwin Press, Inc.

Hunt, G., & Bedwell, L. (1982). An axiom for classroom management. *The High School Journal, 66*(1), 10–13.

Hunt, G., Touzel, T., & Wiseman, D. (1999). *Effective Teaching: Preparation and Implementation* (3rd ed.). Springfield, IL: Charles C Thomas Publisher.

Kohn, A. (1993). *Punished by Rewards: The Trouble with Gold Stars, Incentive Plans., A's, Praise, and Other Bribes.* New York: Houghton Mifflin Company.

Kounin, J. (1970). *Discipline and Group Management in Classrooms.* New York: Holt, Rhinehart, & Winston.

Levin, J., & Nolan, J. (2000). *Principles of Classroom Management: A Professional Decision-making Model.* Boston: Allyn & Bacon.

Marzano, R., Pickering, D., & Pollock, J. (2001). *Classroom Instruction that Works: Research-based Strategies for Increasing Student Achievement.* Alexandria, VA: Association for Supervision and Curriculum Development.

McCormick, C., & Pressley, M. (1997). *Educational Psychology: Learning, Instruction, Assessment.* New York: Longman.

Schlechty, P. (1976). *Teaching and Social Behavior: Toward an Organizational Theory of Instruction.* Boston: Allyn & Bacon.

Weiner, B. (1985). An attributional theory of achievement motivation and emotion. *Psychological Review, 92*(4), 548–573.

Chapter 7

CASE STUDIES FOR ANALYSIS IN STUDENT MOTIVATION AND CLASSROOM MANAGEMENT

As this text has been developed, the foundation has been laid identifying that effective teachers must work as informed reflective educators. Although it is recognized that effective teaching can be defined in different ways, when the term "effective teaching" is used here, effective is in reference to teacher practices that bring about increased levels of student achievement. And, with respect to effective teachers being informed reflective educators, informed in this context includes the teacher's knowledge and/or abilities in five key areas. These are the teacher's:

1. Understanding of his or her students to include their abilities, interests, and background characteristics
2. Understanding of what is known through educational research with respect to the body of knowledge related to student motivation
3. Understanding of what is known through educational research with respect to the body of knowledge related to classroom management
4. Understanding of what is known through educational research with respect to the body of knowledge related to best teaching practices
5. Ability to be a reasoned decision maker who uses relevant information and a logical and systematic approach to solving problems of student motivation and classroom management that will result in higher levels of student achievement

Considerable information has been presented through the previous chapters in this text regarding each of these five areas of knowledge and/or ability. Of special importance has been reference to the use of the Model for Reflection and Inquiry introduced in Chapter 1. This model has been referred to throughout the text to reinforce and illustrate the importance of effective teachers being logical problem solvers. It is included again in this chapter in Figure 7.1. The focus of the remainder of the text will be on using the model in exploring specific student problem behavior situations in the classroom that represent problems of student motivation and/or classroom management.

Figure 7.1
Model for Reflection and Inquiry

Statement of the Problem

The problem is identified and clarified; the problem should be meaningful and manageable.

Development of a Hypothesis(es)

A hypothesis or educated guess regarding a solution to the problem is formulated; there may be more than one hypothesis.

Collection of Relevant Data

Data or pertinent information relevant to the problem are collected and/or identified; references or sources of information are considered and reviewed.

Analysis of Data

Clarifications are made as to information collected; sources of data are considered and perhaps reconsidered. Relationships should be identified among data collected, and data should be clearly organized and analyzed as to how this information relates to the problem.

Interpretation and Reporting of Results, Drawing Conclusions, and Making Generalizations

Conclusions should be drawn and relevant generalizations made related to the accuracy of the original hypothesis.

Reflective educators are able to use information in a logical manner to solve the problems that they encounter in working with their students. In cases in which additional information is needed for the problem to be solved beyond that which is immediately available, reflective educators also have the ability to acquire this additional information and appropriately apply it to the decision-making process. Teachers without question are confronted with numerous problems needing resolutions on a daily basis. It is their ability to solve these problems efficiently and effectively, and learn from the problems that they have solved, which in large measure determines their effectiveness as teachers.

The remainder of Chapter 7 will focus on the application of the Model for Reflection and Inquiry as a systematic problem-solving approach recommended for use in addressing eight different types of student misbehaviors commonly found in the classroom. These types of misbehaviors were introduced and discussed at some length in the previous chapter. They are *inattention, disruptive talking, chronic avoidance of work, unruliness, aggression, attention-seeking, defiance,* and *dishonesty.* Two case studies for analysis are presented for each type of misbehavior. One case study focuses on the problem encountered at the lower level of the PreK–12 continuum with the second case study illustrating the problem at the upper level. Looking on logical problem solving as representing a reasoning process that involves asking and then finding answers to a series of questions, the following questions are offered as a guide to the analysis of each case study presented. Read through the following questions that a teacher should ask himself or herself and then apply them to the case studies that follow:

1. Exactly what is the problem that I am dealing with?

2. What might be a possible solution that I could use to effectively address the problem?

3. What additional information do I need to have that will impact the effectiveness of my solution? For example:
   a. What information is needed about the student(s)?
   b. What information is needed about my teaching?
   c. What information is needed bout the specific problem in general?
   d. What information is needed from other teachers?
   e. What information is needed from family members?

4. How will I know if my solution was really effective?

5. What should I do if my solution is not effective?

6. How can I best decide when or perhaps where this particular solution will work in the future?

After reading each case study that follows and keeping the questions listed here in mind, apply the Model for Reflection and Inquiry to develop an acceptable solution to each problem situation.

INATTENTION (PRIMARY-ELEMENTARY GRADES)

Jimmy's Inattention

Jimmy is a fifth-grade student who does not care for school; school seems boring to him. At least that is how Ms. Graves, Jimmy's fifth grade teacher sees it. According to Ms. Graves, what Jimmy seems to do best is sit next to the window and watch other students on the playground as they play games and enjoy other activities. He likes going to the playground for Ms. White's physical education class, and she says that he has good physical abilities. When the students select teams, he is usually one of the first ones chosen. He also enjoys arts and crafts class taught once a week by Mr. Brown. Mr. Brown indicates that Jimmy has a kind of "creative flair" in art. He is especially good in sketching with his pencil and working with clay. Mr. Brown says that he has the ability to envision things on his own rather than only do the assignments that he is given.

However, Ms. Graves sees Jimmy as someone who just cannot stay focused in class. This is especially the case when she is talking to the entire class. In her opinion, a fifth-grade student should be acting more maturely. Besides looking out the window, sometimes he just draws or doodles at his desk. He also has an annoying habit of tapping his pencil on his desk and humming quietly to himself. Jimmy has a history of poor grades and lately has shown some behaviors that are not acceptable to Ms. Graves. Jimmy's inattentive behavior can also be distracting to the other students as well. She is sorry to admit it, but she has come to a point where she prefers Jimmy's daydreaming rather than some other misbehaviors that he might exhibit. At least he is not being a disruptive force when "he is in his own world."

Still, Ms. Graves has become especially concerned with Jimmy and a few other students like him, because her school district has become very focused on the importance of raising test scores. Her principal makes more and more frequent visits to her classroom to see just how things are going and to check up on whether or not everyone is on task. Jimmy, sadly, is often not on task.

Ms. Graves spoke to Jimmy's mother about his inattention at the last parent conference, and she said that she would speak to him about it. So far, though, Jimmy's inattentive behavior has not changed at all. She just doesn't know what she should try next, but she knows that she has to do something. What should she do?

INATTENTION (MIDDLE-SECONDARY GRADES)

Javier's Inattention

Ms. Thomas, Javier's seventh grade math teacher, finds Javier to be a polite young man. Javier is always well dressed in the current fashion and quite popular with his classmates. When he answers questions in class, which isn't all that often, he speaks clearly and uses correct grammar. Although she finds Javier to be a pleasant student, she feels strongly that he doesn't pay enough attention to what is going on in the classroom to get the most out of it. She often notices him looking at magazines that he has brought with him to school or writing short poems or song lyrics in his notebook rather than paying attention to what she is saying. She has heard him play his guitar in the lunchroom, and, in her opinion, he is quite talented.

Sometimes, when she is teaching, she observes Javier just staring out into space. He often doesn't seem to know what is expected of him. She doesn't think that he is really misbehaving badly in class, but she does see his inattention as a definite problem. Up to this point Javier's behavior hasn't proven to be a problem for other students, but she is worried that some of them might begin to do what Javier is doing. He is very popular, and some of the other students even seem to look up to him. She has seen other occasions in the classroom when one student began to do something and others then began to follow.

She is aware that Javier has lived in the United States for about four years and that he and his parents moved to this country from Spain. Javier has one older brother in the twelfth grade and a younger sister in the second grade. Javier's older brother has received an academic scholarship to attend the local university next year. It was a very prestigious scholarship, and he plans to major in government in preparation to one day become a lawyer. Javier has made average grades all through elementary school, not excelling or doing poorly in any one subject. In her class he is barely keeping up. Javier's mother stays at home and doesn't work. His father works as a salesman at a local automobile dealership. Ms. Thomas has never had a conversation with Javier's parents, but she has seen them at some of the Parent-Teacher Association meetings.

Although Javier's not paying attention isn't the greatest problem in the world, it is creating difficulty for Ms. Thomas, and she is sure that he isn't learning as much as he can from her teaching. She, however, wants to reach all of her students but isn't sure just what to do in this situation. What should she do?

DISRUPTIVE TALKING (PRIMARY-ELEMENTARY GRADES)

Sally's Disruptive Talking

Sally is a third-grade student in Ms. Jackson's classroom. Sally is an excellent student who has never made a grade below "A" since she began school. She is very proud of her record and seems to be pleased that other students are aware of it as well. She has indicated that her parents always give her a special reward for getting such good grades on her report card. Getting good grades in school seems to come easy for her. Her best friend is Beth, who is also a good student yet not as excelled as Sally. Although Beth is a good student, her grades have been getting worse in recent weeks. She only infrequently completes assignments that Ms. Jackson has made and often does not follow the instructions and examples that Ms. Jackson provides. Ms. Jackson has noticed that Sally usually finishes her work before anyone else in the class and then spends time talking to Beth. She feels that this has been a part of the drop that she has seen in Beth's performance. When it got to the point that Sally was consistently talking while Ms. Jackson was explaining lessons to the class, Beth and Sally were asked to change their seats as far from one another as possible. This bothered Beth a good deal, because Sally now has become best friends with Rachel, who she now sits beside. In fact, Sally now spends much of the class time talking with Rachel whose work is beginning to suffer. In turn, Beth now has begun talking in class with Clifford instead of completing her own work.

Ms. Jackson's effort to help Beth's grades improve by moving her away from Sally has not been effective. On the contrary, Beth has begun her own disruptive talking behavior and is now having a negative impact on Clifford. Also, Sally's disruptive talking has actually continued after the use of the new seating arrangement, because she now talks to Rachel after she completes her assignments.

Ms. Jackson has spoken to her about her problem with talking, and Sally has promised to stop. She told Sally that when she talks, it is distracting to her when she is teaching, and this is frustrating. She also thought about lowering Sally's grade because of her talking but decided not to mention this possibility to her. Ms. Jackson was prepared to speak to Sally's parents about the problem at the last parent-teacher conference meeting that they had scheduled, but they didn't show up for the conference as planned. She isn't sure what step to take next. What should she do?

DISRUPTIVE TALKING (MIDDLE-SECONDARY GRADES)

Kelli's Disruptive Talking

Kelli is one of those students who seems to be happy one day and sad the next. One day she is prepared with her homework, and the next time homework is due, she hasn't done it. The one thing that Mr. Howard, Kelli's tenth grade science teacher can predict, however, is that he can tell every time Kelli is in the classroom, because she seems to be constantly talking when she is there. He has spoken to her about her talking on more than one occasion, because he finds it to be really distracting to his teaching. Sometimes, she talks to other students when he is trying to teach and at times just calls out answers to questions that he is asking even when he is about to call on another student for an answer. She even makes remarks about what he is talking about during his lesson to seemingly no one at all. It is as though when an idea comes into her head, she just says whatever comes to mind. When she talks, he focuses on her talking and loses track of where he is. This upsets him, and he thinks that Kelli and the other students can tell when he gets upset.

To Mr. Howard, Kelli hasn't outgrown a behavior that he thought was more common to elementary school students. One thing that adds to his frustration is that Kelli almost always receives some of the highest grades in the class. He really can't figure out how she does it when he knows that she isn't giving his teaching her undivided attention. Kelli's talking is also distracting to the other students who sit near her. Some students don't want to be her lab partner, because they know that it is difficult for them to concentrate and get their work done when she is nearby.

He has heard that Kelli is from a large family, but he really doesn't know anything about her home life. He can't recall ever speaking to anyone from her family. The more he thinks about it, she is actually somewhat of a mystery to him. He can't remember if he has ever seen Kelli with any other students outside of class on any regular basis.

He knows that he has to do something about Kelli's disruptive talking. He just isn't sure, though, how he can find out what he needs to know and what to do to make things better. What should he do?

CHRONIC AVOIDANCE OF WORK
(PRIMARY-ELEMENTARY GRADES)

Tabitha's Chronic Avoidance of Work

Tabitha can at times be one of the most cooperative students in the class and other times she can just act as though nothing in the class has any importance to her. Mr. Waverly is Tabitha's fourth-grade teacher, and he has observed her behavior with interest. Lately, what has become especially bothersome for him is that Tabitha seldom turns back into him the work that he has assigned. He does a lot of whole group instruction, as well as cooperative learning activities, and it doesn't seem to matter. For the past two months it has been virtually impossible for him to receive any schoolwork from Tabitha. It seems that it is almost weekly that he asks her about her work that is due, and she always has some comment to make about it. Sometimes it is in her mother's car. Other times she and her parents had gone out to eat the night before, and she didn't have a chance to get it done. Frequently, she just shrugs her shoulders and says that she has simply forgotten to do it but that she will bring it in the next day; the next day, Tabitha never seems to have her work.

Mr. Waverly is very concerned about Tabitha's behavior; it has happened before but has not lasted so long. At this point, Tabitha is falling further and further behind the rest of the students in the class. The school has a parent-teacher conference scheduled in about two weeks, but Mr. Waverly isn't sure that he can wait that long to speak to Tabitha's parents. He knows that both of them work and that it might be hard for them to help her regularly with her schoolwork. He has spoken to the teachers who had Tabitha in class in the second and third grades, and they indicated that this was not typical behavior for her. Although they did not remember Tabitha as being a high-performing student, they did remember her as a student who was solidly in the average range and who was cooperative and helpful in class. She also got along well with other students.

This description of Tabitha doesn't remind Mr. Waverly of the Tabitha that he knows. His Tabitha is neither cooperative nor dependable. At times, she seems downright moody. He also doesn't see her getting along well with other students or at times even associating with them. Even with just this brief history, Mr. Waverly knows that he has a problem that he needs to deal with. Tabitha's behavior needs to change in terms of her schoolwork, and, if she is having other problems, he needs to be prepared to help her there as well. But, what should he do next?

CHRONIC AVOIDANCE OF WORK
(MIDDLE-SECONDARY GRADES)

Jay's Chronic Avoidance of Work

Ms. Davis is Jay's ninth-grade English teacher. She has been closely following his progress, or perhaps his lack of progress, for the past three weeks. It is difficult for her to know just what Jay is able to do, because he so seldom completes and turns in the work that she has assigned. To reinforce the high expectations that she has for her students, she regularly gives writing and some other question-completion assignments each week. Jay hardly ever turns in the work that she has assigned.

Ms. Davis knows that things have been pretty rough for Jay. He is in the ninth grade when most of his friends are in the tenth grade. Jay repeated seventh grade. That had been a difficult year for him because his mother died that year. She has thought about pulling his record to see how he did in school before that year, but she hasn't had the time. Jay lives with his father and three younger sisters. She hasn't visited his home, but she knows that Jay's father works at the local electronics plant. It has to be hard for him raising three young girls and Jay.

Still, Jay is behind the other students in the class and falling further behind with each assignment that she gives. She asked him a couple of times why he hadn't completed his work, and all that he said was that he hadn't had the time. Once he said that he didn't understand what he was supposed to do and really didn't see the point in it anyway. She doesn't understand how he can't know what she wants. She gives her assignments in a very regular and predictable way. He has many chances to ask questions if he is not sure what she wants.

Fortunately, Jay's behavior in class doesn't seem to be a problem. He is quiet and keeps to himself. She isn't sure if he has any real friends in the class or not. She usually teaches the class as a large group and hasn't seen him talking to any of the other students for any length of time. She has so many students in her classes throughout the day that she really hasn't had time to get to know Jay very well. She feels bad about this, but this is just the way it is.

She doesn't want to give Jay poor grades, but she can't just ignore his not completing his work. After all, she has her standards to think about. She does recognize that she has a problem. But, she just isn't sure what to do. What should she do?

UNRULINESS (PRIMARY-ELEMENTARY GRADES)

Billy's Unruliness

Billy is a second-grade student who has little self-control. One of his favorite things to do is run down the hallway at school making motor sounds with his mouth while pretending to shift gears with his right hand. Although Billy thinks this is great fun, Ms. Lee, his teacher, finds this behavior unacceptable. So do other teachers in the school. Billy's classmates often find Billy annoying, because he frequently gets too loud and out of control when the class is involved in one of Ms. Lee's many fun activities. Actually, Ms. Lee views Billy as the kind of child who usually means to please; in fact, Billy is a good learner and makes above-average grades as a rule. However, more than once Billy has embarrassed Ms. Lee by his behaviors like running and talking too loudly in the cafeteria and knocking on each teacher's door as he goes by on his way to the restroom.

At first, Billy's behavior seems as though it might just be the behavior of a very energetic boy. Billy almost always seems happy and alert when he comes to school. The fact that he does make good grades has indicated to Ms. Lee that he has a sound mind and is able to comprehend what is expected of him. In science and math, he seems to be one of the stronger students in the class. His repeated behaviors that just seem too loud, too physical at times, and too much playground-like, however, have proven to be a real problem for what Ms. Lee is trying to accomplish in her teaching. His behavior, she feels, also has impacted negatively on the learning of the other students in the class.

Ms. Lee has spoken to Billy on more than one occasion about his overly rambunctious behavior, and his response has always been that he will try to do better. In fact, Ms. Lee feels as though Billy has tried to do better but has just been unsuccessful in his attempts. Her view is that if he can learn science and math, then he can learn to act properly in the classroom and school. She has even thought about having Billy meet with the assistant principal hoping he might be able to offer assistance. So far she hasn't done this nor has she spoken to Billy's parents about his behavior.

Ms. Lee has always been the kind of teacher who desires to "solve her own problems" whenever they occur. Billy's behavior, though, seems to be getting worse and not better. Ms. Lee needs to try something else, but what?

UNRULINESS (MIDDLE-SECONDARY GRADES)

Kendrick's Unruliness

Kendrick is a handful for Ms. Singh. Ms. Singh is Kendrick's eleventh-grade social studies teacher, or at least tries to be. She has all but given up on Kendrick ever being well behaved in class or being a good student. He is too loud and boisterous. He probably thinks that he is funny, but she just thinks that he is trouble to have around. Just about every time that she seems to have things going well, he does something to distract her and the rest of the class. Sometimes, he will just get out of his seat and walk around the room; other times, he will talk to the other students who sit near him. She doesn't think that he knows how to whisper. She can hear him talking all the way from the back of the room where he usually sits. She doesn't use assigned seats for her students, because it is her opinion that students this age should be able to pick where they want to sit in the class.

Ms. Singh considers herself to be a dedicated and flexible teacher, but her way just isn't connecting with Kendrick. She knows that he is popular in school and thinks that this is because he is on the basketball team. She has never been to one of the games, but she has heard other students talk about how many points he always scores. She has even heard that there may be some college scouts looking at him for a basketball scholarship. Her view of him, though, is that he simply is undisciplined.

As a student, Kendrick is struggling. His work is well below average, and his mind seems to be "somewhere else" when she is teaching. Ms. Singh has become very frustrated, because she knows that Kendrick is getting the best of her. His behavior is distracting to her and to the other students; he simply seems immature when compared to the rest of the class. She has looked in his file and knows that he lives with his mother and four brothers and sisters. He has had a poor track record in school over the years and is barely making the grade to be able to play basketball. As she sees it, basketball is one of the only things that keeps him coming to school and doing any work at all.

Ms. Singh feels that when Kendrick acts out in class, this makes her look bad in the eyes of the other students. If she allows him to "get away with it," other students probably will try to do the same thing. She knows that a lot of students just aren't interested in social studies, and this surprises and disappoints her, because she finds social studies very interesting. He certainly isn't learning very much from her teaching up to this point. In her opinion, the situation has to change. What should she do?

AGGRESSION (PRIMARY-ELEMENTARY GRADES)

Julian's Aggression

Julian is a kindergarten student whose behavior has been a concern to both his parents and his teacher, Mr. Woo. Julian seems to be advanced in his learning compared with some of the other students in the class; his mother, a former first-grade teacher, spent a great deal of time with him before he began school, which resulted in his being a very good reader when he started kindergarten. He also does well in beginning writing and in certain computation skills. In fact, Julian's parents wanted to have him placed in the first grade this year with children a year older because of his advanced learning abilities. They both value education highly, and because Julian is their only child, they are very focused on his development and eventual accomplishments. This accelerated placement to first grade, however, was not made.

Although Julian's academic skills are very much like a student in the first grade, Mr. Woo recognizes that Julian's social and emotional characteristics are actually far less developed than those of even the average kindergarten child's. When playing on the playground with other students, Julian often becomes angry and hits or bites his classmates. When Mr. Woo tries to control Julian, Julian frequently screams and even kicks at him. Julian's aggressive behavior is not relegated only to the playground. He displays similar behaviors in the cafeteria, the hallways, and even in the classroom. Although there is room for other students to avoid him on the playground, this is not the case in the classroom. On more than one occasion, classroom activities have had to be adjusted because of his behavior. Over the past month, some parents have even complained to the principal that they did not want their children in the same class with Julian, because they feared for their safety.

When in a conference with Mr. Woo, Julian's parents voiced their opinion that Julian gets frustrated because the other students are not as advanced as he is, which results in his angry outbursts. Since the beginning of the school year, they have continued to feel that Julian should have been placed in the first grade. Mr. Woo shared with them that he has tried to talk to Julian and work closely with him but that his aggressive behavior is a definite problem for him and the other students.

Mr. Woo isn't sure just what to try next; he likes Julian and sees that he certainly has learning potential, but his behavior needs to change. What should he do?

AGGRESSION (MIDDLE-SECONDARY GRADES)

Sebastian's Aggression

Mr. Allen is embarrassed to say it, but he has come to the point where he is glad when Sebastian is absent from school. Mr. Allen teaches seventh-grade math, and Sebastian is one of his students. The school year started out all right, but it started without Sebastian. It is now early December, and Sebastian joined the school and his class in late October. It has been a rough month and a half. Sebastian is just a very aggressive person. He has already been in three fights and come close on a number of other occasions. When Sebastian is around, the tension in the class seems to rise.

Sebastian actually is physically smaller than most of the other students and has had a hard time catching up to them academically. Mr. Allen hasn't had a chance to see the file that has been sent from Sebastian's last school, but, at least in the math area, Sebastian is far behind. Sebastian has had a difficult time adjusting to the rest of the students in the class as well as to his teaching style that Mr. Allen sees as being very straightforward.

He doesn't see Sebastian as being a bully in that Sebastian doesn't regularly start fights with other students. But, he is quick to say things that offend other students or something that most people consider uncalled for. He sees Sebastian as a loner; he doesn't seem to have any friends in the class. Sebastian was always eating by himself the few times that he saw him in the school cafeteria. The more he thinks about it the more he actually feels sorry for him. He is in a new community and a new school and is behind the other students in his class. This must make him feel very out of place. Maybe, he is doing the best that he can do.

One day, all of the good feelings that Mr. Allen had about reaching Sebastian seemed far away as he saw Sebastian and another student standing face-to-face in the back of the room. Class hadn't started, but it was supposed to in just a few minutes. Mr. Allen's attention was attracted to the back of the room when he heard two students say "Sebastian shouldn't have said that to him," and "I'll bet Sebastian is gonna get him good."

Mr. Allen knows that he has at least two problems to deal with. First, what is he going to do about the fight that is about to take place. Second, what can he do to help Sebastian not be involved in such situations in the future? What is the answer to each of these problems?

ATTENTION-SEEKING (PRIMARY-ELEMENTARY GRADES)

Bridget's Attention-seeking

Bridget, although she comes from a very disadvantaged background, makes very good grades in her fifth-grade classroom. Yet, Ms. Wilson, her teacher, is very concerned about Bridget's behavior problems. Although it is easy for her to think of Bridget and recognize that she has what many call a "sound mind," Bridget often acts in a fashion that Ms. Wilson feels is immature for a child her age. Bridget, for example, is known by her classmates as a "tattler" who frequently goes to Ms. Wilson to tell her of some instance when a classmate broke a rule while the teacher was not watching. Not only does this make her classmates angry, this constant behavior, more common to younger children, has started to get on Ms. Wilson's nerves. It certainly interrupts her instruction when Bridget does this. Moreover, Bridget tries to dominate Ms. Wilson's time even to the extent to which she has pretended not to understand things just so Ms. Wilson would come and sit beside her desk. At the beginning of the school year, Bridget "clowned around" and tried to be funny in class seemingly as a way to get attention. She hasn't done this for some time, though, because many of the other students laughed at her in a way that was not the "type of laugh" that she was seeking.

Ms. Wilson finds it difficult to give the necessary attention to the other students in the class because of Bridget's constant demands. During a conference, Ms. Wilson found that although Bridget is living with an aunt who seems to care for her very much, she has been in three different homes over the past five years. Bridget's birth father, who didn't live with her long, has now left the area and has not been heard from for more than a year. Bridget's birth mother has four other children and has asked her sister, Bridget's aunt, if she could care for her. She has tried to care for Bridget, but her circumstances are also difficult; and, she is away at work in the late afternoons and evenings during the week. In all, Ms. Wilson has discovered that Bridget is one of those many children who, in large part, are raising themselves. It is no wonder that Bridget craves attention from her, because she gets little positive attention away from school. Still, Bridget's behaviors are both interrupting to her instruction and not age-appropriate, she feels, for a student in the fifth grade.

Ms. Wilson wants to help Bridget as she does all of her students, and she recognizes her learning potential; however, she cannot continue to accept Bridget's attention-seeking behaviors. She is uncertain about how to approach the problem. What should she do?

ATTENTION-SEEKING (MIDDLE-SECONDARY GRADES)

Jennifer's Attention-seeking

Jennifer is in Mr. Winslow's tenth-grade Spanish II class; this is an unusual class, because of the twenty-four students in the class only six are girls. Mr. Winslow noticed early on in the term that Jennifer frequently did things to bring attention to herself. Sometimes she would just act out in a disturbing way, and other times she would do something to try to look funny. Once or twice, she even came to Mr. Winslow to tell him something that seemed unnecessary about another student in the class. Not only is her behavior annoying, it is also disturbing to him and the rest of the students in the class.

Mr. Winslow thinks that Jennifer is really struggling to keep up with the other students and wonders if maybe this could be a reason for her attention-seeking. Maybe, she is trying to hide that she isn't doing very well. But, when he asked some of the other teachers in the school who had Jennifer in class, he learned that this was how she acted in their classes too. One of the other teachers added that Jennifer lived with her mother and a younger brother who attended the middle school.

Mr. Winslow is worried about Jennifer for a number of reasons. First, her clowning around and drawing attention to herself is distracting to him and other students. Second, her coming to him and telling him things about other students, he thinks, is not really a typical behavior for a student her age. It certainly isn't earning her any friends in the class. Finally, he is concerned that Jennifer isn't being successful as a student in his class. Except for trying to draw attention to herself, she is friendly, attractive, dresses well, speaks clearly, uses good grammar, and gets along fairly well with the other students. Through some of his investigation, he learned that Jennifer is a cheerleader and that she has been in some of the school plays. On the surface, she seems far better off, at least financially, than some of the other students that he is teaching. But, he has been teaching long enough to know that what might be apparent on the surface might not represent the real situation. He knows that when students seek attention on a regular basis, this can represent a problem.

He wants to help Jennifer, but he just doesn't know how to go about it. One thing he knows for sure is that he needs to know more about her. What should he do?

DEFIANCE (PRIMARY-ELEMENTARY GRADES)

Maggie's Defiance

Maggie is a third-grade student who has had a personal problem during the current school year. Mr. Ray, her teacher, is aware that Maggie's parents recently divorced and that Maggie has become very upset by the fact that her father has moved to a new dwelling with another women and her children. Maggie continues to live with her mother and her older sister, who will graduate from high school at the end of the year. The source of Maggie's frustrations seems obvious. Immediately after the divorce, there seemed to be little change in Maggie's behavior. Over the past month, however, her behavior has changed significantly in a negative fashion.

Mr. Ray is concerned that on three occasions in the last two weeks Maggie has refused to do as Mr. Ray has requested and has told him in front of other students that she did not have to do what he told her to do. These incidents have taken place in such a way that Mr. Ray feels his ability to control his class has been threatened or at least definitely challenged. The public nature of this challenge has been especially bothersome to him. At first, he was shocked at Maggie's behavior and her remarks and just tried to coax her to do what he had asked. Fortunately, she did. On another occasion when he asked his students to work together in pairs, Maggie and the student that she was paired with got into a big argument about who was going to do what on the project that he assigned. When he talked to them about it, the other student just said that Maggie didn't want to cooperate and share the materials that he had passed out.

Mr. Ray feels sorry for Maggie and knows that she is suffering. The changes in her home conditions must be traumatic for her. Still, he does not feel that he can continue to allow her to talk to him as she has and defy his authority, especially in front of other students. With Maggie's parents' divorce being final, there is no chance that her lifestyle will return to being the way it was. Mr. Ray, who is a first-year teacher, is uneasy about going to his principal for advice, because he wants to appear as though he can manage his own classroom problems.

He recalls some discussions in college that dealt with managing classrooms but doesn't remember that this particular kind of situation was presented. He recognizes that he has a problem. Now, he must find the solution. What should he do?

DEFIANCE (MIDDLE-SECONDARY GRADES)

Eric's Defiance

Ms. Hutton is in her first year of teaching. She feels fortunate that she has been able to get a job given that she graduated in December and that there are not as many teaching positions open in the middle of the school year as there are at the beginning of the year. The part that she doesn't feel so fortunate about is that the position that she has accepted is at the high school level when she wanted to teach younger students. The school is also in a rather rough neighborhood. Still, she pledged to herself that she was going to be the best health teacher that she could be. One thing that she learned early on is that some of the students in the school come from very difficult home backgrounds. At times, some of them are hard to manage.

Eric is one such student. Up to this point, Ms. Hutton has not had any major problems with Eric, although she has made every effort to avoid them too. Eric seems to be one of those students who tries to push the envelope, as the popular expression goes. He hardly ever acts as though he wants to be involved in the activities that she has planned and almost dares her to see if she can get him involved. Once or twice he even has made what she thinks are "smart remarks" about what she is having the students do. Even though she has a good relationship with most of the students, she still feels very new to being a teacher. Maybe things have gone fairly well up to this point just because she has shown a lot of flexibility in what she asks her students to do and when she asks them to do it. From listening to some of the other teachers talk, she wonders if she is being too flexible.

Today, Ms. Hutton has given her students what she thinks will be an interesting assignment that her students will enjoy doing. When Eric gets the assignment sheet, Ms. Hutton can tell that he doesn't want to do it. As she is walking by his desk, he just wads it up and throws it on the floor. He says, "this is the most stupid thing I have ever been asked to do, and I'm not gonna do it." Ms. Hutton knows that she is facing one the most difficult moments in her short career. She can't let Eric talk to her like this in the classroom, and she also knows the problem is bigger than just this one assignment.

How can she best deal with the problem of the moment and help things be better in the long run? What should she do?

DISHONESTY (PRIMARY-ELEMENTARY GRADES)

Thom's Dishonesty

Ms. Gore has been teaching fourth grade for ten years and is considered an excellent teacher by both parents and fellow educators. However, never in her ten years of teaching has she had the type of problem that she has had this year. The problem began when Terry reported that he had some money missing from his desk. He said that it was a couple of dollars. Two days later Lakisha said that part of her lunch had been taken. Within the next week, almost every student in the classroom reported that they had been the victim of something having been taken. Ms. Gore knows that some of the reports are not factual. Some children are simply mistaken, and others have gotten caught up in the moment. However, she is certain some objects are being taken; in fact, someone went so far as to steal money from her own desk. But now, students are accusing other students without having any proof.

Ms. Gore finds it amazing that a fourth-grade class can take on all the primary characteristics of what she thinks of as an unruly mob. Fingers are being pointed, and innocent students are being hurt by false accusations. She even got two calls one evening and one e-mail last week from parents asking what was going on in the class. Their children had said that some things had been taken from them. The parents didn't actually seem angry, but she could tell that they wanted to know more about the problem and what was being done about it. All she could say was that she was looking into it. Getting calls from parents makes her think that things are truly getting out of control.

Then, a most amazing thing happens. Ms. Gore finds some of the things that have been taken in Thom's desk. When confronted in private by Ms. Gore, Thom admits to taking everything. Ms. Gore is very confused because Thom's parents are known to be wealthy and generous people. Thom does not "need" to steal. Thom tells Ms. Gore that he is sorry he has stolen and that it will never happen again. He also begs her not to tell his parents about what he has done.

Ms. Gore, although an experienced teacher, is not sure just how to handle the situation. It won't take long for the other students in the class to find out that it is Thom who has been taking things. After that, their parents will soon know. She has a lot to think about and some important decisions to make. What should she do?

DISHONESTY (MIDDLE-SECONDARY GRADES)

Karen's Dishonesty

Mr. Gallagher sees himself as someone who can handle most any problem in the classroom. He teaches eighth-grade social studies and tries to have his class operate as though it is a small community. Everyone has a chance for input into making the "rules" and deciding how the community will operate. He has the class meet regularly to talk about how things are going. Communities are governed by laws, and he thinks that having his students meet on a regular basis will help reinforce this fact. This also helps him see what is on the minds of his students and shows them that he cares about their ideas and their lives. He is glad that he has a positive relationship with his students, because he has a difficult problem that he is dealing with. Over the past month, some students have told him that they have had things missing. Some of this has been pens and pencils, but some of it also has been makeup kits, perfume, and even money. He also thinks that he has had some cheating on his last two tests. The students who told him about the stealing even named another student in the class, Karen, as the thief. He also thinks that Karen has been cheating on his tests. Stealing affects other students in that their property is lost. Cheating on a test also affects other students in that it can make a difference in the grades that they receive.

Mr. Gallagher doesn't know much about Karen except that she doesn't seem to him like someone who would steal and cheat. She has only been in his class for about a month, because she has just recently started attending the school. She interacts well with the other students in the class and seems bright and alert. He has seen both of her parents at school functions, and they both came for the parent-teacher conferences that had been held just two weeks ago. Stealing and cheating are very serious problems. The class meetings that he has held so far have not gotten into anything like this. Should he bring up the problem of stealing and cheating to the students at a class meeting? Maybe, he is wrong about Karen. But, what if he is right, and she really is doing these things? This is a problem that has to be dealt with.

There are issues here that are important not only because of the acts that have been committed but also because they have been formally brought to his attention by some of the students. The problem is pretty much out in the open and needs to be dealt with. He has to take action, but it has to be the right action. What should he do?

CONCLUSION

Many of the problems that teachers face each day have no one right answer or solution. Most are specific to the particular situation where they arise and to the student or students involved and require analysis within that context. Through guided problem solving based on a strong knowledge base of information related to best practice in teaching, student motivation, and classroom management, however, teachers can identify patterns in the various problems that they are called on to deal with and learn from one problem to another. Although each situation needs to be analyzed individually, common patterns and plausible solutions will emerge. It is because of this that it is critical that teachers learn from each situation that they encounter, so that they can more quickly find effective solutions to the problems that they will be faced with in the future.

The case studies presented here for analysis serve to illustrate this point. Teachers can learn from their successes, as well as from their mistakes if they are willing and able to analyze them in a systematic and informed manner. Whether the teacher is dealing with a problem of dishonesty in the second grade or defiance in the tenth grade, a logical pattern to address the problem should be followed. Chapter 7 offered a number of realistic problems for review. By addressing each problem as a situation in which certain questions must be answered for the problem to be resolved effectively, the positive impact of the use of a logical problem-solving model in problem resolution can be seen. Through the disciplined use of the model in these hypothetical situations, the transfer can be more easily and successfully made to the real-life problems that teachers face each day in their schools and classrooms.

GLOSSARY OF TERMS

academic learning time. That portion of the classroom time during which students are engaged in meaningful learning activities and are successful during this engagement.

academic organization. The teacher's means of ordering and arranging information for instruction so that students will be better able to understand the information communicated, e.g., diagrams, outlines, hierarchies.

active listening. Specific approach to listening in which the teacher gives full attention to both the emotional and intellectual meaning of what the student is saying; often involves mirroring back what a student has said or otherwise confirming that one is attentive, interested and nonjudgmental.

advance organizer. Described by David Ausubel as the teacher's use of introductory statements or activities that frame the new content to be taught as a part of the lesson focus.

advancework. The process of preventing problems before they begin rather than reacting to problems after they have already occurred.

aggression. A serious behavior problem in that the possibility exists that one or more students may be injured; fighting is the ultimate form of aggression although aggression may also include pushing and shoving, overly physical play, name-calling, or other verbal attacks.

allocated time. The amount of time a particular teacher or school designates to an identified course topic or activity.

anticipatory set. Mental or attitudinal foundation established by the teacher for the students at the beginning of the instructional experience that helps students to understand what they may anticipate in the instruction that will follow.

Applied Behavior Analysis. An approach to behavior management based on the work of B.F. Skinner's operant conditioning theory; a rewards-based approach to modifying student behavior.

anxiety. Feeling of apprehension, worry, tension, or nervousness.

Assertive Discipline. Management theory promoted by Lee and Marlene Canter that focuses on the tenet that teachers have the right to teach, and students have the right to learn, and no one has the right to disrupt the learning environment; clear rules are established along with clear conse-quences for students who choose to break established rules.

attention-seeking. Student behavior problem often exhibited by tattling and showing off; teachers are advised that there are reasons behind displaying attention-seeking behaviors and these reasons need to be ascertained by the teacher to appropriately deal with the behavior.

attribution theory. Cognitive theory that involves the student's views of the causes of outcomes and how these views influence his or her expectations and behaviors.

behavior modification. Associated with the work of B.F. Skinner, now more popularly called Applied Behavior Analysis; management approach that uses rewards for modifying student behavior.

Behaviorism. Theory of motivation that focuses on the use of reinforcements or rewards to modify student behavior.

chronic avoidance of work. Potentially a serious student behavior problem in which a student consistently fails to complete his or her assigned work after repeated teacher effort to get the work completed.

clarity. Important teacher characteristic in being able to be clear in commu-nications with students so that they understand the different teacher mes-sages used during instruction, how the instruction will be conducted and what is expected of them.

class meeting. Management strategy recommended by William Glasser in which the teacher meets regularly with students as a way to involve stu-dents in establishing guidelines for acceptable behavior and as a forum for collaborative problem solving.

closure. Type of review that occurs at the end of the instructional episode or period that enables the student to end the lesson with a better under-standing of the topic and a place to build on in the future.

coercive strategies. Behavior strategies used by the teacher in maintaining a well-managed classroom that are based on the power of punishment.

cognitive memory level question. Question at the lowest level of cognition that asks students to recall previously learned and memorized informa-tion; behaviors such as recalling, recognizing, and reporting are typically involved.

cognitive theories. Theories of motivation that stress the student's need for order, predictability, and the understanding of events around him.

Conflict Resolution. Management strategy developed by David and Roger Johnson that relies on training students to deal with their own problems and those of their fellow students; peer mediation is an important part of this strategy.

connected discourse. Ability to communicate so that it is clear to students that the teacher's presentation is thematically well connected and leads to a goal, going point by point.

convergent level question. Question at the second lowest level of cognition that asks students to put facts or concepts together to obtain the single correct answer; questions may require students to make comparisons, explain facts or concepts, state or describe relationships, or solve problems using learned procedures.

criterion material. The information that students will be held accountable for that has been communicated to them before instruction; the criteria or standard upon which the teacher will base student success.

debilitating anxiety. Anxiety so extreme that it gets in the way of successful student performance.

defiance. A serious form of student misbehavior in which the student refuses to do what the teacher asks or boldly talks back to the teacher in a hostile or threatening way.

deficiency needs. Needs at the lower levels of Abraham Maslow's Hierarchy of Needs including survival, safety, belonging, and self-esteem.

desists. Remarks made by teachers for the purpose of stopping student misconduct or misbehavior.

discipline. Action taken on the part of the teacher to enforce rules and respond to student misbehavior.

disequilibrium. State of being out of balance.

dishonesty. Considered by some to be the most serious form of student misconduct often exhibited through cheating and/or stealing and telling untruths and lying.

disruptive talking. Student behavior problem through talking that interferes with the learning process by interrupting the teacher while teaching, students as they are listening to the teacher, or as they are involved in completing activities that the teacher has assigned.

divergent level question. A question that asks students to engage in divergence of thought and produce a response that is original for that student; questions may require students to predict, hypothesize, or infer.

diversity. In the school or classroom, that pertains to the variety of backgrounds or circumstances from which students come as they enter the schooling environment.

emphasis. An element of communication in which the teacher specifically identifies for students important points to be remembered, e.g., through the use of such statements as "this is important" or "be sure to remember this".

engaged time. The portion of instructional time that students actually spend directly involved in learning activities; often referred to as time on task.

enthusiasm. The amount of energy and vigor shown by the teacher; believed to communicate to students the degree to which the teacher enjoys teaching and the degree to which the teacher believes that the students will be successful in their learning.

equilibration. The process of searching for order or balance, i.e., equilibrium, and, in so doing, testing one's understanding against the real world.

equilibrium. Being in a state of balance.

equitable distribution. A recommended approach to asking questions in which all students are called on as equally as possible.

expectancy X value theory. Theory that students are motivated to engage in a learning task to the extent that they expect to succeed on the task and the degree to which they value achievement on the task or other potential outcomes that may come as a result of task achievement.

expulsion. Process exercised by a school district's governing authority, generally the school board, of banning a student from attending school for the remainder of the school year or the remainder of the school year plus an additional period of time carried over into the next school year.

external locus of control. When students feel that forces external to or outside themselves control their lives.

extrinsic motivation. Motivation to become involved in an activity as a means to an end; to receive a reward, praise, or some other recognition.

evaluation level question. Question at the highest level of cognition that asks students to make judgments based on logically derived evidence; students must defend or explain their judgments based on criteria that they designate or that have been established by others.

facilitating anxiety. Anxiety in such a small amount that it may actually help to improve student performance.

feedback. Information provided students by teachers, generally in oral or written form, that lets them know the status of their learning progress; the more specific, regular, and in depth the feedback the better.

focus. The attention given to and maintained on the important points to be made during instruction; when teachers have good focus, students clearly understand what will take place during instruction and what will be expected of them as learners.

frequency. Important aspect of question-asking that deals with the number of questions that the teacher asks; generally the more questions the better.

goal. That which an individual is striving to achieve or accomplish; in teaching, goals are generally broader as opposed to narrow and more long term as opposed to short term in nature.

group focus. On-task behavior in which all students in the classroom attend to the teacher or activities that the teacher has assigned.

growth needs. Needs at the higher levels of Abraham Maslow's Hierarchy of Needs including intellectual achievement, aesthetic appreciation, and self-actualization.

Hierarchy of Needs. Humanistic theory of motivation developed by Abraham Maslow that identifies a hierarchy of needs associated with underlying reasons for human behavior; needs are identified as deficiency or growth needs.

Humanism. Theory of motivation that views behavior as an individual's effort to satisfy or fulfill his ultimate potential as a human being.

I message. Three-part communication from the teacher to the student delineating the student's undesired behavior, describing the effect the behavior has on the teacher or the classroom, and relating how the teacher feels when the behavior occurs.

inattention. Student behavior seen as the least severe management problem; students may engage in daydreaming, staring into space, doing unrelated work, etc., as examples of not being involved in the learning process.

indirect teaching. Approach to teaching that focuses heavily on the use of student ideas and student active participation in the learning process.

inquiry. A logical approach to problem solving that includes the statement of the problem, development of a hypothesis, collection and analysis of data, and the drawing of conclusions.

instructional time. The portion of allocated time that is actually devoted to learning activities.

instructional variety. The consistent use of a number of different instructional techniques or strategies by the teacher in instruction rather than relying on only a very few; see also variability.

internal locus of control. When students feel that they are responsible for what happens to them.

intrinsic motivation. Motivation to become involved in an activity for its own sake.

learned helplessness. The feeling on the part of students when they come to believe that no amount of effort on their part will produce success.

learner-focused classroom. A classroom in which emphasis is given to a focus on student learning as opposed to student performance with special attention given to student self-regulation, climate, teacher characteristics, and instruction.

learning goal. Also referred to as mastery goal; goal that emphasizes the challenge of learning and the mastery of a task as opposed to performance.

locus of control. The degree to which students perceive that both positive and negative events in their lives are under their control.

logical consequences. Recommended by both Rudolph Dreikurs and William Glasser as representing understandings on the part of students that when certain behaviors are exhibited certain responses or consequences will follow.

management. A system of organization that addresses all elements of the classroom (i.e., students, space, time, materials, and behavioral rules and procedures) to reach optimum levels of instruction and learning

management organization. The general organizational structure used by the teacher to coordinate the classroom, e.g., starting on time, having specific learning routines.

mastery goal. Also referred to as learning goal; goal that emphasizes the challenge of learning and the mastery of a task as opposed to performance.

misbehavior. Student behavior seen as being unacceptable or inappropriate for the setting or situation in which it occurs.

Model for Reflection and Inquiry. Five-step model for logical problem solving recommended for teachers to use as they analyze problems that they may have with student management and motivation; the model includes the statement of the problem, development of a hypothesis, collection of relevant data, analysis of data, and the interpretation and reporting of results, drawing conclusions, and making generalizations.

motivation. An internal state that arouses students to action, directs them to certain behaviors, and assists them in maintaining their arousal and action with regard to behaviors important and appropriate to the learning environment.

motivation to learn. Motivation represented by the quality of a student's cognitive engagement in a learning task or activity.

no-lose approach. An approach to help students resolve their own conflicts or problems in such a way that all students involved feel positive about the resolution.

normative strategies. Behavior strategies used by the teacher in maintaining a well-managed classroom based on all involved doing what is traditionally expected of them, e.g., teachers are expected to ask certain things of students, and students are expected to do what they are asked by their teachers.

operant conditioning. The process of shaping behavior produced voluntarily by the student through the use of reinforcement.

peer mediation. Important aspect of the Conflict Resolution approach to behavior management in which students, after formal training, lead the problem-solving process by helping each other, i.e., peers, reach acceptable solutions to problems that they have experienced.

performance goal. A goal that emphasizes the demonstration of high ability and the avoidance of failure.

potency. The strength or power of a reinforcer, reward, praise, or even criticism, to change behavior.

power-seeking. Student behavior problem in which the student seeks to control the teacher instead of being directed by the teacher; the student could use such strategies as refusing to follow directions, lying, arguing, and throwing temper tantrums.

precise terminology. Clarity in communication that eliminates vague and ambiguous words and phrases from presentations and interactions with students.

primary reinforcer. A reinforcer that meets a basic physiological need such as food, water, and safety.

proactive teacher. A teacher who, through prior planning and knowledge gained, has the ability to "head off" most management problems before they occur and respond to management problems when they occur in such a way that sets the stage for learning to continue in the future.

probing behaviors. Verbal techniques used by teachers, typically through question-asking, that request in a non-threatening way that a student go deeper into an answer given or comment made and reflect on his or her ideas.

prompting. Question-asking strategy that helps students respond to questions by providing cues after an incorrect or incomplete answer or silence.

proximity control. Control exercised by the teacher based on the teacher's nearness to or distance from the student; generally, the nearer the teacher is to a student the less likelihood there will be for the student to display inappropriate behaviors.

psychological membership. The feeling of membership in a group that is determined by the degree to which students feel personally accepted, respected, included, and supported.

Reality Therapy. Management approach recommended by William Glasser in which students play an active role in the decision-making processes in the classroom.

reactive teacher. A teacher whose behavior is characterized by reacting or responding to classroom management and motivation problems after they have occurred rather than ascertaining the causes of such problems and, through prior planning and the use of relevant information, reducing the likelihood that they will ever take place.

reflective practitioner. An educator who regularly uses formal problem-solving strategies to develop solutions to problems related to motivation, management, and instruction.

reinforcer. Something given or a consequence that, depending on whether it is positive or negative, either adds to or reduces the frequency or length of a behavior.

remunerative strategies. Behavior strategies used by the teacher in maintaining a well-managed classroom that is based on the power of rewards.

revenge-seeking. A student behavior problem in which a student may do something to cause other students to be punished to "get back at them."

review. An instructional procedure that may occur at different points during a lesson in which the teacher summarizes important information from previous work in helping students to link what has been learned to what will be taught in the future.

ripple effect. The effect on other students in the classroom when the teacher reinforces or corrects students for their behavior.

sane messages. Recommended by Hiam Ginott as a way for teachers to communicate to students by focusing on their undesired behaviors and not on them as individuals on a personal level.

secondary reinforcer. A reinforcer that may address a particular psychological need such as praise, grades, and money.

self-actualization. The full development or use of one's potential.

self-efficacy. Learners' beliefs about their capability of succeeding on specific tasks.

self-fulfilling prophecy. A phenomenon that a student's performance is greatly influenced when a teacher holds certain beliefs about the student's ability to perform.

self-regulation. The process or ability of students to use their own thoughts and actions to reach academic learning goals and to govern their own behaviors.

shaping. The practice of gradually changing a student's unwanted actions to more acceptable behavior over time through the use of reinforcements.

state anxiety. Anxiety brought about through the presence of a certain situation that typically results in a sense of fear, concern, or threat.

structuring comments. Verbal statements used by the teacher normally at the beginning of the instructional experience that alerts students to the events that are to follow and the important points that they should focus on during the instruction.

student success rate. The rate at which students gain an understanding of and correctly complete their work.

suspension. Removal of a student from the regular school environment for a stated period of time for the breaking identified school rules; most schools have both in-school and out-of-school suspension programs.

task oriented/business-like behavior. A manner of conducting classroom instruction in which the teacher is businesslike and task oriented in his or her demeanor and approach to teaching communicating to students that there is a clear and important goal to be achieved and that students will stay on task during that period of time needed to reach the goal.

teacher burnout. The point of extreme stress at which a teacher has lost his or her enthusiasm for teaching and has little energy to focus on helping students learn.

Teacher Effectiveness Training (TET). Developed by Thomas Gordon as a model for classroom management focusing on problem solving, active listening, and assisting students to resolve their own conflicts through no-lose processes.

teacher efficacy. The teacher's belief in his or her ability to be successful in getting students to learn.

teacher expectation. What a teacher expects or thinks a particular student will be able to accomplish.

time-on-task. See engaged time.

trait anxiety. Type of anxiety in which students seem to be anxious even in circumstances that should not normally be thought of as threatening.

transition signals. The use of specific communication signals in blending one topic with the next that follows so that the flow of the instruction will be smooth and not abrupt.

You message. As opposed to an *I message*, a statement used by a teacher with a student that blames or attacks the student personally for a problem that has been identified whereas the *I message* focuses on the behavior as the problem, not on the student as the problem.

unruliness. Serious behavior problem in which the student exhibits a lack of self-control; unruliness may be exhibited by talking loudly, running in hallways, using unacceptable language, etc.

variability. Important teacher quality related to student achievement that is represented by the teacher's diversity of information-sending techniques or strategies used during the presentation of lessons; see also instructional variety.

wait-time. The amount of time the teacher allows after asking a question before speaking again; average wait time is about one second; a minimum of three seconds is recommended to increase student achievement.

withitness. When a teacher displays the ability to have an ongoing awareness of events throughout the entire classroom and not just one area of the setting.

zero tolerance. Policy for managing student behavior, usually adopted on a school district–wide basis, represented by the use of certain predetermined consequences when particular rules are broken; the consequences are applied automatically, regardless of the circumstances surrounding the rule being broken.

zone of proximal development. A range of tasks that a student cannot yet do alone but can accomplish when assisted by a more skilled partner.

INDEX